Cyber Law and IT Protection

CYBER LAW AND IT PROTECTION

Monika Selva

AMIGA PRESS INC.
Delhi: - 110002 (India)

AMIGA PRESS INC.

Regd. Office :- 19, DBS Building, Ansari Road, Darya Ganj
Delhi- :- 110002, India
Tel :- 01123283333
Email :- amigapress@gmail.com
info@amigapress.co.in
Website :- www.amigapress.co.in

This edition is published by Amiga Press Inc.

ISBN: 978-93-84533-53-3 (pbk)

First Published 2019

First Reprint 2021

Printed and bound by Replika Press Pvt. Ltd.

Preface

This book has been written to meet the requirement of students getting knowledge in the field of cyber law

"cyberlaw" concerns the law of information technology, including computing and the internet. It is related to legal informatics, and governs the digital dissemination of both (digitalized) information and software, information security and electronic commerce. aspects and it have been described as "paper laws" for a "paperless environment". It raises specific issues of intellectual property in computing and online, contract law, privacy, freedom of expression, and jurisdiction.

A keen attempt has been made to make the book useful and interesting. Leaving aside all the unnecessary things, only the essential facts have been discussed in this book. It has a direct link with practical work , that all the common and complicated troubles have been explained clearly.

This book has been written in such a way that it may equip the students with basic knowledge of cyber law.

Any suggestions towards its further improvement will be thankfully acknowledged and incorporated in the next edition.

—Author

Contents

1

Introduction to Computers

A computer is a device that can be instructed to carry out sequences of arithmetic or logical operations automatically via computer programming. Modern computers have the ability to follow generalized sets of operations, called programs. These programs enable computers to perform an extremely wide range of tasks. A "complete" computer including the hardware, the operating system (main software), and peripheral equipment required and used for "full" operation can be referred to as a computer system. This term may as well be used for a group of computers that are connected and work together, in particular a computer network or computer cluster.

Computers are used as control systems for a wide variety of industrial and consumer devices. This includes simple special purpose devices like microwave ovens and remote controls, factory devices such as industrial robots and computer-aided design, and also general purpose devices like personal computers and mobile devices such as smartphones.

Early computers were only conceived as calculating devices. Since ancient times, simple manual devices like the abacusaided people in doing calculations. Early in the Industrial Revolution, some mechanical devices were built to automate long tedious tasks, such as guiding patterns for looms. More sophisticated electrical machines did specialized analogcalculations in the early 20th century. The first digital electronic calculating machines were developed during World War II. The speed, power, and versatility of computers have been increasing dramatically ever since then.

Conventionally, a modern computer consists of at least one processing element, typically a central processing unit (CPU), and some form of memory. The processing element carries out arithmetic and logical operations, and a sequencing and control unit can change the order of operations in response to stored information. Peripheral devices include input devices (keyboards, mice, joystick, etc.), output devices (monitor screens, printers, etc.), and input/output devices that perform both functions (e.g., the 2000s-era touchscreen). Peripheral devices allow information to be retrieved from an external source and they enable the result of operations to be saved and retrieved.

According to the Oxford English Dictionary, the first known use of the word "computer" was in 1613 in a book called The Yong Mans Gleanings by English writer Richard Braithwait: "I haue [sic] read the truest computer of Times, and the best Arithmetician that euer [sic] breathed, and he reduceth thy dayes into a short number." This usage of the term referred to a human computer, a person who carried out calculations or computations. The word continued with the same meaning until the middle of the 20th century. Originally, women were often hired as "human computers" because they could be paid less than their male counterparts. By 1943, most human computers were women. From the end of the 19th century the word began to take on its more familiar meaning, a machine that carries out computations.

The Online Etymology Dictionary gives the first attested use of "computer" in the "1640s, [meaning] "one who calculates,"; this is an "... agent noun from compute (v.)". The Online Etymology Dictionary states that the use of the term to mean "calculating machine" (of any type) is from 1897." The Online Etymology Dictionary indicates that the "modern use" of the term, to mean "programmable digital electronic computer" dates from "... 1945 under this name; [in a] theoretical [sense] from 1937, as Turing machine".

History

Pre-20th century

Devices have been used to aid computation for thousands of years, mostly using one-to-one correspondence with fingers. The earliest counting device was probably a form of tally stick. Later record keeping aids throughout the Fertile Crescent included calculi (clay spheres, cones, etc.) which represented counts of items, probably livestock or grains, sealed in hollow unbaked clay containers. The use of counting rods is one example.

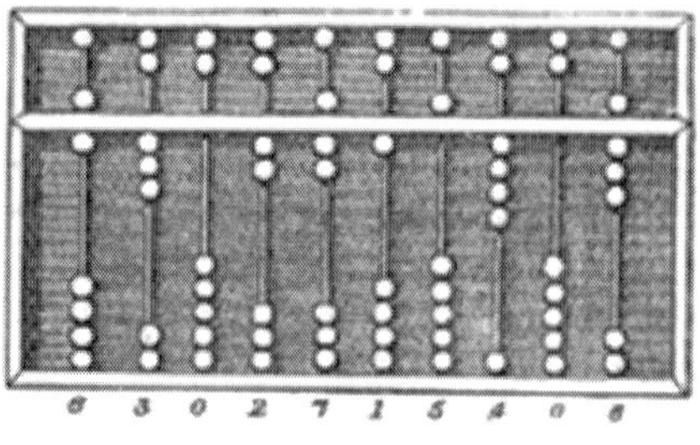

The Chinese Suanpan (□□) (the number represented on this abacus is 6,302,715,408)

The abacus was initially used for arithmetic tasks. The Roman abacus was developed from devices used in Babyloniaas early as 2400 BC. Since then, many other forms of reckoning boards or tables have been invented. In a medieval European counting house, a checkered cloth would be placed on a table, and markers moved around on it according to certain rules, as an aid to calculating sums of money.

The ancient Greek-designed Antikythera mechanism, dating between 150 and 100 BC, is the world's oldest analog computer.

The Antikythera mechanism is believed to be the earliest mechanical analog "computer", according to Derek J. de Solla Price. It was designed to calculate astronomical positions. It was discovered in 1901 in the Antikythera wreck off the Greek island of Antikythera, between Kythera and Crete, and has been dated to c. 100 BC. Devices of a level of complexity comparable to that of the Antikythera mechanism would not reappear until a thousand years later.

Many mechanical aids to calculation and measurement were constructed for astronomical and navigation use. The planisphere was a star chart invented by Abū Rayhān al-Bīrūnī in the early 11th century. The astrolabe was invented in the Hellenistic world in either the 1st or 2nd centuries BC and is often attributed to Hipparchus. A combination of the planisphere and dioptra, the astrolabe was effectively an analog computer capable of working out several different kinds of problems in spherical astronomy. An astrolabe incorporating a mechanical calendar computer and gear-wheels was invented by Abi Bakr of Isfahan, Persia in 1235. Abū Rayhān al-Bīrūnī invented the first mechanical geared lunisolar calendar astrolabe, an early fixed-wired knowledge processing machine with a gear train and gear-wheels, c. 1000 AD.

The sector, a calculating instrument used for solving problems in proportion, trigonometry, multiplication and division, and for various functions, such as squares and cube roots, was developed in the late 16th century and found application in gunnery, surveying and navigation.

The planimeter was a manual instrument to calculate the area of a closed figure by tracing over it with a mechanical linkage.

The slide rule was invented around 1620–1630, shortly after the publication of the concept of the logarithm. It is a hand-operated analog computer for doing multiplication and division. As slide rule development progressed, added scales provided reciprocals, squares and square roots, cubes and cube roots, as well as transcendental functions such as logarithms and exponentials, circular and hyperbolic trigonometryand other functions. Slide rules with special scales are still used for quick performance of routine calculations, such as the E6B circular slide rule used for time and distance calculations on light aircraft.

In the 1770s, Pierre Jaquet-Droz, a Swiss watchmaker, built a mechanical doll (automaton) that could write holding a quill pen. By switching the number and order of its internal wheels different letters, and hence different messages, could be produced. In effect, it could be mechanically "programmed" to read instructions. Along with two other complex machines, the doll is at the Musée d'Art et d'Histoire of Neuchâtel, Switzerland, and still operates.

The tide-predicting machine invented by Sir William Thomson in 1872 was of great utility to navigation in shallow waters. It used a system of pulleys and wires to automatically calculate predicted tide levels for a set period at a particular location.

The differential analyser, a mechanical analog computer designed to solve differential equations by integration, used wheel-and-disc mechanisms to perform the integration. In 1876, Lord Kelvin had already discussed the possible construction of such calculators, but he had been stymied by the limited output torque of the ball-and-disk integrators. In a differential analyzer, the output of one integrator drove the input of the next integrator, or a graphing output. The torque amplifier was the advance that allowed these machines to work. Starting in the 1920s, Vannevar Bush and others developed mechanical differential analyzers.

First computing device

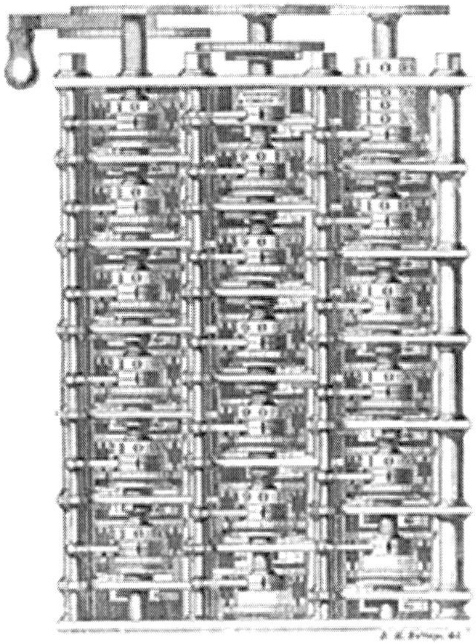

A portion of Babbage's Difference engine.

Charles Babbage, an English mechanical engineer and polymath, originated the concept of a programmable computer. Considered the "father of the computer", he conceptualized and invented the first mechanical computer in the early 19th century. After working on his revolutionary difference engine, designed to aid in navigational calculations, in 1833 he realized that a much more general design, an Analytical Engine, was possible. The input of programs and data was to be provided to the machine via punched cards, a method being used at the time to direct mechanical looms such as the Jacquard loom. For output, the machine would have a printer, a curve plotter and a bell. The machine would also be able to punch numbers onto cards to be read in later. The Engine incorporated an arithmetic logic unit, control flow in the form of conditional branching and loops, and integrated memory, making it the first design for a general-purpose computer that could be described in modern terms as Turing-complete.

The machine was about a century ahead of its time. All the parts for his machine had to be made by hand – this was a major problem for a device with thousands of parts. Eventually, the project was dissolved with the decision of the British Government to cease funding. Babbage's failure to complete the analytical engine can be chiefly attributed to difficulties not only of politics and financing, but also to his desire to develop an increasingly sophisticated computer and to move ahead faster than anyone else could follow. Nevertheless, his son, Henry Babbage, completed a simplified version of the analytical engine's computing unit (the mill) in 1888. He gave a successful demonstration of its use in computing tables in 1906.

Analog computers

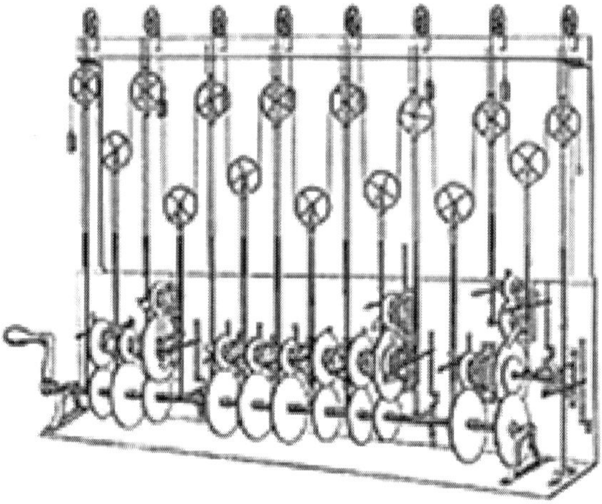

Sir William Thomson's third tide-predicting machine design, 1879–81

During the first half of the 20th century, many scientific computing needs were met by increasingly sophisticated analog computers, which used a direct mechanical or electrical model of the problem as a basis for computation. However, these were not programmable and generally lacked the versatility and accuracy of modern digital computers. The first modern analog computer was a tide-predicting machine, invented by Sir William Thomson in 1872. The differential analyser, a mechanical analog computer designed to solve differential equations by integration using wheel-and-disc mechanisms, was conceptualized in 1876 by James Thomson, the brother of the more famous Lord Kelvin.

The art of mechanical analog computing reached its zenith with the differential analyzer, built by H. L. Hazen and Vannevar Bush at MIT starting in 1927. This built on the mechanical integrators of James Thomson and the torque amplifiers invented by H. W. Nieman. A dozen of these devices were built before their obsolescence became obvious. By the 1950s, the success of digital electronic computers had spelled the end for most analog computing machines, but analog computers remained in use during the 1950s in some specialized applications such as education (control systems) and aircraft (slide rule).

Digital computers

Electromechanical

By 1938, the United States Navy had developed an electromechanical analog computer small enough to use aboard a submarine. This was the

Torpedo Data Computer, which used trigonometry to solve the problem of firing a torpedo at a moving target. During World War II similar devices were developed in other countries as well.

Replica of Zuse's Z3, the first fully automatic, digital (electromechanical) computer.

Early digital computers were electromechanical; electric switches drove mechanical relays to perform the calculation. These devices had a low operating speed and were eventually superseded by much faster all-electric computers, originally using vacuum tubes. The Z2, created by German engineer Konrad Zuse in 1939, was one of the earliest examples of an electromechanical relay computer.

In 1941, Zuse followed his earlier machine up with the Z3, the world's first working electromechanical programmable, fully automatic digital computer. The Z3 was built with 2000 relays, implementing a 22 bit word length that operated at a clock frequency of about 5–10 Hz.Program code was supplied on punched film while data could be stored in 64 words of memory or supplied from the keyboard. It was quite similar to modern machines in some respects, pioneering numerous advances such as floating point numbers. Rather than the harder-to-implement decimal system (used in Charles Babbage's earlier design), using a binary system meant that Zuse's machines were easier to build and potentially more reliable, given the technologies available at that time. The Z3 was Turing complete.

Vacuum tubes and digital electronic circuits

Purely electronic circuit elements soon replaced their mechanical and electromechanical equivalents, at the same time that digital calculation replaced analog. The engineer Tommy Flowers, working at the Post Office Research Station in London in the 1930s, began to explore the possible use of electronics for the telephone exchange. Experimental equipment that he built in 1934 went into operation five years later, converting a portion of the telephone exchange network into an electronic data processing system, using thousands of vacuum tubes. In the US, John Vincent Atanasoff and Clifford E. Berry of Iowa State University developed and tested the Atanasoff–Berry Computer (ABC) in 1942, the first "automatic electronic digital computer". This design was also all-electronic and used about 300 vacuum tubes, with capacitors fixed in a mechanically rotating drum for memory.

Colossus, the first electronic digitalprogrammable computing device, was used to break German ciphers during World War II.

During World War II, the British at Bletchley Park achieved a number of successes at breaking encrypted German military communications. The German encryption machine, Enigma, was first attacked with the help of the electro-mechanical bombes which were often run by women. To crack the more sophisticated German Lorenz SZ 40/42 machine, used for high-level Army communications, Max Newmanand his colleagues commissioned Flowers to build the Colossus. He spent eleven months from early February 1943 designing and building the first Colossus. After a functional test in December 1943, Colossus was shipped to Bletchley Park, where it was delivered on 18 January 1944 and attacked its first message on 5 February.

Colossus was the world's first electronic digital programmable computer. It used a large number of valves (vacuum tubes). It had paper-tape input and was capable of being configured to perform a variety of boolean logical operations on its data, but it was not Turing-complete. Nine Mk II Colossi were built (The Mk I was converted to a Mk II making ten machines in total). Colossus Mark I contained 1,500 thermionic valves (tubes), but Mark II with 2,400 valves, was both 5 times faster and simpler to operate than Mark I, greatly speeding the decoding process.

ENIAC was the first electronic, Turing-complete device, and performed ballistics trajectory calculations for the United States Army.

The U.S.-built ENIAC (Electronic Numerical Integrator and Computer) was the first electronic programmable computer built in the US. Although the ENIAC was similar to the Colossus, it was much faster, more flexible, and it was Turing-complete. Like the Colossus, a "program" on the ENIAC was defined by the states of its patch cables and switches, a far cry from the stored program electronic machines that came later. Once a program was written, it had to be mechanically set into the machine with manual resetting of plugs and switches. The programmers of the ENIAC were six women, often known collectively as the "ENIAC girls".

It combined the high speed of electronics with the ability to be programmed for many complex problems. It could add or subtract 5000 times a second, a thousand times faster than any other machine. It also had modules to multiply, divide, and square root. High speed memory was limited to 20 words (about 80 bytes). Built under the direction of John Mauchly and J. Presper Eckert at the University of Pennsylvania, ENIAC's development and construction lasted from 1943 to full operation at the end of 1945. The machine was huge, weighing 30 tons, using 200 kilowatts of electric power and contained over 18,000 vacuum tubes, 1,500 relays, and hundreds of thousands of resistors, capacitors, and inductors.

Modern computers

Concept of modern computer

The principle of the modern computer was proposed by Alan Turing in his seminal 1936 paper, On Computable Numbers. Turing proposed a simple device that he called "Universal Computing machine" and that is now known as a universal Turing machine. He proved that such a machine is capable of computing anything that is computable by executing instructions (program) stored on tape, allowing the machine to be programmable. The fundamental concept of Turing's design is the stored program, where all the instructions for computing are stored in memory. Von Neumann acknowledged that the central concept of the modern computer was due to this paper. Turing machines are to this day a central object of study in theory of computation. Except for the limitations imposed by their finite memory stores, modern computers are said to be Turing-complete, which is to say, they have algorithm execution capability equivalent to a universal Turing machine.

Stored programs

A section of the Manchester Baby, the first electronic stored-program computer

Early computing machines had fixed programs. Changing its function required the re-wiring and re-structuring of the machine. With the proposal of the stored-program computer this changed. A stored-program computer includes by design an instruction set and can store in memory a set of instructions (a program) that details the computation. The theoretical basis for the stored-program computer was laid by Alan Turing in his 1936 paper. In 1945, Turing joined the National Physical Laboratory and began work on developing an electronic stored-program digital computer. His 1945 report "Proposed Electronic Calculator" was the first specification for such a device. John von Neumann at the University of Pennsylvania also circulated his First Draft of a Report on the EDVAC in 1945.

The Manchester Baby was the world's first stored-program computer. It was built at the Victoria University of Manchester by Frederic C. Williams, Tom Kilburn and Geoff Tootill, and ran its first program on 21 June 1948. It was designed as a testbed for the Williams tube, the first random-access digital storage device. Although the computer was considered "small and primitive" by the standards of its time, it was the first working machine to contain all of the elements essential to a modern electronic computer. As soon as the Baby had demonstrated the feasibility of its design, a project was initiated at the university to develop it into a more usable computer, the Manchester Mark 1. Grace Hopper was the first person to develop a compiler for programming language.

The Mark 1 in turn quickly became the prototype for the Ferranti Mark 1, the world's first commercially available general-purpose computer. Built by Ferranti, it was delivered to the University of Manchester in February 1951. At least seven of these later machines were delivered between 1953 and 1957, one of them to Shell labs in Amsterdam. In October 1947, the directors of British catering company J. Lyons & Company decided to take an active role in promoting the commercial development of computers. The LEO I computer became operational in April 1951 and ran the world's first regular routine office computer job.

Transistors

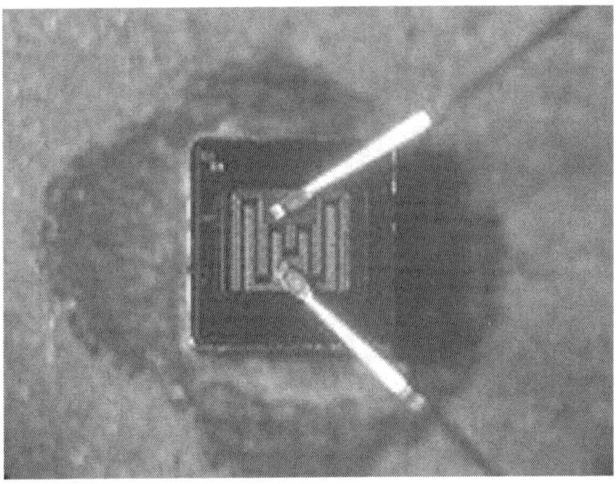

A bipolar junction transistor

The bipolar transistor was invented in 1947. From 1955 onwards transistors replaced vacuum tubes in computer designs, giving rise to the "second generation" of computers. Compared to vacuum tubes, transistors have many advantages: they are smaller, and require less power than vacuum tubes, so give off less heat. Silicon junction transistors were much more reliable than vacuum tubes and had longer, indefinite, service life. Transistorized computers could contain tens of thousands of binary logic circuits in a relatively compact space.

At the University of Manchester, a team under the leadership of Tom Kilburn designed and built a machine using the newly developed transistors instead of valves. Their first transistorised computer and the first in the world, was operational by 1953, and a second version was completed there in April

1955. However, the machine did make use of valves to generate its 125 kHz clock waveforms and in the circuitry to read and write on its magnetic drum memory, so it was not the first completely transistorized computer. That distinction goes to the Harwell CADET of 1955, built by the electronics division of the Atomic Energy Research Establishment at Harwell.

Integrated circuits

The next great advance in computing power came with the advent of the integrated circuit. The idea of the integrated circuit was first conceived by a radar scientist working for the Royal Radar Establishment of the Ministry of Defence, Geoffrey W.A. Dummer. Dummer presented the first public description of an integrated circuit at the Symposium on Progress in Quality Electronic Components in Washington, D.C. on 7 May 1952.

The first practical ICs were invented by Jack Kilby at Texas Instruments and Robert Noyce at Fairchild Semiconductor. Kilby recorded his initial ideas concerning the integrated circuit in July 1958, successfully demonstrating the first working integrated example on 12 September 1958. In his patent application of 6 February 1959, Kilby described his new device as "a body of semiconductor material ... wherein all the components of the electronic circuit are completely integrated". Noyce also came up with his own idea of an integrated circuit half a year later than Kilby. His chip solved many practical problems that Kilby's had not. Produced at Fairchild Semiconductor, it was made of silicon, whereas Kilby's chip was made of germanium.

This new development heralded an explosion in the commercial and personal use of computers and led to the invention of the microprocessor. While the subject of exactly which device was the first microprocessor is contentious, partly due to lack of agreement on the exact definition of the term "microprocessor", it is largely undisputed that the first single-chip microprocessor was the Intel 4004, designed and realized by Ted Hoff, Federico Faggin, and Stanley Mazor at Intel.

Mobile computers

The first mobile computers were heavy and ran from mains power. The 50lb IBM 5100 was an early example. Later portables such as the Osborne 1 and Compaq Portable were considerably lighter, but still needed to be plugged in. The first laptops, such as the Grid Compass, removed this requirement by incorporating batteries – and with the continued miniaturization of computing resources and advancements in portable battery life, portable computers grew in popularity in the 2000s. The same developments allowed manufacturers to integrate computing resources into cellular phones.

These smartphones and tablets run on a variety of operating systems and soon became the dominant computing device on the market, with manufacturers reporting having shipped an estimated 237 million devices in 2Q 2013.

Types

Computers are typically classified based on their uses:

Based on uses

- Analog computer
- Digital computer
- Hybrid computer

Based on sizes

- Smartphone
- Microcomputer
- Workstation
- Personal computer
- Laptop
- Minicomputer
- Mainframe computer
- Supercomputer
- Tablet computer

Hardware

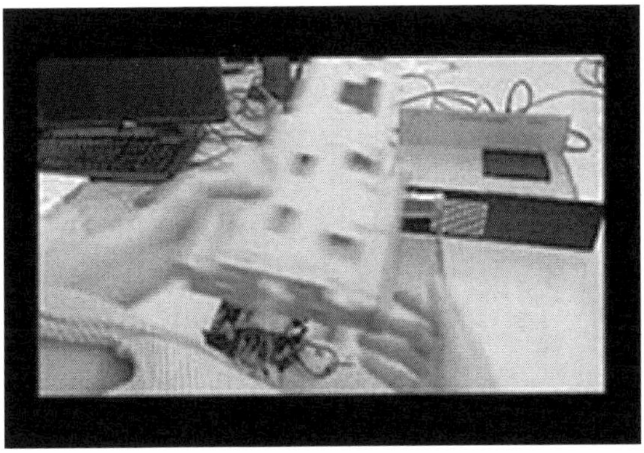

Video demonstrating the standard components of a "slimline" computer

The term hardware covers all of those parts of a computer that are tangible physical objects. Circuits, computer chips, graphic cards, sound cards, memory (RAM), motherboard, displays, power supplies, cables, keyboards, printers and "mice" input devices are all hardware.

History of computing hardware

A general purpose computer has four main components: the arithmetic logic unit (ALU), the control unit, the memory, and the input and output devices (collectively termed I/O). These parts are interconnected by buses, often made of groups of wires. Inside each of these parts are thousands to trillions of small electrical circuits which can be turned off or on by means of an electronic switch. Each circuit represents a bit (binary digit) of information so that when the circuit is on it represents a "1", and when off it represents a "0" (in positive logic representation). The circuits are arranged in logic gates so that one or more of the circuits may control the state of one or more of the other circuits.

Input devices

When unprocessed data is sent to the computer with the help of input devices, the data is processed and sent to output devices. The input devices may be hand-operated or automated. The act of processing is mainly regulated by the CPU. Some examples of input devices are:

- Computer keyboard
- Digital camera
- Digital video
- Graphics tablet
- Image scanner
- Joystick
- Microphone
- Mouse
- Overlay keyboard
- Real-time clock
- Trackball
- Touchscreen

Output devices

The means through which computer gives output are known as output devices. Some examples of output devices are:

- Computer monitor
- Printer
- PC speaker
- Projector

- Sound card
- Video card

Control unit

Diagram showing how a particular MIPS architecture instruction would be decoded by the control system

The control unit (often called a control system or central controller) manages the computer's various components; it reads and interprets (decodes) the program instructions, transforming them into control signals that activate other parts of the computer. Control systems in advanced computers may change the order of execution of some instructions to improve performance.

A key component common to all CPUs is the program counter, a special memory cell (a register) that keeps track of which location in memory the next instruction is to be read from.

The control system's function is as follows—note that this is a simplified description, and some of these steps may be performed concurrently or in a different order depending on the type of CPU:

1. Read the code for the next instruction from the cell indicated by the program counter.

2. Decode the numerical code for the instruction into a set of commands or signals for each of the other systems.

3. Increment the program counter so it points to the next instruction.

4. Read whatever data the instruction requires from cells in memory (or perhaps from an input device). The location of this required data is typically stored within the instruction code.

5. Provide the necessary data to an ALU or register.

6. If the instruction requires an ALU or specialized hardware to complete, instruct the hardware to perform the requested operation.

7. Write the result from the ALU back to a memory location or to a register or perhaps an output device.

8. Jump back to step (1).

Since the program counter is (conceptually) just another set of memory cells, it can be changed by calculations done in the ALU. Adding 100 to the program counter would cause the next instruction to be read from a place 100 locations further down the program. Instructions that modify the program counter are often known as "jumps" and allow for loops (instructions that are repeated by the computer) and often conditional instruction execution (both examples of control flow).

The sequence of operations that the control unit goes through to process an instruction is in itself like a short computer program, and indeed, in some more complex CPU designs, there is another yet smaller computer called a microsequencer, which runs a microcode program that causes all of these events to happen.

Central processing unit (CPU)

The control unit, ALU, and registers are collectively known as a central processing unit (CPU). Early CPUs were composed of many separate components but since the mid-1970s CPUs have typically been constructed on a single integrated circuit called a microprocessor.

Arithmetic logic unit (ALU)

The ALU is capable of performing two classes of operations: arithmetic and logic. The set of arithmetic operations that a particular ALU supports may be limited to addition and subtraction, or might include multiplication, division, trigonometry functions such as sine, cosine, etc., and square roots. Some can only operate on whole numbers (integers) while others use floating point to represent real numbers, albeit with limited precision. However, any computer that is capable of performing just the simplest operations can be programmed to break down the more complex operations into simple steps that it can perform. Therefore, any computer can be programmed to perform any arithmetic operation—although it will take more time to do so if its ALU does not directly support the operation. An ALU may also compare numbers and return boolean truth values (true or false) depending on whether one is equal to, greater than or less than the other ("is 64 greater than 65?"). Logic operations involve Boolean logic: AND, OR, XOR, and NOT. These can be useful for creating complicated conditional statements and processing boolean logic.

Superscalar computers may contain multiple ALUs, allowing them to process several instructions simultaneously. Graphics processors and computers with SIMD and MIMDfeatures often contain ALUs that can perform arithmetic on vectors and matrices.

Memory

A computer's memory can be viewed as a list of cells into which numbers can be placed or read. Each cell has a numbered "address" and can store a single number. The computer can be instructed to "put the number 123 into the cell numbered 1357" or to "add the number that is in cell 1357 to the number that is in cell 2468 and put the answer into cell 1595." The information stored in memory may represent practically anything. Letters, numbers, even computer instructions can be placed into memory with equal ease. Since the CPU does not differentiate between different types of information, it is the software's responsibility to give significance to what the memory sees as nothing but a series of numbers.

In almost all modern computers, each memory cell is set up to store binary numbers in groups of eight bits (called a byte). Each byte is able to represent 256 different numbers (2 = 256); either from 0 to 255 or −128 to +127. To store larger numbers, several consecutive bytes may be used (typically, two, four or eight). When negative numbers are required, they are usually stored in two's complement notation. Other arrangements are possible, but are usually not seen outside of specialized applications or historical contexts. A computer can store any kind of information in memory if it can be represented numerically. Modern computers have billions or even trillions of bytes of memory.

The CPU contains a special set of memory cells called registers that can be read and written to much more rapidly than the main memory area. There are typically between two and one hundred registers depending on the type of CPU. Registers are used for the most frequently needed data items to avoid having to access main memory every time data is needed. As data is constantly being worked on, reducing the need to access main memory (which is often slow compared to the ALU and control units) greatly increases the computer's speed.

Computer main memory comes in two principal varieties:

- random-access memory or RAM
- read-only memory or ROM

RAM can be read and written to anytime the CPU commands it, but ROM is preloaded with data and software that never changes, therefore the CPU can only read from it. ROM is typically used to store the computer's initial start-up instructions. In general, the contents of RAM are erased when the power to the computer is turned off, but ROM retains its data indefinitely. In a PC, the ROM contains a specialized program called the BIOS that orchestrates loading the computer's operating system from the hard disk drive into RAM whenever the computer is turned on or reset. In embedded computers, which frequently do not have disk drives, all of the required software may be stored in ROM. Software stored in ROM is often called firmware, because it is notionally more like hardware than software. Flash memory blurs the distinction between ROM and RAM, as it retains its data when turned off but is also rewritable. It is typically much slower than conventional ROM and RAM however, so its use is restricted to applications where high speed is unnecessary.

In more sophisticated computers there may be one or more RAM cache memories, which are slower than registers but faster than main memory. Generally computers with this sort of cache are designed to move frequently needed data into the cache automatically, often without the need for any intervention on the programmer's part.

Hard disk drives are common storage devices used with computers.

I/O is the means by which a computer exchanges information with the outside world. Devices that provide input or output to the computer are called peripherals. On a typical personal computer, peripherals include input devices like the keyboard and mouse, and output devices such as the display and printer. Hard disk drives, floppy disk drives and optical disc drives serve as both input and output devices. Computer networking is another form of I/O. I/O devices are often complex computers in their own right, with their own CPU and memory. A graphics processing unit might contain fifty or more tiny computers that perform the calculations necessary to display 3D graphics. Modern desktop computers contain many smaller computers that assist the main CPU in performing I/O. A 2016-era flat screen display contains its own computer circuitry.

Multitasking

While a computer may be viewed as running one gigantic program stored in its main memory, in some systems it is necessary to give the appearance of running several programs simultaneously. This is achieved by multitasking i.e. having the computer switch rapidly between running each program in turn. One means by which this is done is with a special signal called an interrupt, which can periodically cause the computer to stop executing instructions where it was and do something else instead. By remembering where it was executing prior to the interrupt, the computer can return to that task later. If several programs are running "at the same time". then the interrupt generator might be causing several hundred interrupts per second, causing a program switch each time. Since modern computers typically execute instructions several orders of magnitude faster than human perception, it may appear that many programs are running at the same time even though only one is ever executing in any given instant. This method of multitasking is sometimes termed "time-sharing" since each program is allocated a "slice" of time in turn.

Before the era of inexpensive computers, the principal use for multitasking was to allow many people to share the same computer. Seemingly, multitasking would cause a computer that is switching between several programs to run more slowly, in direct proportion to the number of programs it is running, but most programs spend much of their time waiting for slow input/output devices to complete their tasks. If a program is waiting for the user to click on the mouse or press a key on the keyboard, then it will not take a "time slice" until the event it is waiting for has occurred. This frees up time for other programs to execute so that many programs may be run simultaneously without unacceptable speed loss.

Multiprocessing

Cray designed many supercomputers that used multiprocessing heavily.

Some computers are designed to distribute their work across several CPUs in a multiprocessing configuration, a technique once employed only in large and powerful machines such as supercomputers, mainframe computers and servers. Multiprocessor and multi-core (multiple CPUs on a single integrated circuit) personal and laptop computers are now widely available, and are being increasingly used in lower-end markets as a result.

Supercomputers in particular often have highly unique architectures that differ significantly from the basic stored-program architecture and from general purpose computers. They often feature thousands of CPUs, customized high-speed interconnects, and specialized computing hardware. Such designs tend to be useful only for specialized tasks due to the large scale of program organization required to successfully utilize most of the available resources at once. Supercomputers usually see usage in large-scale simulation, graphics rendering, and cryptography applications, as well as with other so-called "embarrassingly parallel" tasks.

Software

Software refers to parts of the computer which do not have a material form, such as programs, data, protocols, etc. Software is that part of a computer system that consists of encoded information or computer instructions, in contrast to the physical hardware from which the system is built. Computer software includes computer programs, libraries and related non-executable data, such as online documentation or digital media. It is often divided into system software and application software]] Computer hardware and software require each other and neither can be realistically used on its own. When software is stored in hardware that cannot easily be modified, such as with BIOS ROM in an IBM PC compatible computer, it is sometimes called "firmware".

There are thousands of different programming languages—some intended to be general purpose, others useful only for highly specialized applications.

Programs

The defining feature of modern computers which distinguishes them from all other machines is that they can be programmed. That is to say that some type of instructions (the program) can be given to the computer, and it will process them. Modern computers based on the von Neumann architecture often have machine code in the form of an imperative programming language. In practical terms, a computer program may be just a few instructions or extend to many millions of instructions, as do the programs for word processors and web browsers for example. A typical modern computer can execute billions of instructions per second (gigaflops) and rarely makes a mistake over many years of operation. Large computer programs consisting of several million instructions may take teams of programmers years to write, and due to the complexity of the task almost certainly contain errors.

Stored program architecture

Replica of the Manchester Baby, the world's first electronic stored-program computer, at the Museum of Science and Industry in Manchester, England

This section applies to most common RAM machine–based computers.

In most cases, computer instructions are simple: add one number to another, move some data from one location to another, send a message to some external device, etc. These instructions are read from the computer's memory and are generally carried out (executed) in the order they were given. However, there are usually specialized instructions to tell the computer to jump ahead or backwards to some other place in the program and to carry on executing from there. These are called "jump" instructions (or branches). Furthermore, jump instructions may be made to happen conditionally so that different sequences of instructions may be used depending on the result of some previous calculation or some external event. Many computers directly support subroutines by providing a type of jump that "remembers" the location it jumped from and another instruction to return to the instruction following that jump instruction.

Program execution might be likened to reading a book. While a person will normally read each word and line in sequence, they may at times jump back to an earlier place in the text or skip sections that are not of interest. Similarly, a computer may sometimes go back and repeat the instructions in some section of the program over and over again until some internal condition is met. This is called the flow of control within the program and it is what allows the computer to perform tasks repeatedly without human intervention.

Comparatively, a person using a pocket calculator can perform a basic arithmetic operation such as adding two numbers with just a few button presses. But to add together all of the numbers from 1 to 1,000 would take thousands of button presses and a lot of time, with a near certainty of making a mistake. On the other hand, a computer may be programmed to do this with just a few simple instructions. The following example is written in the MIPS assembly language:

Once told to run this program, the computer will perform the repetitive addition task without further human intervention. It will almost never make a mistake and a modern PC can complete the task in a fraction of a second.

Machine code

In most computers, individual instructions are stored as machine code with each instruction being given a unique number (its operation code or opcode for short). The command to add two numbers together would have one opcode; the command to multiply them would have a different opcode, and so on. The simplest computers are able to perform any of a handful of different instructions; the more complex computers have several hundred to choose from, each with a unique numerical code. Since the computer's memory is able to store numbers, it can also store the instruction codes. This leads to the important fact that entire programs (which are just lists of these instructions) can be represented as lists of numbers and can themselves be manipulated inside the computer in the same way as numeric data. The fundamental concept of storing programs in the computer's memory alongside the data they operate on is the crux of the von Neumann, or stored program, architecture. In some cases, a computer might store some or all of its program in memory that is kept separate from the data it operates on. This is called the Harvard architecture after the Harvard Mark I computer. Modern von Neumann computers display some traits of the Harvard architecture in their designs, such as in CPU caches.

While it is possible to write computer programs as long lists of numbers (machine language) and while this technique was used with many early computers, it is extremely tedious and potentially error-prone to do so in practice, especially for complicated programs. Instead, each basic instruction can be given a short name that is indicative of its function and easy to remember – a mnemonic such as ADD, SUB, MULT or JUMP. These mnemonics are collectively known as a computer's assembly language. Converting programs written in assembly language into something the computer can actually understand (machine language) is usually done by a computer program called an assembler.

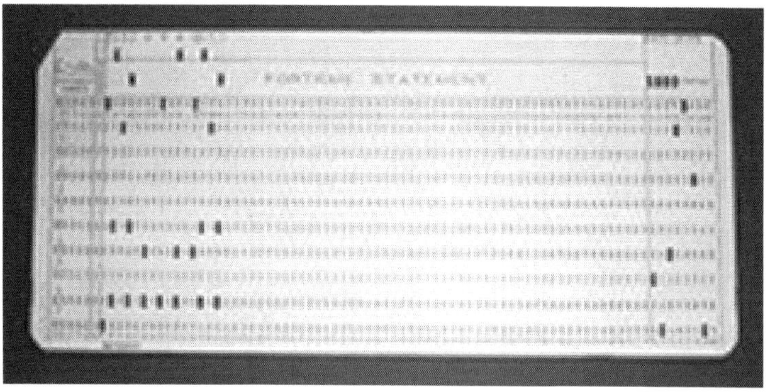

A 1970s punched card containing one line from a Fortran program. The card reads: "Z(1) = Y + W(1)" and is labeled "PROJ039" for identification purposes.

Programming language

Programming languages provide various ways of specifying programs for computers to run. Unlike natural languages, programming languages are designed to permit no ambiguity and to be concise. They are purely written languages and are often difficult to read aloud. They are generally either translated into machine code by a compiler or an assembler before being run, or translated directly at run time by an interpreter. Sometimes programs are executed by a hybrid method of the two techniques.

Low-level languages

Machine languages and the assembly languages that represent them (collectively termed low-level programming languages) tend to be unique to a particular type of computer. For instance, an ARM architecture computer (such as may be found in a smartphone or a hand-held videogame) cannot understand the machine language of an x86 CPU that might be in a PC.

High-level languages

Although considerably easier than in machine language, writing long programs in assembly language is often difficult and is also error prone. Therefore, most practical programs are written in more abstract high-level programming languages that are able to express the needs of the programmer more conveniently (and thereby help reduce programmer error). High level languages are usually "compiled" into machine language (or sometimes into assembly language and then into machine language) using another computer program called a compiler. High level languages are less related to the workings of the target computer than assembly language, and more related to the language and structure of the problem(s) to be solved by the final program. It is therefore often possible to use different compilers to translate the same high level language program into the machine language of many different types of computer. This is part of the means by which software like video games may be made available for different computer architectures such as personal computers and various video game consoles.

Program design

Program design of small programs is relatively simple and involves the analysis of the problem, collection of inputs, using the programming constructs within languages, devising or using established procedures and algorithms, providing data for output devices and solutions to the problem as applicable. As problems become larger and more complex, features such as subprograms, modules, formal documentation, and new paradigms such as object-oriented programming are encountered. Large programs involving thousands of line of code and more require formal software methodologies. The task of developing large software systems presents a significant intellectual challenge. Producing software with an acceptably high reliability within a predictable schedule and budget has historically been difficult; the academic and professional discipline of software engineering concentrates specifically on this challenge.

Bugs

Errors in computer programs are called "bugs". They may be benign and not affect the usefulness of the program, or have only subtle effects. But in some cases, they may cause the program or the entire system to "hang", becoming unresponsive to input such as mouse clicks or keystrokes, to completely fail, or to crash. Otherwise benign bugs may sometimes be harnessed for malicious intent by an unscrupulous user writing an exploit, code designed to take advantage of a bug and disrupt a computer's proper execution. Bugs are usually not the fault of the computer. Since computers merely execute the instructions they are given, bugs are nearly always the result of programmer error or an oversight made in the program's design. Admiral Grace Hopper, an American computer scientist and developer of the first compiler, is credited for having first used the term "bugs" in computing after a dead moth was found shorting a relay in the Harvard Mark II computer in September 1947.

Networking and the Internet

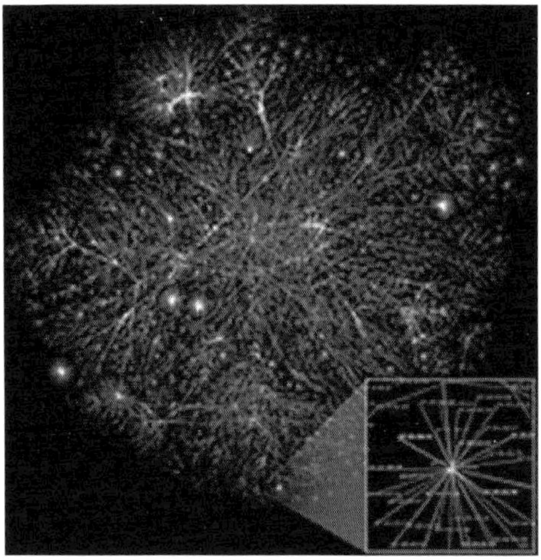

Visualization of a portion of the routes on the Internet

Computers have been used to coordinate information between multiple locations since the 1950s. The U.S. military's SAGE system was the first large-scale example of such a system, which led to a number of special-purpose commercial systems such as Sabre. In the 1970s, computer engineers at research institutions throughout the United States began to link their computers together using telecommunications technology. The effort was funded by ARPA (now DARPA), and the computer network that resulted was called the ARPANET. The technologies that made the Arpanet possible spread and evolved.

In time, the network spread beyond academic and military institutions and became known as the Internet. The emergence of networking involved a redefinition of the nature and boundaries of the computer. Computer operating systems and applications were modified to include the ability to define and access the resources of other computers on the network, such as peripheral devices, stored information, and the like, as extensions of the resources of an individual computer. Initially these facilities were available primarily to people working in high-tech environments, but in the 1990s the spread of applications like e-mail and the World Wide Web, combined with the development of cheap, fast networking technologies like Ethernet and ADSL saw computer networking become almost ubiquitous. In fact, the number of computers that are networked is growing phenomenally. A very large proportion of personal computers regularly connect to the Internet to communicate and receive information. "Wireless" networking, often utilizing mobile phone networks, has meant networking is becoming increasingly ubiquitous even in mobile computing environments.

Unconventional computers

A computer does not need to be electronic, nor even have a processor, nor RAM, nor even a hard disk. While popular usage of the word "computer" is synonymous with a personal electronic computer, the modern definition of a computer is literally: "A device that computes, especially a programmable [usually] electronic machine that performs high-speed mathematical or logical operations or that assembles, stores, correlates, or otherwise processes information." Any device which processes information qualifies as a computer, especially if the processing is purposeful.

Future

There is active research to make computers out of many promising new types of technology, such as optical computers, DNA computers, neural computers, and quantum computers. Most computers are universal, and are able to calculate any computable function, and are limited only by their memory capacity and operating speed. However different designs of computers can give very different performance for particular problems; for example quantum computers can potentially break some modern encryption algorithms (by quantum factoring) very quickly.

Computer architecture paradigms

There are many types of computer architectures:

- Quantum computer vs. Chemical computer
- Scalar processor vs. Vector processor
- Non-Uniform Memory Access (NUMA) computers
- Register machine vs. Stack machine
- Harvard architecture vs. von Neumann architecture
- Cellular architecture

Of all these abstract machines, a quantum computer holds the most promise for revolutionizing computing. Logic gates are a common abstraction which can apply to most of the above digital or analog paradigms. The ability to store and execute lists of instructions called programs makes computers extremely versatile, distinguishing them from calculators. The Church–Turing thesis is a mathematical statement of this versatility: any computer with a minimum capability (being Turing-complete) is, in principle, capable of performing the same tasks that any other computer can perform. Therefore, any type of computer (netbook, supercomputer, cellular automaton, etc.) is able to perform the same computational tasks, given enough time and storage capacity.

Artificial intelligence

A computer will solve problems in exactly the way it is programmed to, without regard to efficiency, alternative solutions, possible shortcuts, or possible errors in the code. Computer programs that learn and adapt are part of the emerging field of artificial intelligence and machine learning. Artificial intelligence based products generally fall into two major categories: rule based systems and pattern recognition systems. Rule based systems attempt to represent the rules used by human experts and tend to be expensive to develop. Pattern based systems use data about a problem to generate conclusions. Examples of pattern based systems include voice recognition, font recognition, translation and the emerging field of on-line marketing.

2

Internet and Cyber Laws

In Simple way we can say that cyber crime is unlawful acts wherein the computer is either a tool or a target or both. Cyber crimes can involve criminal activities that are traditional in nature, such as theft, fraud, forgery, defamation and mischief, all of which are subject to the Indian Penal Code. The abuse of computers has also given birth to a gamut of new age crimes that are addressed by the Information Technology Act, 2000.

We can categorize Cyber crimes in two ways

- The Computer as a Target :-using a computer to attack other computers.

e.g. Hacking,Virus/Worm attacks,DOS attack etc.

- The computer as a weapon :-using a computer to commit real world crimes.

e.g. Cyber Terrorism, IPR violations,Credit card frauds,EFT frauds, Pornography etc.

Cyber law (also referred to as cyberlaw) is a term used to describe the legal issues related to use of communications technology, particularly "cyberspace", i.e. the Internet. It is less a distinct field of law in the way that property or contract are as it is an intersection of many legal fields, including intellectual property, privacy, freedom of expression, and jurisdiction. In essence, cyber law is an attempt to integrate the challenges presented by human activity on the Internet with legacy system of laws applicable to the physical world.

When Internet was developed, the founding fathers of Internet hardly had any inclination that Internet could transform itself into an all pervading revolution which could be misused for criminal activities and which required regulation. Today, there are many disturbing things happening in cyberspace. Due to the anonymous nature of the Internet, it is possible to engage into a variety of criminal activities with impunity and people with intelligence, have been grossly misusing this aspect of the Internet to perpetuate criminal activities in cyberspace. Hence the need for Cyberlaws in India.

Cyberlaw is important because it touches almost all aspects of transactions and activities on and concerning the Internet, the World Wide Web and Cyberspace. Initially it may seem that Cyberlaws is a very technical field and that it does not have any bearing to most activities in Cyberspace. But the actual truth is that nothing could be further than the truth. Whether we realize it or not, every action and every reaction in Cyberspace has some legal and Cyber legal perspectives.

. As the nature of Internet is changing and this new medium is being seen as the ultimate medium ever evolved in human history, every activity of yours in Cyberspace can and will have a Cyberlegal perspective. From the time you register your Domain Name, to the time you set up your web site, to the time you promote your website, to the time when you send and receive emails , to the time you conduct electronic commerce transactions on the said site, at every point of time, there are various Cyberlaw issues involved. You may not be bothered about these issues today because you may feel that they are very distant from you and that they do not have an impact on your Cyber activities. But sooner or later, you will have to tighten your belts and take note of Cyberlaw for your own benefit.

Advantages of Cyber Laws

The IT Act 2000 attempts to change outdated laws and provides ways to deal with cyber crimes. We need such laws so that people can perform purchase transactions over the Net through credit cards without fear of misuse. The Act offers the much-needed legal framework so that information is not denied legal effect, validity or enforceability, solely on the ground that it is in the form of electronic records.

In view of the growth in transactions and communications carried out through electronic records, the Act seeks to empower government departments to accept filing, creating and retention of official documents in the digital format. The Act has also proposed a legal framework for the authentication and origin of electronic records / communications through digital signature.

- From the perspective of e-commerce in India, the IT Act 2000 and its provisions contain many positive aspects. Firstly, the implications of these provisions for the e-businesses would be that email would now be a valid and legal form of communication in our country that can be duly produced and approved in a court of law.

• Companies shall now be able to carry out electronic commerce using the legal infrastructure provided by the Act.

• Digital signatures have been given legal validity and sanction in the Act.

• The Act throws open the doors for the entry of corporate companies in the business of being Certifying Authorities for issuing Digital Signatures Certificates.

• The Act now allows Government to issue notification on the web thus heralding e-governance.

• The Act enables the companies to file any form, application or any other document with any office, authority, body or agency owned or controlled by the appropriate Government in electronic form by means of such electronic form as may be prescribed by the appropriate Government.

• The IT Act also addresses the important issues of security, which are so critical to the success of electronic transactions. The Act has given a legal definition to the concept of secure digital signatures that would be required to have been passed through a system of a security procedure, as stipulated by the Government at a later date.

• Under the IT Act, 2000, it shall now be possible for corporates to have a statutory remedy in case if anyone breaks into their computer systems or network and causes damages or copies data. The remedy provided by the Act is in the form of monetary damages, not exceeding Rs. 1 crore.

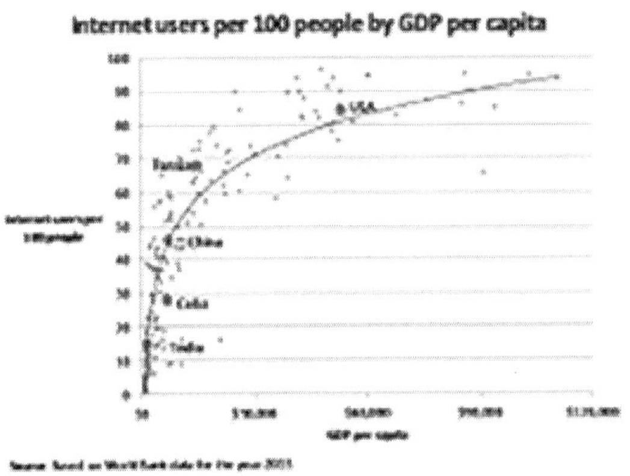

Internet users per 100 population members and GDP per capita for selected countries.

The Internet (contraction of interconnected network) is the global system of interconnected computer networks that use the Internet protocol suite (TCP/IP) to link devices worldwide. It is a network of networks that consists of private, public, academic, business, and government networks of local to global scope, linked by a broad array of electronic, wireless, and optical networking technologies. The Internet carries a vast range of information resources and services, such as the inter-linked hypertext documents and applications of the World Wide Web (WWW), electronic mail, telephony, and file sharing.

The origins of the Internet date back to research commissioned by the federal government of the United States in the 1960s to build robust, fault-tolerant communication with computer networks. The primary precursor network, the ARPANET, initially served as a backbone for interconnection of regional academic and military networks in the 1980s. The funding of the National Science Foundation Network as a new backbone in the 1980s, as well as private funding for other commercial extensions, led to worldwide participation in the development of new networking technologies, and the merger of many networks. The linking of commercial networks and enterprises by the early 1990s marked the beginning of the transition to the modern Internet, and generated a sustained exponential growth as generations of institutional, personal, and mobile computers were connected to the network. Although the Internet was widely used by academia since the 1980s, commercialization incorporated its services and technologies into virtually every aspect of modern life.

Most traditional communications media, including telephony, radio, television, paper mail and newspapers are reshaped, redefined, or even bypassed by the Internet, giving birth to new services such as email, Internet telephony, Internet television, online music, digital newspapers, and video streaming websites. Newspaper, book, and other print publishing are adapting to website technology, or are reshaped into blogging, web feeds and online news aggregators. The Internet has enabled and accelerated new forms of personal interactions through instant messaging, Internet forums, and social networking. Online shopping has grown exponentially both for major retailers and small businesses and entrepreneurs, as it enables firms to extend their "brick and mortar" presence to serve a larger market or even sell goods and services entirely online. Business-to-business and financial services on the Internet affect supply chainsacross entire industries.

The Internet has no centralized governance in either technological implementation or policies for access and usage; each constituent network sets its own policies. Only the overreaching definitions of the two principal name spaces in the Internet, the Internet Protocol address (IP address) space and the Domain Name System (DNS), are directed by a maintainer organization, the Internet Corporation for Assigned Names and Numbers (ICANN). The technical underpinning and standardization of the core protocols is an activity of the Internet Engineering Task Force (IETF), a non-profit organization of loosely affiliated international participants that anyone may associate with by contributing technical expertise. In November 2006, the Internet was included on USA Today's list of New Seven Wonders.

The Internet Messenger by Buky Schwartz, located in Holon, Israel

When the term Internet is used to refer to the specific global system of interconnected Internet Protocol (IP) networks, the word is a proper noun that should be written with an initial capital letter. In common use and the media, it is often erroneously not capitalized, viz. the internet. Some guides specify that the word should be capitalized when used as a noun, but not capitalized when used as an adjective. The Internet is also often referred to as the Net, as a short form of network. Historically, as early as 1849, the word internetted was used uncapitalized as an adjective, meaning interconnected or interwoven. The designers of early computer networks used internet both as a noun and as a verb in shorthand form of internetwork or internetworking, meaning interconnecting computer networks.

The terms Internet and World Wide Web are often used interchangeably in everyday speech; it is common to speak of "going on the Internet" when using a web browser to view web pages. However, the World Wide Web or the Web is only one of a large number of Internet services. The Web is a collection of interconnected documents (web pages) and other web resources, linked by hyperlinks and URLs. As another point of comparison, Hypertext Transfer Protocol, or HTTP, is the language used on the Web for information transfer, yet it is just one of many languages or protocols that can be used for communication on the Internet. The term Interweb is a portmanteau of Internet and World Wide Web typically used sarcastically to parody a technically unsavvy user.

History

Main articles: History of the Internet and History of the World Wide Web

Research into packet switching, one of the fundamental Internet technologies started in the early 1960s in the work of Paul Baran, and packet switched networks such as the NPL network by Donald Davies, ARPANET, Tymnet, the Merit Network, Telenet, and CYCLADES, were developed in the late 1960s and 1970s using a variety of protocols.The ARPANET project led to the development of protocols for internetworking, by which multiple separate networks could be joined into a network of networks. ARPANET development began with two network nodes which were interconnected between the Network Measurement Center at the University of California, Los Angeles (UCLA) Henry Samueli School of Engineering and Applied Science directed by Leonard Kleinrock, and the NLS system at SRI International (SRI) by Douglas Engelbart in Menlo Park, California, on 29 October 1969. The third site was the Culler-Fried Interactive Mathematics Center at the University of California, Santa Barbara, followed by the University of Utah Graphics Department. In an early sign of future growth, fifteen sites were connected to the young ARPANET by the end of 1971. These early years were documented in the 1972 film Computer Networks: The Heralds of Resource Sharing.

Early international collaborations on the ARPANET were rare. European developers were concerned with developing the X.25 networks. Notable exceptions were the Norwegian Seismic Array (NORSAR) in June 1973, followed in 1973 by Sweden with satellite links to the Tanum Earth Station and Peter T. Kirstein's research group in the United Kingdom, initially at the Institute of Computer Science, University of London and later at University College London. In December 1974, RFC 675 (Specification of Internet Transmission Control Program), by Vinton Cerf, Yogen Dalal, and Carl Sunshine, used the term internet as a shorthand for internetworking and later RFCs repeated this use.Access to the ARPANET was expanded in 1981 when the National Science Foundation (NSF) funded the Computer Science Network (CSNET). In 1982, the Internet Protocol Suite(TCP/IP) was standardized, which permitted worldwide proliferation of interconnected networks.

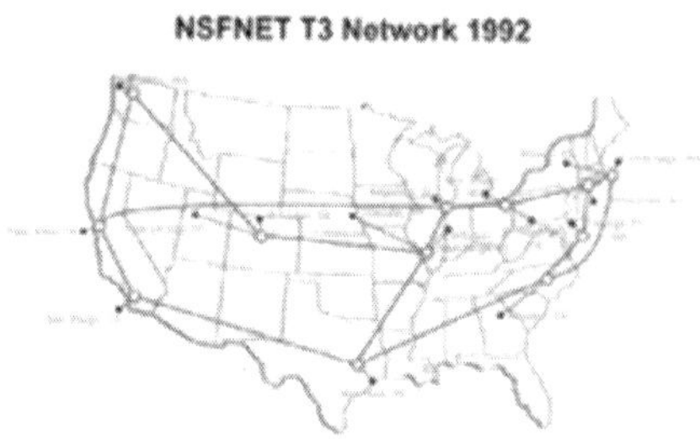

T3 NSFNET Backbone, c. 1992.

TCP/IP network access expanded again in 1986 when the National Science Foundation Network (NSFNet) provided access to supercomputer sites in the United States for researchers, first at speeds of 56 kbit/s and later at 1.5 Mbit/s and 45 Mbit/s. Commercial Internet service providers (ISPs) emerged in the late 1980s and early 1990s. The ARPANET was decommissioned in 1990. Stanford Federal Credit Union was the first financial institution to offer online internet banking services to all of its members in October 1994. In 1996 OP Financial Group, also a cooperative bank, became the second online bank in the world and the first in Europe. By 1995, the Internet was fully commercialized in the U.S. when the NSFNet was decommissioned, removing the last restrictions on use of the Internet to carry commercial traffic. The Internet rapidly expanded in Europe and Australia in the mid to late 1980s and to Asia in the late 1980s and early 1990s. The beginning of dedicated transatlantic communication between the NSFNET and networks in Europe was established with a low-speed satellite relay between Princeton University and Stockholm, Sweden in December 1988. Although other network protocols such as UUCP had global reach well before this time, this marked the beginning of the Internet as an intercontinental network.

Public commercial use of the Internet began in mid-1989 with the connection of MCI Mail and Compuserve's email capabilities to the 500,000 users of the Internet. Just months later on 1 January 1990, PSInet launched an alternate Internet backbone for commercial use; one of the networks that would grow into the commercial Internet we know today. In March 1990, the first high-speed T1 (1.5 Mbit/s) link between the NSFNET and Europe was installed between Cornell University and CERN, allowing much more robust communications than were capable with satellites. Six months later Tim Berners-Lee would begin writing WorldWideWeb, the first web browser after two years of lobbying CERN management. By Christmas 1990, Berners-Lee had built all the tools necessary for a working Web: the HyperText Transfer Protocol (HTTP) 0.9, the HyperText Markup Language(HTML), the first Web browser (which was also a HTML editor and could access Usenet newsgroups and FTP files), the first HTTP server software (later known as CERN httpd), the first web server, and the first Web pages that described the project itself. In 1991 the Commercial Internet eXchange was founded, allowing PSInet to communicate with the other commercial networks CERFnet and Alternet. Since 1995 the Internet has tremendously impacted culture and commerce, including the rise of near instant communication by email, instant messaging, telephony (Voice over Internet Protocol or VoIP), two-way interactive video calls, and the World Wide Web with its discussion forums, blogs, social networking, and online shopping sites. Increasing amounts of data are transmitted at higher and higher speeds over fiber optic networks operating at 1-Gbit/s, 10-Gbit/s, or more.

The Internet continues to grow, driven by ever greater amounts of online information and knowledge, commerce, entertainment and social networking. During the late 1990s, it was estimated that traffic on the public Internet grew by 100 percent per year, while the mean annual growth in the number of Internet users was thought to be between 20% and 50%. This growth is often attributed to the lack of central administration, which allows organic growth of the network, as well as the non-proprietary nature of the Internet protocols, which encourages vendor interoperability and prevents any one company from exerting too much control over the network. As of 31 March 2011, the estimated total number of Internet users was 2.095 billion (30.2% of world population). It is estimated that in 1993 the Internet carried only 1% of the information flowing through two-way telecommunication, by 2000 this figure had grown to 51%, and by 2007 more than 97% of all telecommunicated information was carried over the Internet.

Governance

ICANN headquarters in the Playa Vista neighborhood of Los Angeles, California, United States.

The Internet is a global network that comprises many voluntarily interconnected autonomous networks. It operates without a central governing body. The technical underpinning and standardization of the core protocols (IPv4 and IPv6) is an activity of the Internet Engineering Task Force (IETF), a non-profit organization of loosely affiliated international participants that anyone may associate with by contributing technical expertise. To maintain interoperability, the principal name spaces of the Internet are administered by the Internet Corporation for Assigned Names and Numbers (ICANN). ICANN is governed by an international board of directors drawn from across the Internet technical, business, academic, and other non-commercial communities. ICANN coordinates the assignment of unique identifiers for use on the Internet, including domain names, Internet Protocol (IP) addresses, application port numbers in the transport protocols, and many other parameters. Globally unified name spaces are essential for maintaining the global reach of the Internet. This role of ICANN distinguishes it as perhaps the only central coordinating body for the global Internet.

Regional Internet Registries (RIRs) allocate IP addresses:

- African Network Information Center (AfriNIC) for Africa
- American Registry for Internet Numbers (ARIN) for North America
- Asia-Pacific Network Information Centre (APNIC) for Asia and the Pacific region
- Latin American and Caribbean Internet Addresses Registry (LACNIC) for Latin America and the Caribbean region
- Réseaux IP Européens – Network Coordination Centre (RIPE NCC) for Europe, the Middle East, and Central Asia

The National Telecommunications and Information Administration, an agency of the United States Department of Commerce, had final approval over changes to the DNS root zoneuntil the IANA stewardship transition on 1 October 2016. The Internet Society (ISOC) was founded in 1992 with a mission to "assure the open development, evolution and use of the Internet for the benefit of all people throughout the world". Its members include individuals (anyone may join) as well as corporations, organizations, governments, and universities. Among other activities ISOC provides an administrative home for a number of less formally organized groups that are involved in developing and managing the Internet, including: the Internet Engineering Task Force (IETF), Internet Architecture Board (IAB), Internet Engineering Steering Group (IESG), Internet Research Task Force (IRTF), and Internet Research Steering Group (IRSG). On 16 November 2005, the United Nations-sponsored World Summit on the Information Society in Tunis established the Internet Governance Forum (IGF) to discuss Internet-related issues.

Infrastructure

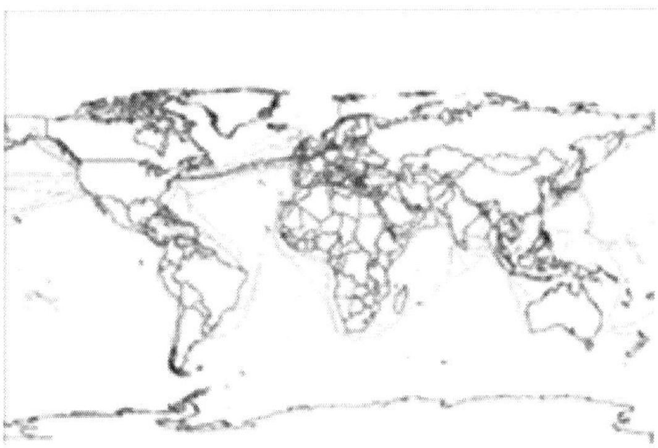

2007 map showing submarine fiberoptic telecommunication cables around the world.

The communications infrastructure of the Internet consists of its hardware components and a system of software layers that control various aspects of the architecture.

Routing and service tiers

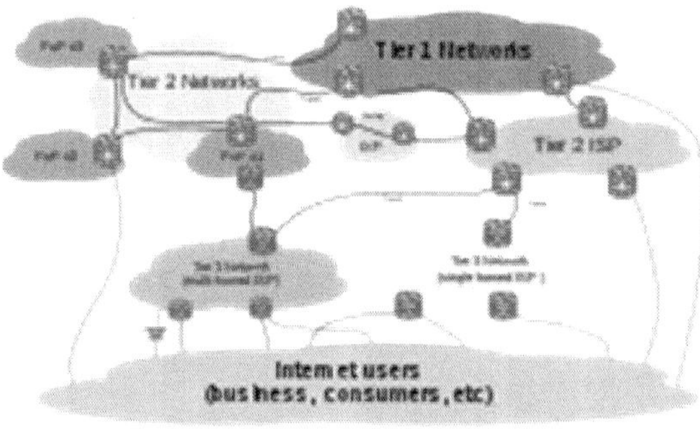

Packet routing across the Internet involves several tiers of Internet service providers.

Internet service providers (ISPs) establish the worldwide connectivity between individual networks at various levels of scope. End-users who only access the Internet when needed to perform a function or obtain information, represent the bottom of the routing hierarchy. At the top of the routing hierarchy are the tier 1 networks, large telecommunication companies that exchange traffic directly with each other via very high speed fibre optic cables and governed by peering agreements. Tier 2 and lower level networks buy Internet transit from other providers to reach at least some parties on the global Internet, though they may also engage in peering. An ISP may use a single upstream provider for connectivity, or implement multihoming to achieve redundancy and load balancing. Internet exchange points are major traffic exchanges with physical connections to multiple ISPs. Large organizations, such as academic institutions, large enterprises, and governments, may perform the same function as ISPs, engaging in peering and purchasing transit on behalf of their internal networks. Research networks tend to interconnect with large subnetworks such as GEANT, GLORIAD, Internet2, and the UK's national research and education network, JANET. Both the Internet IP routing structure and hypertext links of the World Wide Web are examples of scale-free networks. Computers and routers use routing tables in their operating system to direct IP packets to the next-hop router or destination. Routing tables are maintained by manual configuration or automatically by routing protocols. End-nodes typically use a default route that points toward an ISP providing transit, while ISP routers use the Border Gateway Protocol to establish the most efficient routing across the complex connections of the global Internet.

An estimated 70 percent of the world's Internet traffic passes through Ashburn, Virginia.

Access

Common methods of Internet access by users include dial-up with a computer modem via telephone circuits, broadband over coaxial cable, fiber optics or copper wires, Wi-Fi, satellite, and cellular telephone technology (e.g. 3G, 4G). The Internet may often be accessed from computers in libraries and Internet cafes. Internet access points exist in many public places such as airport halls and coffee shops. Various terms are used, such as public Internet kiosk, public access terminal, and Web payphone. Many hotels also have public terminals that are usually fee-based. These terminals are widely accessed for various usages, such as ticket booking, bank deposit, or online payment. Wi-Fi provides wireless access to the Internet via local computer networks. Hotspots providing such access include Wi-Fi cafes, where users need to bring their own wireless devices such as a laptop or PDA. These services may be free to all, free to customers only, or fee-based.

Grassroots efforts have led to wireless community networks. Commercial Wi-Fi services covering large city areas are in many cities, such as New York, London, Vienna, Toronto, San Francisco, Philadelphia, Chicago and Pittsburgh. The Internet can then be accessed from places, such as a park bench. Apart from Wi-Fi, there have been experiments with proprietary mobile wireless networks like Ricochet, various high-speed data services over cellular phone networks, and fixed wireless services. High-end mobile phones such as smartphones in general come with Internet access through the phone network. Web browsers such as Opera are available on these advanced handsets, which can also run a wide variety of other Internet software. Internet usage by mobile and tablet devices exceeded desktop worldwide for the first time in October 2016. An Internet access provider and protocol matrix differentiates the methods used to get online.

Internet and mobile

Number of mobile cellular subscriptions 2012–2016, World Trends in Freedom of Expression and Media Development Global Report 2017/2018

According to the International Telecommunication Union (ITU), by the end of 2017, an estimated 48 per cent of individuals regularly connect to the internet, up from 34 per cent in 2012. Mobile internet connectivity has played an important role in expanding access in recent years especially in Asia and the Pacific and in Africa. The number of unique mobile cellular subscriptions increased from 3.89 billion in 2012 to 4.83 billion in 2016, two-thirds of the world's population, with more than half of subscriptions located in Asia and the Pacific. The number of subscriptions is predicted to rise to 5.69 billion users in 2020. As of 2016, almost 60 per cent of the world's population had access to a 4G broadband cellular network, up from almost 50 per cent in 2015 and 11 per cent in 2012. The limits that users face on accessing information via mobile applications coincide with a broader process of fragmentation of the internet. Fragmentation restricts access to media content and tends to affect poorest users the most.

Zero-rating, the practice of internet providers allowing users free connectivity to access specific content or applications for free, has offered some opportunities for individuals to surmount economic hurdles, but has also been accused by its critics as creating a 'two-tiered' internet. To address the issues with zero-rating, an alternative model has emerged in the concept of 'equal rating' and is being tested in experiments by Mozilla and Orange in Africa. Equal rating prevents prioritization of one type of content and zero-rates all content up to a specified data cap. A study published by Chatham House, 15 out of 19 countries researched in Latin America had some kind of hybrid or zero-rated product offered. Some countries in the region had a handful of plans to choose from (across all mobile network operators) while others, such as Colombia, offered as many as 30 pre-paid and 34 post-paid plans.

A study of eight countries in the Global South found that zero-rated data plans exist in every country, although there is a great range in the frequency with which they are offered and actually used in each. Across the 181 plans examined, 13 per cent were offering zero-rated services. Another study, covering Ghana, Kenya, Nigeria and South Africa, found Facebook's Free Basics and Wikipedia Zero to be the most commonly zero-rated content.

Protocols

While the hardware components in the Internet infrastructure can often be used to support other software systems, it is the design and the standardization process of the software that characterizes the Internet and provides the foundation for its scalability and success. The responsibility for the architectural design of the Internet software systems has been assumed by the Internet Engineering Task Force (IETF). The IETF conducts standard-setting work groups, open to any individual, about the various aspects of Internet architecture. Resulting contributions and standards are published as Request for Comments (RFC) documents on the IETF web site. The principal methods of networking that enable the Internet are contained in specially designated RFCs that constitute the Internet Standards. Other less rigorous documents are simply informative, experimental, or historical, or document the best current practices (BCP) when implementing Internet technologies.

The Internet standards describe a framework known as the Internet protocol suite. This is a model architecture that divides methods into a layered system of protocols, originally documented in RFC 1122 and RFC 1123. The layers correspond to the environment or scope in which their services operate. At the top is the application layer, space for the application-specific networking methods used in software applications. For example, a web browser program uses the client-server application model and a specific protocol of interaction between servers and clients, while many file-sharing systems use a peer-to-peer paradigm. Below this top layer, the transport layer connects applications on different hosts with a logical channel through the network with appropriate data exchange methods.

Underlying these layers are the networking technologies that interconnect networks at their borders and exchange traffic across them. The Internet layer enables computers ("hosts") to identify each other via Internet Protocol (IP) addresses, and route their traffic to each other via any intermediate (transit) networks. Last, at the bottom of the architecture is the link layer, which provides logical connectivity between hosts on the same network link, such as a local area network (LAN) or a dial-up connection. The model, also known as TCP/IP, is designed to be independent of the underlying hardware used for the physical connections, which the model does not concern itself with in any detail. Other models have been developed, such as the OSI model, that attempt to be comprehensive in every aspect of communications. While many similarities exist between the models, they are not compatible in the details of description or implementation. Yet, TCP/IP protocols are usually included in the discussion of OSI networking.

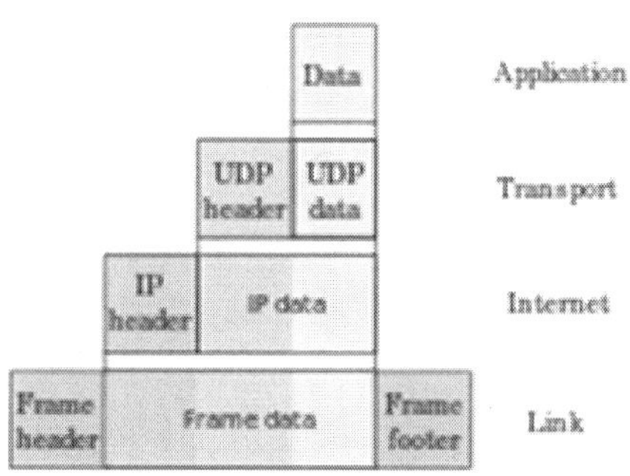

As user data is processed through the protocol stack, each abstraction layer adds encapsulation information at the sending host. Data is transmitted over the wire at the link level between hosts and routers. Encapsulation is removed by the receiving host. Intermediate relays update link encapsulation at each hop, and inspect the IP layer for routing purposes.

The most prominent component of the Internet model is the Internet Protocol (IP), which provides addressing systems, including IP addresses, for computers on the network. IP enables internetworking and, in essence, establishes the Internet itself. Internet Protocol Version 4 (IPv4) is the initial version used on the first generation of the Internet and is still in dominant use. It was designed to address up to ~4.3 billion (10) hosts. However, the explosive growth of the Internet has led to IPv4 address exhaustion, which entered its final stage in 2011, when the global address allocation pool was exhausted. A new protocol version, IPv6, was developed in the mid-1990s, which provides vastly larger addressing capabilities and more efficient routing of Internet traffic. IPv6 is currently in growing deployment around the world, since Internet address registries (RIRs) began to urge all resource managers to plan rapid adoption and conversion.

IPv6 is not directly interoperable by design with IPv4. In essence, it establishes a parallel version of the Internet not directly accessible with IPv4 software. Thus, translation facilities must exist for internetworking or nodes must have duplicate networking software for both networks. Essentially all modern computer operating systems support both versions of the Internet Protocol. Network infrastructure, however, has been lagging in this development. Aside from the complex array of physical connections that make up its infrastructure, the Internet is facilitated by bi- or multi-lateral commercial contracts, e.g., peering agreements, and by technical specifications or protocols that describe the exchange of data over the network. Indeed, the Internet is defined by its interconnections and routing policies.

Services

Many people use, erroneously, the terms Internet and World Wide Web, or just the Web, interchangeably, but the two terms are not synonymous. The World Wide Web is a primary application program that billions of people use on the Internet, and it has changed their lives immeasurably. However, the Internet provides many network services, most prominently include mobile apps such as social media apps, the World Wide Web, electronic mail, multiplayer online games, Internet telephony, and file sharing and streaming media services.

World Wide Web

This NeXT Computer was used by Tim Berners-Lee at CERN and became the world's first Web server.

World Wide Web browser software, such as Microsoft's Internet Explorer/Edge, Mozilla Firefox, Opera, Apple's Safari, and Google Chrome, lets users navigate from one web page to another via hyperlinks embedded in the documents. These documents may also contain any combination of computer data, including graphics, sounds, text, video, multimedia and interactive content that runs while the user is interacting with the page. Client-side software can include animations, games, office applications and scientific demonstrations. Through keyword-driven Internet research using search engines like Yahoo!, Bing and Google, users worldwide have easy, instant access to a vast and diverse amount of online information. Compared to printed media, books, encyclopedias and traditional libraries, the World Wide Web has enabled the decentralization of information on a large scale.

The Web is therefore a global set of documents, images and other resources, logically interrelated by hyperlinks and referenced with Uniform Resource Identifiers (URIs). URIs symbolically identify services, servers, and other databases, and the documents and resources that they can provide. Hypertext Transfer Protocol (HTTP) is the main access protocol of the World Wide Web. Web services also use HTTP to allow software systems to communicate in order to share and exchange business logic and data.

The Web has enabled individuals and organizations to publish ideas and information to a potentially large audience online at greatly reduced expense and time delay. Publishing a web page, a blog, or building a website involves little initial cost and many cost-free services are available. However, publishing and maintaining large, professional web sites with attractive, diverse and up-to-date information is still a difficult and expensive proposition. Many individuals and some companies and groups use web logs or blogs, which are largely used as easily updatable online diaries. Some commercial organizations encourage staff to communicate advice in their areas of specialization in the hope that visitors will be impressed by the expert knowledge and free information, and be attracted to the corporation as a result.

Advertising on popular web pages can be lucrative, and e-commerce, which is the sale of products and services directly via the Web, continues to grow. Online advertising is a form of marketing and advertising which uses the Internet to deliver promotional marketing messages to consumers. It includes email marketing, search engine marketing (SEM), social media marketing, many types of display advertising (including web banner advertising), and mobile advertising. In 2011, Internet advertising revenues in the United States surpassed those of cable television and nearly exceeded those of broadcast television. Many common online advertising practices are controversial and increasingly subject to regulation.

When the Web developed in the 1990s, a typical web page was stored in completed form on a web server, formatted in HTML, complete for transmission to a web browser in response to a request. Over time, the process of creating and serving web pages has become dynamic, creating a flexible design, layout, and content. Websites are often created using content management software with, initially, very little content. Contributors to these systems, who may be paid staff, members of an organization or the public, fill underlying databases with content using editing pages designed for that purpose while casual visitors view and read this content in HTML form. There may or may not be editorial, approval and security systems built into the process of taking newly entered content and making it available to the target visitors.

Communication

Email is an important communications service available on the Internet. The concept of sending electronic text messages between parties in a way analogous to mailing letters or memos predates the creation of the Internet. Pictures, documents, and other files are sent as email attachments. Emails can be cc-ed to multiple email addresses.

Internet telephony is another common communications service made possible by the creation of the Internet. VoIP stands for Voice-over-Internet Protocol, referring to the protocol that underlies all Internet communication. The idea began in the early 1990s with walkie-talkie-like voice applications for personal computers. In recent years many VoIP systems have become as easy to use and as convenient as a normal telephone. The benefit is that, as the Internet carries the voice traffic, VoIP can be free or cost much less than a traditional telephone call, especially over long distances and especially for those with always-on Internet connections such as cable or ADSL and mobile data. VoIP is maturing into a competitive alternative to traditional telephone service. Interoperability between different providers has improved and the ability to call or receive a call from a traditional telephone is available. Simple, inexpensive VoIP network adapters are available that eliminate the need for a personal computer.

Voice quality can still vary from call to call, but is often equal to and can even exceed that of traditional calls. Remaining problems for VoIP include emergency telephone numberdialing and reliability. Currently, a few VoIP providers provide an emergency service, but it is not universally available. Older traditional phones with no "extra features" may be line-powered only and operate during a power failure; VoIP can never do so without a backup power source for the phone equipment and the Internet access devices. VoIP has also become increasingly popular for gaming applications, as a form of communication between players. Popular VoIP clients for gaming include Ventrilo and Teamspeak. Modern video game consoles also offer VoIP chat features.

Data transfer

File sharing is an example of transferring large amounts of data across the Internet. A computer file can be emailed to customers, colleagues and friends as an attachment. It can be uploaded to a website or File Transfer Protocol (FTP) server for easy download by others. It can be put into a "shared location" or onto a file server for instant use by colleagues. The load of bulk downloads to many users can be eased by the use of "mirror" servers or peer-to-peer networks. In any of these cases, access to the file may be controlled by user authentication, the transit of the file over the Internet may be obscured by encryption, and money may change hands for access to the file. The price can be paid by the remote charging of funds from, for example, a credit card whose details are also passed – usually fully encrypted – across the Internet. The origin and authenticity of the file received may be checked by digital signatures or by MD5 or other message digests. These simple features of the Internet, over a worldwide basis, are changing the production, sale, and distribution of anything that can be reduced to a computer file for transmission. This includes all manner of print publications, software products, news, music, film, video, photography, graphics and the other arts. This in turn has caused seismic shifts in each of the existing industries that previously controlled the production and distribution of these products.

Streaming media is the real-time delivery of digital media for the immediate consumption or enjoyment by end users. Many radio and television broadcasters provide Internet feeds of their live audio and video productions. They may also allow time-shift viewing or listening such as Preview, Classic Clips and Listen Again features. These providers have been joined by a range of pure Internet "broadcasters" who never had on-air licenses. This means that an Internet-connected device, such as a computer or something more specific, can be used to access on-line media in much the same way as was previously possible only with a television or radio receiver. The range of available types of content is much wider, from specialized technical webcasts to on-demand popular multimedia services. Podcasting is a variation on this theme, where – usually audio – material is downloaded and played back on a computer or shifted to a portable media player to be listened to on the move. These techniques using simple equipment allow anybody, with little censorship or licensing control, to broadcast audio-visual material worldwide.

Digital media streaming increases the demand for network bandwidth. For example, standard image quality needs 1 Mbit/s link speed for SD 480p, HD 720p quality requires 2.5 Mbit/s, and the top-of-the-line HDX quality needs 4.5 Mbit/s for 1080p.

Webcams are a low-cost extension of this phenomenon. While some webcams can give full-frame-rate video, the picture either is usually small or updates slowly. Internet users can watch animals around an African waterhole, ships in the Panama Canal, traffic at a local roundabout or monitor their own premises, live and in real time. Video chat rooms and video conferencing are also popular with many uses being found for personal webcams, with and without two-way sound. YouTube was founded on 15 February 2005 and is now the leading website for free streaming video with a vast number of users. It uses a HTML5 based web player by default to stream and show video files. Registered users may upload an unlimited amount of video and build their own personal profile. YouTube claims that its users watch hundreds of millions, and upload hundreds of thousands of videos daily.

Social impact

The Internet has enabled new forms of social interaction, activities, and social associations. This phenomenon has given rise to the scholarly study of the sociology of the Internet.

Users

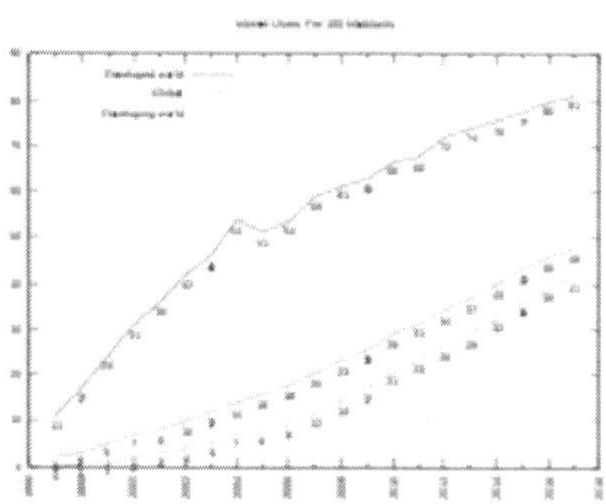

Internet users per 100 inhabitants

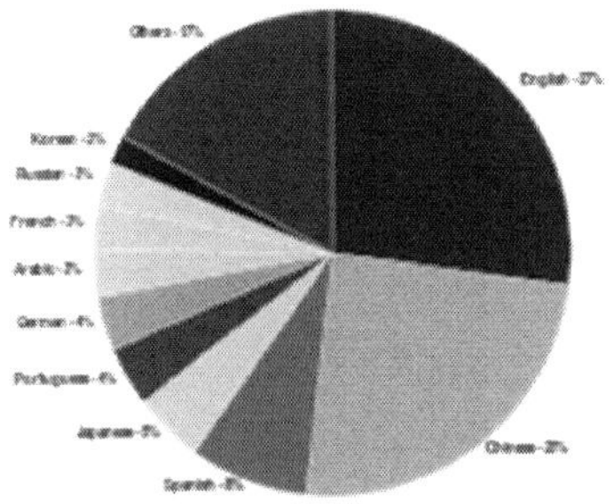

Internet users by language

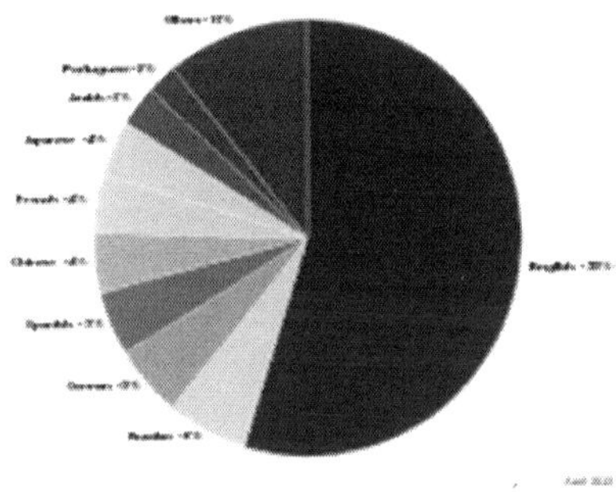

Website content languages

Internet usage has seen tremendous growth. From 2000 to 2009, the number of Internet users globally rose from 394 million to 1.858 billion. By 2010, 22 percent of the world's population had access to computers with 1 billion Google searches every day, 300 million Internet users reading blogs, and 2 billion videos viewed daily on YouTube. In 2014 the world's Internet users surpassed 3 billion or 43.6 percent of world population, but two-thirds of the users came from richest countries, with 78.0 percent of Europe countries population using the Internet, followed by 57.4 percent of the Americas.

The prevalent language for communication on the Internet has been English. This may be a result of the origin of the Internet, as well as the language's role as a lingua franca. Early computer systems were limited to the characters in the American Standard Code for Information Interchange (ASCII), a subset of the Latin alphabet.

After English (27%), the most requested languages on the World Wide Web are Chinese (25%), Spanish (8%), Japanese (5%), Portuguese and German (4% each), Arabic, French and Russian (3% each), and Korean (2%). By region, 42% of the world's Internet users are based in Asia, 24% in Europe, 14% in North America, 10% in Latin America and the Caribbean taken together, 6% in Africa, 3% in the Middle East and 1% in Australia/Oceania. The Internet's technologies have developed enough in recent years, especially in the use of

Unicode, that good facilities are available for development and communication in the world's widely used languages. However, some glitches such as mojibake (incorrect display of some languages' characters) still remain.

In an American study in 2005, the percentage of men using the Internet was very slightly ahead of the percentage of women, although this difference reversed in those under 30. Men logged on more often, spent more time online, and were more likely to be broadband users, whereas women tended to make more use of opportunities to communicate (such as email). Men were more likely to use the Internet to pay bills, participate in auctions, and for recreation such as downloading music and videos. Men and women were equally likely to use the Internet for shopping and banking. More recent studies indicate that in 2008, women significantly outnumbered men on most social networking sites, such as Facebook and Myspace, although the ratios varied with age. In addition, women watched more streaming content, whereas men downloaded more. In terms of blogs, men were more likely to blog in the first place; among those who blog, men were more likely to have a professional blog, whereas women were more likely to have a personal blog.

Forecasts predict that 44% of the world's population will be users of the Internet by 2020. Splitting by country, in 2012 Iceland, Norway, Sweden, the Netherlands, and Denmark had the highest Internet penetration by the number of users, with 93% or more of the population with access.

Several neologisms exist that refer to Internet users: Netizen (as in "citizen of the net") refers to those actively involved in improving online communities, the Internet in general or surrounding political affairs and rights such as free speech, Internaut refers to operators or technically highly capable users of the Internet, digital citizen refers to a person using the Internet in order to engage in society, politics, and government participation.

Usage

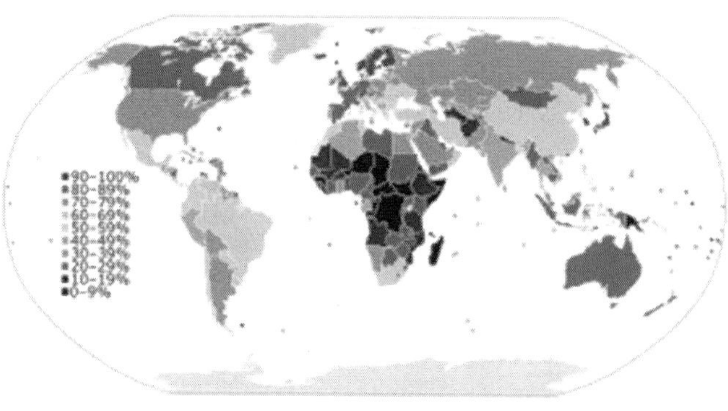

Internet users in 2015 as a percentage of a country's population

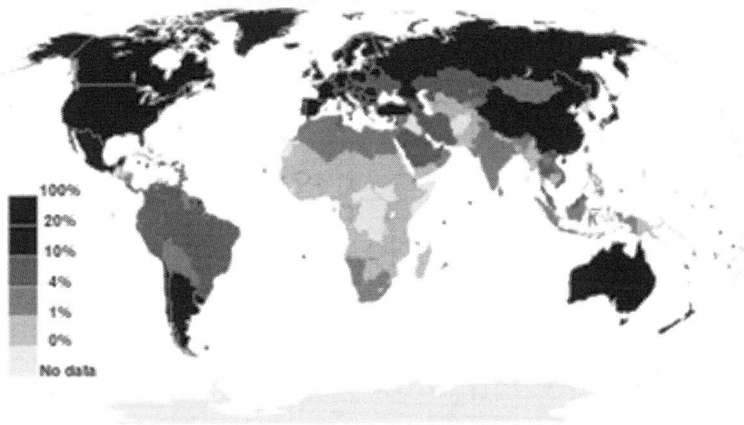

Fixed broadband Internet subscriptions in 2012

The Internet allows greater flexibility in working hours and location, especially with the spread of unmetered high-speed connections. The Internet can be accessed almost anywhere by numerous means, including through mobile Internet devices. Mobile phones, datacards, handheld game consoles and cellular routers allow users to connect to the Internet wirelessly. Within the limitations imposed by small screens and other limited facilities of such pocket-sized devices, the services of the Internet, including email and the web, may be available. Service providers may restrict the services offered and mobile data charges may be significantly higher than other access methods.

Educational material at all levels from pre-school to post-doctoral is available from websites. Examples range from CBeebies, through school and high-school revision guides and virtual universities, to access to top-end scholarly literature through the likes of Google Scholar. For distance education, help with homework and other assignments, self-guided learning, whiling away spare time, or just looking up more detail on an interesting fact, it has never been easier for people to access educational information at any level from anywhere. The Internet in general and the World Wide Web in particular are important enablers of both formal and informal education. Further, the Internet allows universities, in particular, researchers from the social and behavioral sciences, to conduct research remotely via virtual laboratories, with profound changes in reach and generalizability of findings as well as in communication between scientists and in the publication of results.

The low cost and nearly instantaneous sharing of ideas, knowledge, and skills have made collaborative work dramatically easier, with the help of collaborative software. Not only can a group cheaply communicate and share ideas but the wide reach of the Internet allows such groups more easily to form. An example of this is the free software movement, which has produced, among other things, Linux, Mozilla Firefox, and OpenOffice.org (later forked into LibreOffice). Internet chat, whether using an IRC chat room, an instant messaging system, or a social networkingwebsite, allows colleagues to stay in touch in a very convenient way while working at their computers during the day. Messages can be exchanged even more quickly and conveniently than via email. These systems may allow files to be exchanged, drawings and images to be shared, or voice and video contact between team members.

Content management systems allow collaborating teams to work on shared sets of documents simultaneously without accidentally destroying each other's work. Business and project teams can share calendars as well as documents and other information. Such collaboration occurs in a wide variety of areas including scientific research, software development, conference planning, political activism and creative writing. Social and political collaboration is also becoming more widespread as both Internet access and computer literacy spread.

The Internet allows computer users to remotely access other computers and information stores easily from any access point. Access may be with computer security, i.e. authentication and encryption technologies, depending on the requirements. This is encouraging new ways of working from home, collaboration and information sharing in many industries. An accountant sitting at home can audit the books of a company based in another country, on a serversituated in a third country that is remotely maintained by IT specialists in a fourth. These accounts could have been created by home-working bookkeepers, in other remote locations, based on information emailed to them from offices all over the world. Some of these things were possible before the widespread use of the Internet, but the cost of private leased lines would have made many of them infeasible in practice. An office worker away from their desk, perhaps on the other side of the world on a business trip or a holiday, can access their emails, access their data using cloud computing, or open a remote desktop session into their office PC using a secure virtual private network (VPN) connection on the Internet. This can give the worker complete access to all of their normal files and data, including email and other applications, while away from the office. It has been referred to among system administrators as the Virtual Private Nightmare, because it extends the secure perimeter of a corporate network into remote locations and its employees' homes.

Social networking and entertainment

Many people use the World Wide Web to access news, weather and sports reports, to plan and book vacations and to pursue their personal interests. People use chat, messaging and email to make and stay in touch with friends worldwide, sometimes in the same way as some previously had pen pals. Social networking websites such as Facebook, Twitter, and Myspace have created new ways to socialize and interact. Users of these sites are able to add a wide variety of information to pages, to pursue common interests, and to connect with others. It is also possible to find existing acquaintances, to allow communication among existing groups of people. Sites like LinkedIn foster commercial and business connections. YouTube and Flickr specialize in users' videos and photographs. While social networking sites were initially for individuals only, today they are widely used by businesses and other organizations to promote their brands, to market to their customers and to encourage posts to "go viral". "Black hat" social media techniques are also employed by some organizations, such as spam accounts and astroturfing.

A risk for both individuals and organizations writing posts (especially public posts) on social networking websites, is that especially foolish or controversial posts occasionally lead to an unexpected and possibly large-scale backlash on social media from other Internet users. This is also a risk in relation to controversial offline behavior, if it is widely made known. The nature of this backlash can range widely from counter-arguments and public mockery, through insults and hate speech, to, in extreme cases, rape and death threats. The online disinhibition effect describes the tendency of many individuals to behave more stridently or offensively online than they would in person. A significant number of feminist women have been the target of various forms of harassment in response to posts they have made on social media, and Twitter in particular has been criticised in the past for not doing enough to aid victims of online abuse.

For organizations, such a backlash can cause overall brand damage, especially if reported by the media. However, this is not always the case, as any brand damage in the eyes of people with an opposing opinion to that presented by the organization could sometimes be outweighed by strengthening the brand in the eyes of others. Furthermore, if an organization or individual gives in to demands that others perceive as wrong-headed, that can then provoke a counter-backlash.

Some websites, such as Reddit, have rules forbidding the posting of personal information of individuals (also known as doxxing), due to concerns about such postings leading to mobs of large numbers of Internet users directing harassment at the specific individuals thereby identified. In particular, the Reddit rule forbidding the posting of personal information is widely understood to imply that all identifying photos and names must be censored in Facebook screenshots posted to Reddit. However, the interpretation of this rule in relation to public Twitter posts is less clear, and in any case, like-minded people online have many other ways they can use to direct each other's attention to public social media posts they disagree with.

Children also face dangers online such as cyberbullying and approaches by sexual predators, who sometimes pose as children themselves. Children may also encounter material which they may find upsetting, or material which their parents consider to be not age-appropriate. Due to naivety, they may also post personal information about themselves online, which could put them or their families at risk unless warned not to do so. Many parents choose to enable Internet filtering, and/or supervise their children's online activities, in an attempt to protect their children from inappropriate material on the Internet. The most popular social networking websites, such as Facebook and Twitter, commonly forbid users under the age of 13. However, these policies are typically trivial to circumvent by registering an account with a false birth date, and a significant number of children aged under 13 join such sites anyway. Social networking sites for younger children, which claim to provide better levels of protection for children, also exist.

The Internet has been a major outlet for leisure activity since its inception, with entertaining social experiments such as MUDs and MOOs being conducted on university servers, and humor-related Usenet groups receiving much traffic. Many Internet forums have sections devoted to games and funny videos. The Internet pornographyand online gambling industries have taken advantage of the World Wide Web, and often provide a significant source of advertising revenue for other websites. Although many governments have attempted to restrict both industries' use of the Internet, in general, this has failed to stop their widespread popularity.

Another area of leisure activity on the Internet is multiplayer gaming. This form of recreation creates communities, where people of all ages and origins enjoy the fast-paced world of multiplayer games. These range from MMORPG to first-person shooters, from role-playing video games to online gambling. While online gaming has been around since the 1970s, modern modes of online gaming began with subscription services such as GameSpy and MPlayer. Non-subscribers were limited to certain types of game play or certain games. Many people use the Internet to access and download music, movies and other works for their enjoyment and relaxation. Free and fee-based services exist for all of these activities, using centralized servers and distributed peer-to-peer technologies. Some of these sources exercise more care with respect to the original artists' copyrights than others.

Internet usage has been correlated to users' loneliness. Lonely people tend to use the Internet as an outlet for their feelings and to share their stories with others, such as in the "I am lonely will anyone speak to me" thread.

Cybersectarianism is a new organizational form which involves: "highly dispersed small groups of practitioners that may remain largely anonymous within the larger social context and operate in relative secrecy, while still linked remotely to a larger network of believers who share a set of practices and texts, and often a common devotion to a particular leader. Overseas supporters provide funding and support; domestic practitioners distribute tracts, participate in acts of resistance, and share information on the internal situation with outsiders. Collectively, members and practitioners of such sects construct viable virtual communities of faith, exchanging personal testimonies and engaging in the collective study via email, on-line chat rooms, and web-based message boards." In particular, the British government has raised concerns about the prospect of young British Muslims being indoctrinated into Islamic extremism by material on the Internet, being persuaded to join terrorist groups such as the so-called "Islamic State", and then potentially committing acts of terrorism on returning to Britain after fighting in Syria or Iraq.

Cyberslacking can become a drain on corporate resources; the average UK employee spent 57 minutes a day surfing the Web while at work, according to a 2003 study by Peninsula Business Services. Internet addiction disorder is excessive computer use that interferes with daily life. Nicholas G. Carr believes that Internet use has other effects on individuals, for instance improving skills of scan-reading and interfering with the deep thinking that leads to true creativity.

Electronic business

Electronic business (e-business) encompasses business processes spanning the entire value chain: purchasing, supply chain management, marketing, sales, customer service, and business relationship. E-commerce seeks to add revenue streams using the Internet to build and enhance relationships with clients and partners. According to International Data Corporation, the size of worldwide e-commerce, when global business-to-business and -consumer transactions are combined, equate to $16 trillion for 2013. A report by Oxford Economics adds those two together to estimate the total size of the digital economy at $20.4 trillion, equivalent to roughly 13.8% of global sales.

While much has been written of the economic advantages of Internet-enabled commerce, there is also evidence that some aspects of the Internet such as maps and location-aware services may serve to reinforce economic inequality and the digital divide. Electronic commerce may be responsible for consolidation and the decline of mom-and-pop, brick and mortar businesses resulting in increases in income inequality.

Author Andrew Keen, a long-time critic of the social transformations caused by the Internet, has recently focused on the economic effects of consolidation from Internet businesses. Keen cites a 2013 Institute for Local Self-Reliance report saying brick-and-mortar retailers employ 47 people for every $10 million in sales while Amazon employs only 14. Similarly, the 700-employee room rental start-up Airbnb was valued at $10 billion in 2014, about half as much as Hilton Worldwide, which employs 152,000 people. At that time, transportation network company Uber employed 1,000 full-time employees and was valued at $18.2 billion, about the same valuation as Avis Rent a Car and The Hertz Corporation combined, which together employed almost 60,000 people.

Telecommuting

Telecommuting is the performance within a traditional worker and employer relationship when it is facilitated by tools such as groupware, virtual private networks, conference calling, videoconferencing, and voice over IP (VOIP) so that work may be performed from any location, most conveniently the worker's home. It can be efficient and useful for companies as it allows workers to communicate over long distances, saving significant amounts of travel time and cost. As broadband Internet connections become commonplace, more workers have adequate bandwidth at home to use these tools to link their home to their corporate intranet and internal communication networks.

Collaborative publishing

Wikis have also been used in the academic community for sharing and dissemination of information across institutional and international boundaries. In those settings, they have been found useful for collaboration on grant writing, strategic planning, departmental documentation, and committee work. The United States Patent and Trademark Office uses a wiki to allow the public to collaborate on finding prior art relevant to examination of pending patent applications. Queens, New York has used a wiki to allow citizens to collaborate on the design and planning of a local park. The English Wikipedia has the largest user base among wikis on the World Wide Web and ranks in the top 10 among all Web sites in terms of traffic.

Politics and political revolutions

Banner in Bangkok during the 2014 Thai coup d'état, informing the Thaipublic that 'like' or 'share' activities on social media could result in imprisonment (observed June 30, 2014).

The Internet has achieved new relevance as a political tool. The presidential campaign of Howard Dean in 2004 in the United States was notable for its success in soliciting donation via the Internet. Many political groups use the Internet to achieve a new method of organizing for carrying out their mission, having given rise to Internet activism, most notably practiced by rebels in the Arab Spring. The New York Times suggested that social media websites, such as Facebook and Twitter, helped people organize the political revolutions in Egypt, by helping activists organize protests, communicate grievances, and disseminate information.

Many have understood the Internet as an extension of the Habermasian notion of the public sphere, observing how network communication technologies provide something like a global civic forum. However, incidents of politically motivated Internet censorship have now been recorded in many countries, including western democracies.

Philanthropy

The spread of low-cost Internet access in developing countries has opened up new possibilities for peer-to-peer charities, which allow individuals to contribute small amounts to charitable projects for other individuals. Websites, such as DonorsChoose and GlobalGiving, allow small-scale donors to direct funds to individual projects of their choice. A popular twist on Internet-based philanthropy is the use of peer-to-peer lending for charitable purposes. Kiva pioneered this concept in 2005, offering the first web-based service to publish individual loan profiles for funding. Kiva raises funds for local intermediary microfinance organizations which post stories and updates on behalf of the borrowers. Lenders can contribute as little as $25 to loans of their choice, and receive their money back as borrowers repay. Kiva falls short of being a pure peer-to-peer charity, in that loans are disbursed before being funded by lenders and borrowers do not communicate with lenders themselves.

However, the recent spread of low-cost Internet access in developing countries has made genuine international person-to-person philanthropy increasingly feasible. In 2009, the US-based nonprofit Zidisha tapped into this trend to offer the first person-to-person microfinance platform to link lenders and borrowers across international borders without intermediaries. Members can fund loans for as little as a dollar, which the borrowers then use to develop business activities that improve their families' incomes while repaying loans to the members with interest. Borrowers access the Internet via public cybercafes, donated laptops in village schools, and even smart phones, then create their own profile pages through which they share photos and information about themselves and their businesses. As they repay their loans, borrowers continue to share updates and dialogue with lenders via their profile pages. This direct web-based connection allows members themselves to take on many of the communication and recording tasks traditionally performed by local organizations, bypassing geographic barriers and dramatically reducing the cost of microfinance services to the entrepreneurs.

3

Internet Security

Internet security is a branch of computer security specifically related to not only the Internet, often involving browser security, but also network security on as it applies to other applications or operating systems as a whole. Its objective is to establish rules and measures to use against attacks over the Internet. The Internet represents an insecure channel for exchanging information which leads to a high risk of intrusion or fraud, such as phishing, online viruses, trojans, worms and more.

Many methods are used to protect the transfer of data, including encryption and from-the-ground-up engineering. The current focus is on prevention as much as on real time protection against well known and new threats.

Threats

An internet user can be tricked or forced into downloading software onto a computer that is of malicious intent. Such software comes in many forms, such as viruses, Trojan horses, spyware, and worms.

- Malware, short for malicious software, is any software used to disrupt computer operation, gather sensitive information, or gain access to private computer systems. Malware is defined by its malicious intent, acting against the requirements of the computer user, and does not include software that causes unintentional harm due to some deficiency. The term badware is sometimes used, and applied to both true (malicious) malware and unintentionally harmful software.

- A botnet is a network of zombie computers that have been taken over by a robot or bot that performs large-scale malicious acts for the creator of the botnet.

- Computer Viruses are programs that can replicate their structures or effects by infecting other files or structures on a computer. The common use of a virus is to take over a computer to steal data.

- Computer worms are programs that can replicate themselves throughout a computer network, performing malicious tasks throughout.

- Ransomware is a type of malware which restricts access to the computer system that it infects, and demands a ransom paid to the creator(s) of the malware in order for the restriction to be removed.

- Scareware is scam software of usually limited or no benefit, containing malicious payloads, that is sold to consumers via certain unethical marketing practices. The selling approach uses social engineering to cause shock, anxiety, or the perception of a threat, generally directed at an unsuspecting user.

- Spyware refers to programs that surreptitiously monitor activity on a computer system and report that information to others without the user's consent.

- One particular kind of spyware is KeyLogger malware. Keystroke logging, often referred to as keylogging or keyboard capturing, is the action of recording (logging) the keys struck on a keyboard

- A Trojan horse, commonly known as a Trojan, is a general term for malicious software that pretends to be harmless, so that a user willingly allows it to be downloaded onto the computer.

Denial-of-service attacks

A denial-of-service attack (DoS attack) or distributed denial-of-service attack (DDoS attack) is an attempt to make a computer resource unavailable to its intended users. Another way of understanding DDoS is seeing it as attacks in cloud computing environment that are growing due to the essential characteristics of cloud computing. Although the means to carry out, motives for, and targets of a DoS attack may vary, it generally consists of the concerted efforts to prevent an Internet site or service from functioning efficiently or at all, temporarily or indefinitely. According to businesses who participated in an international business security survey, 25% of respondents experienced a DoS attack in 2007 and 16.8% experienced one in 2010. DoS attacks often use bots (or a botnet) to carry out the attack.

Phishing

Phishing is an attack which targets online users for extraction of their sensitive information such as username, password and credit card information.

Phishing occurs when the attacker pretends to be a trustworthy entity, either via email or web page. Victims are directed to fake web pages, which are dressed to look legitimate, via spoof emails, instant messenger/social media or other avenues. Often tactics such as email spoofing are used to make emails appear to be from legitimate senders, or long complex subdomains hide the real website host. Insurance group RSA said that phishing accounted for worldwide losses of $10.8 billion in 2016.

Application vulnerabilities

Applications used to access Internet resources may contain security vulnerabilities such as memory safety bugs or flawed authentication checks. The most severe of these bugs can give network attackers full control over the computer. Most security applications and suites are incapable of adequate defense against these kinds of attacks.

Remedies

Network layer security

TCP/IP protocols may be secured with cryptographic methods and security protocols. These protocols include Secure Sockets Layer (SSL), succeeded by Transport Layer Security(TLS) for web traffic, Pretty Good Privacy (PGP) for email, and IPsec for the network layer security.

Internet Protocol Security (IPsec)

IPsec is designed to protect TCP/IP communication in a secure manner. It is a set of security extensions developed by the Internet Task Force (IETF). It provides security and authentication at the IP layer by transforming data using encryption. Two main types of transformation that form the basis of IPsec: the Authentication Header (AH) and ESP. These two protocols provide data integrity, data origin authentication, and anti-replay service. These protocols can be used alone or in combination to provide the desired set of security services for the Internet Protocol (IP) layer.

The basic components of the IPsec security architecture are described in terms of the following functionalities:

- Security protocols for AH and ESP
- Security association for policy management and traffic processing
- Manual and automatic key management for the Internet key exchange (IKE)
- Algorithms for authentication and encryption

The set of security services provided at the IP layer includes access control, data origin integrity, protection against replays, and confidentiality. The algorithm allows these sets to work independently without affecting other parts of the implementation. The IPsec implementation is operated in a host or security gateway environment giving protection to IP traffic.

Multi-factor authentication

Multi-factor authentication (MFA) is a method of computer access control in which a user is granted access only after successfully presenting several separate pieces of evidence to an authentication mechanism – typically at least two of the following categories: knowledge (something they know), possession (something they have), and inherence (something they are). Internet resources, such as websites and email, may be secured using multi-factor authentication.

Security token

Some online sites offer customers the ability to use a six-digit code which randomly changes every 30–60 seconds on a security token. The keys on the security token have built in mathematical computations and manipulate numbers based on the current time built into the device. This means that every thirty seconds there is only a certain array of numbers possible which would be correct to validate access to the online account. The website that the user is logging into would be made aware of that device's serial number and would know the computation and correct time built into the device to verify that the number given is indeed one of the handful of six-digit numbers that works in that given 30-60 second cycle. After 30–60 seconds the device will present a new random six-digit number which can log into the website.

Electronic mail security

Background

Email messages are composed, delivered, and stored in a multiple step process, which starts with the message's composition. When the user finishes composing the message and sends it, the message is transformed into a standard format: an RFC 2822 formatted message. Afterwards, the message can be transmitted. Using a network connection, the mail client, referred to as a mail user agent (MUA), connects to a mail transfer agent (MTA) operating on the mail server. The mail client then provides the sender's identity to the server. Next, using the mail server commands, the client sends the recipient list to the mail server. The client then supplies the message. Once the mail server receives and processes the message, several events occur: recipient server identification, connection establishment, and message transmission. Using Domain Name System (DNS) services, the sender's mail server determines the mail server(s) for the recipient(s). Then, the server opens up a connection(s) to the recipient mail server(s) and sends the message employing a process similar to that used by the originating client, delivering the message to the recipient(s).

Pretty Good Privacy (PGP)

Pretty Good Privacy provides confidentiality by encrypting messages to be transmitted or data files to be stored using an encryption algorithm such as Triple DES or CAST-128. Email messages can be protected by using cryptography in various ways, such as the following:

- Signing an email message to ensure its integrity and confirm the identity of its sender.
- Encrypting the body of an email message to ensure its confidentiality.
- Encrypting the communications between mail servers to protect the confidentiality of both message body and message header.

The first two methods, message signing and message body encryption, are often used together; however, encrypting the transmissions between mail servers is typically used only when two organizations want to protect emails regularly sent between each other. For example, the organizations could establish a virtual private network (VPN) to encrypt the communications between their mail servers over the Internet. Unlike methods that can only encrypt a message body, a VPN can encrypt entire messages, including email header information such as senders, recipients, and subjects. In some cases, organizations may need to protect header information. However, a VPN solution alone cannot provide a message signing mechanism, nor can it provide protection for email messages along the entire route from sender to recipient.

Multipurpose Internet Mail Extensions (MIME)

MIME transforms non-ASCII data at the sender's site to Network Virtual Terminal (NVT) ASCII data and delivers it to client's Simple Mail Transfer Protocol (SMTP) to be sent through the Internet. The server SMTP at the receiver's side receives the NVT ASCII data and delivers it to MIME to be transformed back to the original non-ASCII data.

Message Authentication Code

A Message authentication code (MAC) is a cryptography method that uses a secret key to encrypt a message. This method outputs a MAC value that can be decrypted by the receiver, using the same secret key used by the sender. The Message Authentication Code protects both a message's data integrity as well as its authenticity.

Firewalls

A computer firewall controls access between networks. It generally consists of gateways and filters which vary from one firewall to another. Firewalls also screen network traffic and are able to block traffic that is dangerous. Firewalls act as the intermediate server between SMTP and Hypertext Transfer Protocol (HTTP) connections.

Role of firewalls in web security

Firewalls impose restrictions on incoming and outgoing Network packets to and from private networks. Incoming or outgoing traffic must pass through the firewall; only authorized traffic is allowed to pass through it. Firewalls create checkpoints between an internal private network and the public Internet, also known as choke points (borrowed from the identical military term of a combat limiting geographical feature). Firewalls can create choke points based on IP source and TCP port number. They can also serve as the platform for IPsec. Using tunnel mode capability, firewall can be used to implement VPNs. Firewalls can also limit network exposure by hiding the internal network system and information from the public Internet.

Types of firewall

Packet filter

A packet filter is a first generation firewall that processes network traffic on a packet-by-packet basis. Its main job is to filter traffic from a remote IP host, so a router is needed to connect the internal network to the Internet. The router is known as a screening router, which screens packets leaving and entering the network.

Stateful packet inspection

In a stateful firewall the circuit-level gateway is a proxy server that operates at the network level of an Open Systems Interconnection (OSI) model and statically defines what traffic will be allowed. Circuit proxies will forward Network packets (formatted unit of data) containing a given port number, if the port is permitted by the algorithm. The main advantage of a proxy server is its ability to provide Network Address Translation (NAT), which can hide the user's IP address from the Internet, effectively protecting all internal information from the Internet.

Application-level gateway

An application-level firewall is a third generation firewall where a proxy server operates at the very top of the OSI model, the IP suite application level. A network packet is forwarded only if a connection is established using a known protocol. Application-level gateways are notable for analyzing entire messages rather than individual packets of data when the data are being sent or received.

Browser choice

Web browser statistics tend to affect the amount a Web browser is exploited. For example, Internet Explorer 6, which used to own a majority of the Web browser market share, is considered extremely insecure because vulnerabilities were exploited due to its former popularity. Since browser choice is now more evenly distributed (Internet Explorer at 28.5%, Firefox at 18.4%, Google Chrome at 40.8%, and so on), vulnerabilities are exploited in many different browsers.

Internet security products

Antivirus

Antivirus software and Internet security programs can protect a programmable device from attack by detecting and eliminating malware; Antivirus software was mainly shareware in the early years of the Internet, but there are now several free security applications on the Internet to choose from for all platforms.

Password managers

A password manager is a software application that helps a user store and organize passwords. Password managers usually store passwords encrypted, requiring the user to create a master password; a single, ideally very strong password which grants the user access to their entire password database from top to bottom.

Security suites

So called security suites were first offered for sale in 2003 (McAfee) and contain a suite of firewalls, anti-virus, anti-spyware and more. They also offer theft protection, portable storage device safety check, private Internet browsing, cloud anti-spam, a file shredder or make security-related decisions (answering popup windows) and several were free of charge.

A social networking service (also social networking site, or SNS or social media) is an online platform which people use to build social networks or social relations with other people who share similar personal or career interests, activities, backgrounds or real-life connections.

The social networks are distributed across various computer networks. The social networks are inherently computer networks, linking people, organization, and knowledge. Social networking services vary in format and the number of features. They can incorporate a range of new information and communication tools, operating on desktops and on laptops, on mobile devices such as tablet computers and smartphones. They may feature digital photo/video/sharing and "web logging" diary entries online (blogging). Online community services are sometimes consideredsocial-network services by programmers and users, though in a broader sense, a social-network service usually provides an individual-centered service whereas online community services are group-centered. Defined as "websites that facilitate the building of a network of contacts in order to exchange various types of content online," social networking sites provide a space for interaction to continue beyond in person interactions. These computer mediated interactions link members of various networks and may help to both maintain and develop new social ties.

Social networking sites allow users to share ideas, digital photos and videos, posts, and to inform others about online or real-world activities and events with people in their network. While in-person social networking – such as gathering in a village market to talk about events – has existed since the earliest development of towns, the Web enables people to connect with others who live in different locations, ranging from across a city to across the world. Depending on the social media platform, members may be able to contact any other member. In other cases, members can contact anyone they have a connection to, and subsequently anyone that contact has a connection to, and so on. The success of social networking services can be seen in their dominance in society today, with Facebook having a massive 2.13 billion active monthly users and an average of 1.4 billion daily active users in 2017. LinkedIn, a career-oriented social-networking service, generally requires that a member personally know another member in real life before they contact them online. Some services require members to have a preexisting connection to contact other members.

The main types of social networking services contain category places (such as age or occupation or religion), means to connect with friends (usually with self-description pages), and a recommendation system linked to trust. One can categorize social-network services into three types:

- socializing social network services used primarily for socializing with existing friends (e.g., Facebook)
- online social networks are decentralized and distributed computer networks where users communicate with each other through internet services.
- networking social network services used primarily for non-social interpersonal communication (e.g., LinkedIn, a career- and employment-oriented site)
- social navigation social network services used primarily for helping users to find specific information or resources (e.g., Goodreads for books)

There have been attempts to standardize these services to avoid the need to duplicate entries of friends and interests (see the FOAF standard). A study reveals that India recorded world's largest growth in terms of social media users in 2013. A 2013 survey found that 73% of U.S. adults use social-networking sites.

There is a variety of social networking services available online. However, most incorporate common features:

- social networking services are Web 2.0, Internet-based applications
- user-generated content (UGC) is the lifeblood of social networking services.

- users create service-specific profiles for the site or app that are designed and maintained by the SNS organization

- social networking services facilitate the development of online social networks by connecting a user's profile with those of other individuals or groups.

A challenge of definition

The variety and evolving range of stand-alone and built-in social networking services in the online space introduces a challenge of definition. Furthermore, the idea that these services are defined by their ability to bring people together and provides too broad a definition. Such a broad definition would suggest that the telegraph and telephone were social networking services – not the Internet technologies scholars are intending to describe. The terminology is also unclear, with some referring to social networking services as social media.

Attempting definition

A recent attempt at providing a clear definition reviewed the prominent literature in the area and identified four commonalities unique to current social networking services:

(1) social networking services are interactive Web 2.0 Internet-based applications,

(2) user-generated content (UGC), such as user-submitted digital photos, text posts, "tagging", online comments, and diary-style "web logs" (blogs), is the lifeblood of the SNS organism,

(3) users create service-specific profiles for the site or app that are designed and maintained by the SNS organization, and

(4) social networking services facilitate the development of social networks online by connecting a user's profile with those of other individuals or groups.

The potential for computer networking to facilitate newly improved forms of computer-mediated social interaction was suggested early on. Efforts to support social networks via computer-mediated communication were made in many early online services, including Usenet, ARPANET, LISTSERV, and bulletin board services (BBS). Many prototypical features of social networking sites were also present in online services such as America Online, Prodigy, CompuServe, ChatNet, and The WELL.

Early social networking on the World Wide Web began in the form of generalized online communities such as Theglobe.com (1995), Geocities (1994) and Tripod.com (1995). Many of these early communities focused on bringing people together to interact with each other through chat rooms, and encouraged users to share personal information and ideas via personal webpages by providing easy-to-use publishing tools and free or inexpensive webspace. Some communities – such as Classmates.com – took a different approach by simply having people link to each other via email addresses. PlanetAll started in 1996.

In the late 1990s, user profiles became a central feature of social networking sites, allowing users to compile lists of "friends" and search for other users with similar interests. New social networking methods were developed by the end of the 1990s, and many sites began to develop more advanced features for users to find and manage friends. Open Diary, a community for online diarists, invented both friends-only content and the reader comment, two features of social networks important to user interaction.

This newer generation of social networking sites began to flourish with the emergence of SixDegrees.com in 1997, followed by Open Diary in 1998, Mixi in 1999, Makeoutclub in 2000, Hub Culture and Friendster in 2002, and soon became part of the Internet mainstream. However, thanks to the nation's high Internet penetration rate, the first mass social networking site was the South Korean service, Cyworld, launched as a blog-based site in 1999 and social networking features added in 2001. It also became one of the first companies to profit from the sale of virtual goods. Friendster was followed by MySpace and LinkedIn a year later, and eventually Bebo. Friendster became very popular in the Pacific Islands. Orkut became the first popular social networking service in Brazil (although most of its very first users were from the United States) and quickly grew in popularity in India (Madhavan, 2007). Attesting to the rapid increase in social networking sites' popularity, by 2005, it was reported that Myspace was getting more page views than Google. Facebook, launched in 2004, became the largest social networking site in the world in early 2009. Facebook was first introduced as a Harvard social networking site, expanding to other universities and eventually, anyone. The term social media was introduced and soon became widespread.

Social impact

Web-based social networking services make it possible to connect people who share interests and activities across political, economic, and geographic borders. Through e-mail and instant messaging, online communities are created where a gift economy and reciprocal altruism are encouraged through cooperation. Information is suited to a gift economy, as information is a nonrival good and can be gifted at practically no cost. Scholars have noted that the term "social" cannot account for technological features of the social network platforms alone. Hence, the level of network sociability should determine by the actual performances of its users. According to the communication theory of uses and gratifications, an increasing number of individuals are looking to the Internet and social media to fulfill cognitive, affective, personal integrative, social integrative, and tension free needs. With Internet technology as a supplement to fulfill needs, it is in turn affecting every day life, including relationships, school, church, entertainment, and family. Companies are using social media as a way to learn about potential employees' personalities and behavior. In numerous situations a candidate who might otherwise have been hired has been rejected due to offensive or otherwise unseemly photos or comments posted to social networks or appearing on a newsfeed.

Facebook and other social networking tools are increasingly the aim of scholarly research. Scholars in many fields have begun to investigate the impact of social networking sites, investigating how such sites may play into issues of identity, privacy, social capital, youth culture, and education. Research has also suggested that individuals add offline friends on Facebook to maintain contact and often this blurs the lines between work and home lives. According to a study in 2015, 63% of the users of Facebook or Twitter in the USA consider these networks to be their main source of news, with entertainment news being the most seen. In the times of breaking news, Twitter users are more likely to stay invested in the story. In some cases when the news story is more political, users may be more likely to voice their opinion on a linked Facebook story with a comment or like, while Twitter users will just follow the sites feed and/ or retweet the article.

A 2015 study shows that 85% of people aged 18 to 34 use social networking sites for their purchase decision making. While over 65% of people aged 55 and over rely on word of mouth. Several websites are beginning to tap into the power of the social networking model for philanthropy. Such models provide a means for connecting otherwise fragmented industries and small organizations without the resources to reach a broader audience with interested users. Social networks are providing a different way for individuals to communicate digitally. These communities of hypertexts allow for the sharing of information and ideas, an old concept placed in a digital environment. In 2011, HCL Technologies conducted research that showed that 50% of British employers had banned the use of social networking sites/ services during office hours.

Research has provided us with mixed results as to whether or not a person's involvement in social networking can affect their feelings of loneliness. Studies have indicated that how a person chooses to use social networking can change their feelings of loneliness in either a negative or positive way. Some companies with mobile workers have encouraged their workers to use social networking to feel connected, educators are using it to keep connected with their students and individuals are benefiting from social networking to keep connect with already close relationships that they've developed under circumstances that would otherwise make it difficult to do so. Each social networking user is able to create a community that centers around a personal identity they choose to create online. In his book Digital Identities: Creating and Communicating the Online Self, Rob Cover argues that social networking's foundation in Web 2.0, high-speed networking shifts online representation to one which is both visual and relational to other people, complexifying the identity process for younger people and creating new forms of anxiety. In 2016, news reports stated that excessive usage of SNS sites may be associated with an increase in the rates of depression, to almost triple the rate for non-SNS users. Experts worldwide have said that 2030 people who use SNS more have higher levels of depression than those who use SNS less. At least one study went as far as to conclude that the negative effects of Facebook usage are equal to or greater than the positive effects of face-to-face interactions.

According to a recent article from Computers in Human Behavior, Facebook has also been shown to lead to issues of social comparison. Users are able to select which photos and status updates to post, allowing them to portray their lives in acclamatory manners. These updates can lead to other users feeling like their lives are inferior by comparison.Users may feel especially inclined to compare themselves to other users with whom they share similar characteristics or lifestyles, leading to a fairer comparison. Motives for these comparisons can be associated with the goals of improving oneself by looking at profiles of people who one feels are superior, especially when their lifestyle is similar and possible. One can also self-compare to make oneself feel superior to others by looking at the profiles of users who one believes to be worser off. However, a study by the Harvard Business Review shows that these goals often lead to negative consequences, as use of Facebook has been linked with lower levels of well-being; mental health has been shown to decrease due to the use of Facebook.Computers in Human Behavior emphasizes that these feelings of poor mental health have been suggested to cause people to take time off from their Facebook accounts; this action is called "Facebook Fatigue" and has been common in recent years.

Usage of social networking has contrubuted to a new form of bullying on social media, the communication model of interpersonal communications motives explains that a person could be embracing the motivation of escape in order to feel more powerful when the person's reality may not reflect the motivation that they are showing when they are online.

Features

Typical features

According to Boyd and Ellison's (2007) article, "Why Youth (Heart) Social Network Sites: The Role of Networked Publics in Teenage Social Life", social networking sites share a variety of technical features that allow individuals to:

construct a public/semi-public profile, articulate a list of other users that they share a connection with, and view their list of connections within the system. The most basic of these are visible profiles with a list of "friends" who are also users of the site. In an article entitled "Social Network Sites: Definition, History, and Scholarship," Boyd and Ellison adopt Sunden's (2003) description of profiles as unique pages where one can "type oneself into being". A profile is generated from answers to questions, such as age, location, interests, etc. Some sites allow users to upload pictures, add multimedia content or modify the look and feel of the profile. Others, e.g., Facebook, allow users to enhance their profile by adding modules or "Applications". Many sites allow users to post blog entries, search for others with similar interests and compile and share lists of contacts. User profiles often have a section dedicated to comments from friends and other users. To protect user privacy, social networks typically have controls that allow users to choose who can view their profile, contact them, add them to their list of contacts, and so on.

Additional features

There is a trend towards more interoperability between social networks led by technologies such as OpenID and OpenSocial. In most mobile communities, mobile phone users can now create their own profiles, make friends, participate in chat rooms, create chat rooms, hold private conversations, share photos and videos, and share blogs by using their mobile phone. Some companies provide wireless services that allow their customers to build their own mobile community and brand it; one of the most popular wireless services for social networking in North America and Nepal is Facebook Mobile.

Emerging trends

" The things you share are things that make you look good, things which you are happy to tie into your identity. "

— Hilary Mason, chief data scientist, bitly, VentureBeat, 2012

While the popularity of social networking consistently rises, new uses for the technology are frequently being observed. Today's technologically savvy population requires convenient solutions to their daily needs. At the forefront of emerging trends in social networking sites is the concept of "real-time web" and "location-based". Real-time allows users to contribute contents, which is then broadcast as it is being uploaded—the concept is analogous to live radio and television broadcasts. Twitter set the trend for "real-time" services, wherein users can broadcast to the world what they are doing, or what is on their minds within a 140-character limit. Facebook followed suit with their "Live Feed" where users' activities are streamed as soon as it happens. While Twitter focuses on words, Clixtr, another real-time service, focuses on group photo sharing wherein users can update their photo streams with photos while at an event. Facebook, however, remains the largest photo sharing site—Facebook application and photo aggregator Pixable estimates that Facebook will have 100 billion photos by Summer 2012. In April 2012, the image-based social media network Pinterest had become the third largest social network in the United States.

Companies have begun to merge business technologies and solutions, such as cloud computing, with social networking concepts. Instead of connecting individuals based on social interest, companies are developing interactive communities that connect individuals based on shared business needs or experiences. Many provide specialized networking tools and applications that can be accessed via their websites, such as LinkedIn. Others companies, such as Monster.com, have been steadily developing a more "socialized" feel to their career center sites to harness some of the power of social networking sites. These more business related sites have their own nomenclature for the most part but the most common naming conventions are "Vocational Networking Sites" or "Vocational Media Networks", with the former more closely tied to individual networking relationships based on social networking principles.

Foursquare gained popularity as it allowed for users to check into places that they are frequenting at that moment. Gowalla is another such service that functions in much the same way that Foursquare does, leveraging the GPS in phones to create a location-based user experience. Clixtr, though in the real-time space, is also a location-based social networking site, since events created by users are automatically geotagged, and users can view events occurring nearby through the Clixtr iPhone app. Recently, Yelp announced its entrance into the location-based social networking space through check-ins with their mobile app; whether or not this becomes detrimental to Foursquare or Gowalla is yet to be seen, as it is still considered a new space in the Internet technology industry.

One popular use for this new technology is social networking between businesses. Companies have found that social networking sites such as Facebook and Twitter are great ways to build their brand image. According to Jody Nimetz, author of Marketing Jive, there are five major uses for businesses and social media: to create brand awareness, as an online reputation management tool, for recruiting, to learn about new technologies and competitors, and as a lead generation tool to intercept potential prospects. These companies are able to drive traffic to their own online sites while encouraging their consumers and clients to have discussions on how to improve or change products or services. As of September 2013, 71% of online adults use Facebook, 17% use Instagram, 21% use Pinterest, and 22% use LinkedIn.

Niche networks

In 2012, it was reported that in the past few years, the niche social network has steadily grown in popularity, thanks to better levels of user interaction and engagement. In 2012, a survey by Reuters and research firm Ipsos found that one in three users were getting bored with Facebook and in 2014 the GlobalWebIndex found that this figured had risen to almost 50%. The niche social network offers a specialized space that's designed to appeal to a very specific market with a clearly defined set of needs. Where once the streams of social minutia on networks such as Facebook and Twitter were the ultimate in online voyeurism, now users are looking for connections, community and shared experiences. Social networks that tap directly into specific activities, hobbies, tastes and lifestyles are seeing a consistent rise in popularity. Niche social networks such as Fishbrain for fishing and Stravafor cycling. These social platforms offer brands a rich space in which to engage with their target market and build awareness.

Science

One other use that is being discussed is the use of social networks in the science communities. Julia Porter Liebeskind et al. have published a study on how new biotechnology firms are using social networking sites to share exchanges in scientific knowledge. They state in their study that by sharing information and knowledge with one another, they are able to "increase both their learning and their flexibility in ways that would not be possible within a self-contained hierarchical organization". Social networking is allowing scientific groups to expand their knowledge base and share ideas, and without these new means of communicating their theories might become "isolated and irrelevant". Researchers use social networks frequently to maintain and develop professional relationships. They are interested in consolidating social ties and professional contact, keeping in touch with friends and colleagues and seeing what their own contacts are doing. This can be related to their need to keep updated on the activities and events of their friends and colleagues in order to establish collaborations on common fields of interest and knowledge sharing. Social networks are used also to communicate scientists research results and as a public communication tool and to connect people who share the same professional interests, their benefits can vary according to the discipline. The most interesting aspects of social networks for professional purposes are their potentialities in terms of dissemination of information and the ability to reach and multiply professional contacts exponentially. Social networks like Academia.edu, LinkedIn, Facebook, and ResearchGate give the possibility to join professional groups and pages, to share papers and results, publicize events, to discuss issues and create debates. Academia.edu is extensively used by researchers, where they follow a combination of social networking and scholarly norms.ResearchGate is also widely used by researchers, especially to disseminate and discuss their publications, where it seems to attract an audience that it wider than just other scientists. The usage of Research Gate and Academia in different academic communities has increasingly been studied in recent years.

Education

The European Southern Observatory uses social networks to engage people in astronomical observations.

The advent of social networking platforms may also be impacting the way(s) in which learners engage with technology in general. For a number of years, Prensky's (2001) dichotomy between Digital Natives and Digital Immigrants has been considered a relatively accurate representation of the ease with which people of a certain age range—in particular those born before and after 1980—use technology. Prensky's theory has been largely disproved, however, and not least on account of the burgeoning popularity of social networking sites and other metaphors such as White and Le Cornu's "Visitors" and "Residents" (2011) are greater currency. The use of online social networks by school libraries is also increasingly prevalent and they are being used to communicate with potential library users, as well as extending the services provided by individual school libraries. Social networks and their educational uses are of interest to many researchers. According to Livingstone and Brake (2010), "Social networking sites, like much else on the Internet, represent a moving target for researchers and policy makers." Pew Research Center project, called Pew Internet, did a USA-wide survey in 2009 and in 2010 February published that 47% of American adults use a social networking website. Same survey found that 73% of online teenagers use SNS, which is an increase from 65% in 2008, 55% in 2006. Recent studies have shown that social network services provide opportunities within professional education, curriculum education, and learning. However, there are constraints in this area. Researches, especially in Africa, have disclosed that the use of social networks among students have been known to negatively affect their academic life. This is buttressed by the fact that their use constitutes distractions, as well as that the students tend to invest a good deal of time in the use of such technologies.

Albayrak and Yildirim (2015) examined the educational use of social networking sites. They investigated students' involvement in Facebook as a Course Management System (CMS) and the findings of their study support that Facebook as a CMS has the potential to increase student involvement in discussions and out-of-class communication among instructors and students.

Professional use

Professional use of social networking services refers to the employment of a network site to connect with other professionals within a given field of interest. SNSs like LinkedIn, a social networking website geared towards companies and industry professionals looking to make new business contacts or keep in touch with previous co-workers, affiliates, and clients. Not only does LinkedIn provide a professional social use, but it also encourages people to inject their personality into their profile–making it more personal than a resume. Other network sites are now being used in this manner, Twitter has become [a] mainstay for professional development as well as promotion and online SNSs support both the maintenance of existing social ties and the formation of new connections. Much of the early research on online communities assume that individuals using these systems would be connecting with others outside their preexisting social group or location, liberating them to form communities around shared interests, as opposed to shared geography. Other researchers have suggested that the professional use of network sites produce "social capital". For individuals, social capital allows a person to draw on resources from other members of the networks to which he or she belongs. These resources can take the form of useful information, personal relationships, or the capacity to organize groups. As well, networks within these services also can be established or built by joining special interest groups that others have made, or creating one and asking others to join.

Curriculum use

According to Doering, Beach and O'Brien, a future English curriculum needs to recognize a major shift in how adolescents are communicating with each other. Curriculum uses of social networking services also can include sharing curriculum-related resources. Educators tap into user-generated content to find and discuss curriculum-related content for students. Responding to the popularity of social networking services among many students, teachers are increasingly using social networks to supplement teaching and learning in traditional classroom environments as they can provide new opportunities for enriching existing curriculum through creative, authentic and flexible, non-linear learning experiences. Some social networks, such as English, baby! and LiveMocha, are explicitly education-focused and couple instructional content with an educational peer environment. The new Web 2.0 technologies built into most social networking services promote conferencing, interaction, creation, research on a global scale, enabling educators to share, remix, and repurpose curriculum resources. In short, social networking services can become research networks as well as learning networks.

Learning use

Educators and advocates of new digital literacies are confident that social networking encourages the development of transferable, technical, and social skills of value in formal and informal learning. In a formal learning environment, goals or objectives are determined by an outside department or agency. Tweeting, instant messaging, or blogging enhances student involvement. Students who would not normally participate in class are more apt to partake through social network services. Networking allows participants the opportunity for just-in-time learning and higher levels of engagement. The use of SNSs allow educators to enhance the prescribed curriculum. When learning experiences are infused into a website students utilize everyday for fun, students realize that learning can and should be a part of everyday life. It does not have to be separate and unattached.Informal learning consists of the learner setting the goals and objectives. It has been claimed that media no longer just influence human culture; they are human culture. With such a high number of users between the ages of 13–18, a number of skills are developed. Participants hone technical skills in choosing to navigate through social networking services. This includes elementary items such as sending an instant message or updating a status. The development of new media skills are paramount in helping youth navigate the digital world with confidence. Social networking services foster learning through what Jenkins (2006) describes as a "participatory culture". A participatory culture consists of a space that allows engagement, sharing, mentoring, and an opportunity for social interaction. Participants of social network services avail of this opportunity. Informal learning, in the forms of participatory and social learning online, is an excellent tool for teachers to sneak in material and ideas that students will identify with and therefore, in a secondary manner, students will learn skills that would normally be taught in a formal setting in the more interesting and engaging environment of social learning. Sites like Twitter provide students with the opportunity to converse and collaborate with others in real time. Social networking services provide a virtual "space" for learners. James Gee (2004) suggests that affinity spacesinstantiate participation, collaboration, distribution, dispersion of expertise, and relatedness. Registered users share and search for knowledge which contributes to informal learning.

Constraints

In the past, social networking services were viewed as a distraction and offered no educational benefit. Blocking these social networks was a form of protection for students against wasting time, bullying, and invasions of privacy. In an educational setting, Facebook, for example, is seen by many instructors and educators as a frivolous, time-wasting distraction from schoolwork, and it is not uncommon to be banned in junior high or high school computer labs. Cyberbullying has become an issue of concern with social networking services. According to the UK Children Go Online survey of 9- to 19-year-olds, it was found that a third have received bullying comments online. To avoid this problem, many school districts/boards have blocked access to social networking services such as Facebook, MySpace, and Twitter within the school environment. Social networking services often include a lot of personal information posted publicly, and many believe that sharing personal information is a window into privacy theft. Schools have taken action to protect students from this. It is believed that this outpouring of identifiable information and the easy communication vehicle that social networking services opens the door to sexual predators, cyberbullying, and cyberstalking. In contrast, however, 70% of social media using teens and 85% of adults believe that people are mostly kind to one another on social network sites. Recent research suggests that there has been a shift in blocking the use of social networking services. In many cases, the opposite is occurring as the potential of online networking services is being realized. It has been suggested that if schools block them [social networking services], they are preventing students from learning the skills they need. Banning social networking [...] is not only inappropriate but also borderline irresponsible when it comes to providing the best educational experiences for students.Schools and school districts have the option of educating safe media usage as well as incorporating digital media into the classroom experience, thus preparing students for the literacy they will encounter in the future.

Positive correlates

A cyberpsychology research study conducted by Australian researchers demonstrated that a number of positive psychological outcomes are related to Facebook use. These researchers established that people can derive a sense of social connectedness and belongingness in the online environment. Importantly, this online social connectedness was associated with lower levels of depression and anxiety, and greater levels of subjective well-being. These findings suggest that the nature of online social networking determines the outcomes of online social network use.

Grassroots organizing

Social networks are being used by activists as a means of low-cost grassroots organizing. Extensive use of an array of social networking sites enabled organizers of the 2009 National Equality March to mobilize an estimated 200,000 participants to march on Washington with a cost savings of up to 85% per participant over previous methods. The August 2011 England riots were similarly considered to have escalated and been fuelled by this type of grassroots organization.

Employment

A rise in social network use is being driven by college students using the services to network with professionals for internship and job opportunities. Many studies have been done on the effectiveness of networking online in a college setting, and one notable one is by Phipps Arabie and Yoram Wind published in Advances in Social Network Analysis. Many schools have implemented online alumni directories which serve as makeshift social networks that current and former students can turn to for career advice. However, these alumni directories tend to suffer from an oversupply of advice-seekers and an undersupply of advice providers. One new social networking service, Ask-a-peer, aims to solve this problem by enabling advice seekers to offer modest compensation to advisers for their time. LinkedIn is also another great resource. It helps alumni, students and unemployed individuals look for work. They are also able to connect with others professionally and network with companies.

In addition, employers have been found to use social network sites to screen job candidates.

Hosting service

A social network hosting service is a web hosting service that specifically hosts the user creation of web-based social networking services, alongside related applications.

Trading networks

A social trade network is a service that allows traders of financial derivatives such as contracts for difference or foreign exchange contracts to share their trading activity via trading profiles online. There services are created by financial brokers.

Business model

Few social networks charge money for membership. In part, this may be because social networking is a relatively new service, and the value of using them has not been firmly established in customers' minds. Companies such as Myspace and Facebook sell online advertising on their site. Their business model is based upon large membership count, and charging for membership would be counterproductive. Some believe that the deeper information that the sites have on each user will allow much better targeted advertising than any other site can currently provide. In recent times, Apple has been critical of the Google and Facebook model, in which users are defined as product and a commodity, and their data being sold for marketing revenue. Social networks operate under an autonomous business model, in which a social network's members serve dual roles as both the suppliers and the consumers of content. This is in contrast to a traditional business model, where the suppliers and consumers are distinct agents. Revenue is typically gained in the autonomous business model via advertisements, but subscription-based revenue is possible when membership and content levels are sufficiently high.

Social interaction

People use social networking sites for meeting new friends, finding old friends, or locating people who have the same problems or interests they have, called niche networking. More and more relationships and friendships are being formed online and then carried to an offline setting. Psychologist and University of Hamburg professor Erich H. Witte says that relationships which start online are much more likely to succeed. In this regard, there are studies which predict tie strength among the friends on social networking websites. Witte has said that in less than 10 years, online dating will be the predominant way for people to start a relationship. One online dating site claims that 2% of all marriages begin at its site, the equivalent of 236 marriages a day. Other sites claim one in five relationships begin online. Users do not necessarily share with others the content which is of most interest to them, but rather that which projects a good impression of themselves. While everyone agrees that social networking has had a significant impact on social interaction, there remains a substantial disagreement as to whether the nature of this impact is completely positive. A number of scholars have done research on the negative effects of Internet communication as well. These researchers have contended that this form of communication is an impoverished version of conventional face-to-face social interactions, and therefore produce negative outcomes such as loneliness and depression for users who rely on social networking entirely. By engaging solely in online communication, interactions between communities, families, and other social groups are weakened.

Issues

Spamming

Spamming on online social networks is quite prevalent. A primary motivation to spam arises from the fact that a user advertising a brand would like others to see them and they typically publicize their brand over the social network. Detecting such spamming activity has been well studied by developing a semi-automated model to detect spams. For instance, text mining techniques are leveraged to detect regular activity of spamming which reduces the viewership and brings down the reputation (or credibility) of a public pages maintained over Facebook. In some online social networks like Twitter, users have evolved mechanisms to report spammers which has been studied and analyzed.

Privacy

Privacy concerns with social networking services have been raised growing concerns among users on the dangers of giving out too much personal information and the threat of sexual predators. Users of these services also need to be aware of data theft or viruses. However, large services, such as Myspace and Netlog, often work with law enforcement to try to prevent such incidents. In addition, there is a perceived privacy threat in relation to placing too much personal information in the hands of large corporations or governmental bodies, allowing a profile to be produced on an individual's behavior on which decisions, detrimental to an individual, may be taken. Furthermore, there is an issue over the control of data and information that was altered or removed by the user may in fact be retained and passed to third parties. This danger was highlighted when the controversial social networking site Quechup harvested e-mail addresses from users' e-mail accounts for use in a spamming operation.

In medical and scientific research, asking subjects for information about their behaviors is normally strictly scrutinized by institutional review boards, for example, to ensure that adolescents and their parents have informed consent. It is not clear whether the same rules apply to researchers who collect data from social networking sites. These sites often contain a great deal of data that is hard to obtain via traditional means. Even though the data are public, republishing it in a research paper might be considered invasion of privacy.

Privacy on social networking sites can be undermined by many factors. For example, users may disclose personal information, sites may not take adequate steps to protect user privacy, and third parties frequently use information posted on social networks for a variety of purposes. "For the Net generation, social networking sites have become the preferred forum for social interactions, from posturing and role playing to simply sounding off. However, because such forums are relatively easy to access, posted content can be reviewed by anyone with an interest in the users' personal information". The UK government has plans to monitor traffic on social networks. As well, schemes similar to e-mail jamming have been proposed for networks such as Twitter and Facebook. These would involve "friending" and "following" large numbers of random people to thwart attempts at network analysis. Privacy concerns have been found to differ between users according to gender and personality. Women are less likely to publish information that reveals methods of contacting them. Personality measures openness, extraversion, and conscientiousness were found to positively affect the willingness to disclose data, while neuroticism decreases the willingness to disclose personal information.

Another debate lies in the design of algorithmicsystems to target specific audiences on social networking sites. With multiple formats for marketing,

Facebook offers a variety of direct marketing options for advertisers to reach their intended audience. For example, these ads may appear as suggested ad posts on the home News Feed or on the right side of the feed as a banner. Businesses may create a page to outline their company and post related information, promotions and contact information to it, directly reaching their interested audience. Users who "like" a business page will be subscribed to receive these business' updates on their home News Feed. Banner ads and suggested posts are paid for by marketers and advertisers to reach their intended audience. Like other methods of marketing, emotional connections are critical to reaching the user. From the fourth quarter of 2012 to the fourth quarter of 2013, Facebook increased its advertising click through rate by 365%, having 2.5 million promoted suggested posts on user's news feeds. This surge of posts resulted in an influx of information that was difficult to organize. A study of the emotional responses to advertising on Facebook found that Business Pages found the highest appeal to users because they were only recommended when liked by the user or the user's friends. "Liked" pages have a higher credibility to users. However, a change in algorithm announced on April 10, 2014 said that Business Pages were receiving a reduced reach after engaging in "click bait" tactics (fooling users to click links to things other than what discretely said on Facebook). The quantity of engagement on Facebook posts are measured, relaying important information about the user audience and their actions online.

The debate questions to what extent the design of these systems is compromising the needs, privacy and information of the users. More research is needed to evaluate if allowing advertising to access user information to specifically tailor content to their choices and interactions, for example by placing ads within their personal feeds and throughout their use of the site, is compromising the user's information and social wellbeing. John Herrman (2018) compares the function of algorithms in adjusting content to an omniscience and recounts the unpleasant experiences that coincide as a result. He calls to web browsing on Amazon, where products he browsed through briefly reappear on other news feeds, including his Instagram feed. He outlines the experience as if the networks "[have] got eyes everywhere," and suggests that this looming omniscience may alter how we interact online, even "risk driving away followers in the process." This may deter users from engaging in social interactions online and points to how much advertisers are able to tailor information to their intended audience. This debate was further ignited in early 2018. On April 10, 2018 Mark Zuckerberg testified before congress on questions defining Facebook's policy, information handling and data design systems. Congress placed emphasis on addressing Facebook's tracking of user data online, skeptical that the social networking site can regulate itself.

Data mining

Through data mining, companies are able to improve their sales and profitability. With this data, companies create customer profiles that contain customer demographics and online behavior. A recent strategy has been the purchase and production of "network analysis software". This software is able to sort out through the influx of social networking data for any specific company. Facebook has been especially important to marketing strategists. Facebook's controversial "Social Ads" program gives companies access to the millions of profiles in order to tailor their ads to a Facebook user's own interests and hobbies. However, rather than sell actual user information, Facebook sells tracked "social actions". That is, they track the websites a user uses outside of Facebook through a program called Facebook Beacon.

Notifications

There has been a trend for social networking sites to send out only "positive" notifications to users. For example, sites such as Bebo, Facebook, and MySpace will not send notifications to users when they are removed from a person's friends list. Likewise, Bebo will send out a notification if a user is moved to the top of another user's friends list but no notification is sent if they are moved down the list. This allows users to purge undesirables from their list extremely easily and often without confrontation since a user will rarely notice if one person disappears from their friends list. It also enforces the general positive atmosphere of the website without drawing attention to unpleasant happenings such as friends falling out, rejection and failed relationships.

Access to information

Many social networking services, such as Facebook, provide the user with a choice of who can view their profile. This is supposed to prevent unauthorized users from accessing their information. Parents who want to access their child's MySpace or Facebook account have become a big problem for teenagers who do not want their profile seen by their parents. By making their profile private, teens can select who may see their page, allowing only people added as "friends" to view their profile and preventing unwanted viewing of the profile by parents. Most teens are constantly trying to create a structural barrier between their private life and their parents. To edit information on a certain social networking service account, the social networking sites require you to log in or provide a password. This is designed to prevent unauthorized users from adding, changing, or removing personal information, pictures, or other data.

Impact on employability

Social networking sites have created issues among getting hired for jobs and losing jobs because of exposing inappropriate content, posting photos of embarrassing situations or posting comments that contain potentially offensive comments (e.g., racist, homophobic or defamatory comments), or even political comments that are contrary to those of the employer. There are works which recommend friends to social networking users based on their political opinions. Many people use social networking sites to express their personal opinions about current events and news issues to their friends. If a potential applicant expresses personal opinions on political issues or makes potentially embarrassing posts online on a publicly available social networking platform, employers can access their employees' and applicants' profiles, and judge them based on their social behavior or political views. According to Silicon Republic's statistics, 17,000 young people in six countries were interviewed in a survey. 1 in 10 people aged 16 to 34 have been rejected for a job because of comments made on an online profile. This shows the effects that social networks have had on people's lives. There have been numerous cases where employees have lost jobs because their opinions represented their companies negatively. In September 2013, a woman got fired over Facebook because she posted disruptive information about her company stating that military patrons should not receive special treatment or discounts. A manager of the company found her opinion online, disagreed with it, and fired her because it went against the company's mission statement. In November 2012, a woman posted a racist remark about the President of the United States and mentioned a possible assassination. She lost her job, and was put under investigation by the Secret Service.

Not only have employees lost their jobs in the United States, but it has happened with social network users internationally. In April 2011, a Lloyd's banking group employee in the United Kingdom was fired for making a sarcastic post about the higher salary of her boss in relation to hers. In February 2013 there was another case where a flight attendant working for a Russian airline lost her job because she posted a photo of herself giving the middle finger to a plane full of passengers. The photo went viral exposing it all over the Internet. In November 2009, a woman working for IBM in Quebec, Canada, lost her company's health insurance benefits because she posted photos displaying her mental health problem. The company decided to cut her benefits because it was costing them additional funds.

Cases like these have created some privacy implications as to whether or not companies should have the right to look at employees' social network profiles. In March 2012, Facebook decided they might take legal action against employers for gaining access to employee's profiles through their passwords. According to Facebook Chief Privacy Officer for policy, Erin Egan, the company has worked hard to give its users the tools to control who sees their information. He also said users shouldn't be forced to share private information and communications just to get a job. According to the network's Statement of Rights and Responsibilities, sharing or soliciting a password is a violation to Facebook. Employees may still give their password information out to get a job, but according to Erin Egan, Facebook will continue to do their part to protect the privacy and security of their users.

Potential for misuse

The relative freedom afforded by social networking services has caused concern regarding the potential of its misuse by individual patrons. In October 2006, a fake MySpace profile created in the name of Josh Evans by Lori Janine Drew led to the suicide of Megan Meier. The event incited global concern regarding the use of social networking services for bullying purposes. In July 2008, a Briton and a former friend was ordered to pay a total of GBP £22,000 (about US$44,000) for libel and breach of privacy. He had posted a fake page on Facebook purporting to be that of a former school friend Matthew Firsht, with whom he had fallen out in 2000. The page falsely claimed that Firsht was homosexual and that he was dishonest.

At the same time, genuine use of social networking services has been treated with suspicion on the ground of the services' misuse. In September 2008, the profile of Australian Facebook user Elmo Keep was banned by the site's administrators on the grounds that it violated the site's terms of use. Keep is one of several users of Facebook who were banned from the site on the presumption that their names aren't real, as they bear resemblance to the names of characters like Sesame Street's Elmo.

Online social networks have also become a platform for spread of rumors, one such study has analyzed rumors in retrospect. One of the approaches to detect rumors (or misinformation) is to compare the spread of topic over social network (say Twitter) with those spread by reliable and authorized news agencies.

Unauthorized access

There are different forms where user data in social networks are accessed and updated without a user's permission. One study highlighted that the most common incidents included inappropriate comments posted on social networking sites (43%), messages sent to contacts that were never authored (25%) and change of personal details (24%). The most incidents are carried out by the victim's friends (36%) or partners (21%) and one in ten victims say their ex-partner has logged into their account without prior consent. The survey found that online social network accounts had been subject to unauthorized access in 60 million cases in 2011.

Risk for child safety

Citizens and governments have been concerned with misuse of social networking services by children and teenagers, in particular in relation to online sexual predators. For instance, there is a study which suggests the children are not too far from inappropriate content on YouTube. Overuse of social networking may also make children more susceptible to depression and anxiety. Governments are taking action to better understand the problem and find some solutions. A 2008 panel concluded that technological fixes such as age verification and scans are relatively ineffective means of apprehending online predators. In May 2010, a child pornography social networking site with hundreds of members was dismantled by law enforcement. It was deemed "the largest crimes against children case brought anywhere by anyone". Girls in particular are also known to be at more of a risk online using social networks than boys. According to the article, High Tech or High Risks: Moral Panics About Girls Online, it suggests that young girls are more at risks because they are often represented through "products of play" in transgressive poses because they often manipulate other users online by making themselves look older than what they actually appear which can attract sexual predators. Many parents of teenage girls worry about their safety online because of the many manipulations there are online and on social networking sites.

Social networking can also be a risk to child safety in another way; parents can get addicted to games and neglect their children. One instance in South Korea resulted in the death of a child from starvation. Law enforcement agencies have published articles with their recommendations to parents about their children's use of social networking sites.

Trolling

Social networking sites such as Facebook are occasionally used to emotionally abuse, harass or bully individuals, either by posting defamatory statements or by forwarding private digital photos or videos that can have an adverse impact on the individuals depicted in the videos. Such actions are often referred to as "trolling". Confrontations in the real world can also be transferred to the online world. Trolling can occur in many different forms, such as (but not limited to) defacement of deceased person(s) tribute pages, name-calling, playing online pranks on individuals and making controversial or inflammatory comments with the intention to cause anger and cause arguments. Individuals troll for many reasons. The psychology behind why people troll according to Psychology Today is due to anonymity, perceived obscurity, and a perceived lack of consequences for online misbehavior. Trolls may also do their activities due to a perceived majority status, social identity salience and due to a sense by the troll that she or he is surrounded by online 'friends'. Trolls may also engage in harmful acts due to desensitization or negative personality traits (Fox, 2014). As these eight reasons behind the thought processes of trolls suggest individuals thrive behind being able to create a false identity or pseudonym to hide behind and the premise that they have 'friends' on social networks that agree with their outlook on certain topics, thus join in on trolling. The reason for the perceived lack of consequences is that they believe they have created an identity in which they can not be seen as a real life human and more of a persona/avatar that they have created, which leads them to feel that they will not face the consequences of being an online troll.

Trolling is a prominent issue in the 2010s, and as the Internet and social media is consistently expanding and more individuals sign up to social networking sites, more people come under fire and become the target of trolls. As more people sign up to social networking sites, more celebrities are also becoming more prominent on these sites. With a variety of celebrities joining social networking sites, trolls tend to target abuse towards them. With some famous people gaining an influx of negative comments and slew of abuse from trolls it causes them to 'quit' social media. One prime example of a celebrity quitting social media is Stephen Fry. He left Twitter due to "too much aggression and unkindness around" emphasizing how trolls can negatively impact people's lives (Cohen, 2014). As celebrities face trolls and backlash on social media forcing them to quit, it can mean that they become less in touch with their fans, potentially losing a fan base, as they are not as relevant as people enjoy interacting with celebrities and makes them feel as though they are valued. As trolling can lead to celebrities deleting their social networks such as Twitter, it emphasizes how trolls can win, and can ruin people's lives.

While trolls believe that they do not face consequences and can troll others on the Internet without repercussions, in the 2000s, due to high-profile cases where cyberbullies have allegedly been factors in suicides attributed to bullying, more laws have been put in place by governments. Trolls can face going to prison for certain actions that they take on the Internet, such as spreading hate speech such as racist messages. One of the highest profile cases is racist trolling. Racist trolling has seen individuals been sent to prison for Tweets they have sent that to them may have seemed harmless and not racist. One case of this in recent years is Liam Stacey who was jailed for fifty-six days for tweeting offensive messages such as 'Muamba is dead, hahahaha', referring to when footballer Fabrice Muamba collapsed during a professional football game for Bolton Wanders (Williams, 2012).This highlights how offensive tweets and messages sent on any social networking platform does have repercussions for individuals and they have to be aware that they have to face the consequences of their actions.

Online bullying

Online bullying, also called cyberbullying, is a relatively common occurrence and it can often result in emotional trauma for the victim. Depending on the networking outlet, up to 39% of users admit to being "cyber-bullied". In her article, "Why Youth (Heart) Social Network Sites", danah boyd, published in December 2007, a researcher of social networks, quotes a teenager. The teenager expresses frustration towards networking sites like MySpace because it causes drama and too much emotional stress. There are not many limitations as to what individuals can post when online. Individuals are given the power to post offensive remarks or pictures that could potentially cause a great amount of emotional pain for another individual.

Interpersonal communication

Interpersonal communication has been a growing issue as more and more people have turned to social networking as a means of communication. "Benniger (1987) describes how mass media has gradually replaced interpersonal communication as a socializing force. Further, social networking sites have become popular sites for youth culture to explore themselves, relationships, and share cultural artifacts". Many teens and social networking users may be harming their interpersonal communication by using sites such as Facebook and MySpace. Stated by Baroness Greenfield, an Oxford University neuroscientist, "My fear is that these technologies are infantilizing the brain into the state of small children who are attracted by buzzing noises and bright lights, who have a small attention span and who live for the moment".

The convenience that social network sites give users to communicate with one another can also damage their interpersonal communication. Sherry Turkle, the founder and director of the MIT Initiative on Technology and Self, stated, "Networked, we are together, but so lessened are our expectations of each other that we feel utterly alone. And there is the risk that we come to see others as objects to be accessed--and only for the parts we find useful, comforting, or amusing". Furthermore, social network sites can create insincere friendships, Turkle also noted, "They nurture friendships on social-networking sites and then wonder if they are among friends. They become confused about companionship".

Psychological effects of social networking

As social networking sites have risen in popularity over the past years, people have been spending an excessive amount of time on the Internet in general and social networking sites in specific. This has led researchers to debate the establishment of Internet addiction as an actual clinical disorder. Social networking can also affect the extent to which a person feels lonely. In a Newsweek article, Johannah Cornblatt explains "Social-networking sites like Facebook and MySpace may provide people with a false sense of connection that ultimately increases loneliness in people who feel alone." John T. Cacioppo, a neuroscientist at the University of Chicago, claims that social networking can foster feelings of sensitivity to disconnection, which can lead to loneliness. Fabio Sabatini and Francesco Sarracino found that if an individual tends to (a) trust people and (b) have a significant number of face-to-face interactions, the individual is likely to assess their own well-being as relatively high. The researchers found that online social networking plays a positive role in subjective well-being when the networking is used to facilitate physical interactions, but networking activities that do not facilitate face-to-face interactions tend to erode trust, and this erosion can then negatively affect subjective well-being (independent of the online social interaction itself).

Sabatini and Sarracino conclude that "The overall effect of networking on individual welfare is significantly negative." However, some scholars have expressed that concerns about social networking are often exaggerated and poorly researched.

Patents

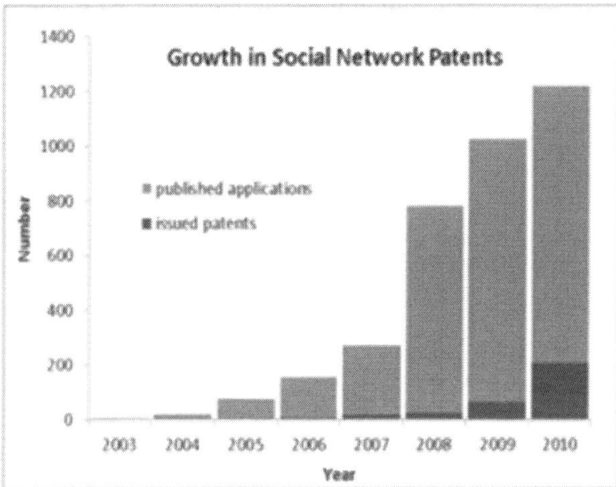

Number of US social network patent applications published per year and patents issued per year

There has been rapid growth in the number of U.S. patent applications that cover new technologies related to social networking. The number of published applications has been growing rapidly since 2003. There are now over 3,500 published applications. As many as 7,000 applications may be currently on file including those that haven't been published yet. Only about 400 of these applications have issued as patents, however, due largely to the multi-year backlog in examination of business method patents and the difficulty in getting these patent applications allowed.

It has been reported that social networking patents are important for the establishment of new start-up companies. It has also been reported, however, that social networking patents inhibit innovation. On June 15, 2010, the United States Patent and Trademark Office awarded Amazon.com a patent for a "Social Networking System" based on its ownership of PlanetAll.The patent describes a Social Networking System as

A networked computer system provides various services for assisting users in locating, and establishing contact relationships with, other users. For example, in one embodiment, users can identify other users based on their affiliations with particular schools or other organizations. The system also provides a mechanism for a user to selectively establish contact relationships or connections with other users, and to grant permissions for such other users to view personal information of the user. The system may also include features for enabling users to identify contacts of their respective contacts. In addition, the system may automatically notify users of personal information updates made by their respective contacts.

The patent has garnered attention due to its similarity to the popular social networking site Facebook.

Worker's rights

What types of speech workers are protected from being fired for on social networking websites has been an issue for American companies with over 100 complaints as of 2011 on this topic having been made to the National Labor Relations Board (NLRB). The National Labor Relations Act protects workers from being fired for "protected concerted activity", which prevents workers from being fired for collective action, while allowing companies the right to fire workers for individual actions they take against the company. Companies are concerned with the potential damage comments online can do to public image due to their visibility and accessibility, but despite over 100 cases being presented thus far to NLRB only one has led to a formal ruling, leaving uncertainty as to the boundaries of what types of speech the NLRB will ultimately protect or condemn.

Decentralized architecture

Most of the existing SNS sites use one or multiple dedicated data centers to serve all its users. Such infrastructure-based systems faces over-provisioning during non-peak hours, while may encounter service outage during peak hours, due to the highly dynamic of SNS users' activities. There are several proposals, leveraging a decentralized architecture to ensure the scalability of SNS sites with low infrastructure cost. These proposals include Fethr, uaOSN, and Cuckoo.

Virtual identity suicide

There is a growing number of social network users who decide to quit their user account by committing a so-called virtual identity suicide or Web 2.0 suicide. A 2013 study in the journal Cyberpsychology, Behavior, and Social Networking investigated this phenomenon from the perspective of Facebook users. The number one reason for these users was privacy concerns (48%), being followed by a general dissatisfaction with the social networking website (14%), negative aspects regarding social network friends (13%) and the feeling of getting addicted to the social networking website (6%). Facebook quitters were found to be more concerned about privacy, more addicted to the Internet and more conscientious.

Breaking up

Sites such as Facebook are becoming increasingly popular tools for methods of ending relationships and friendships, proving that although new media is being used as a tool for connecting with individuals, it is now creating new problems associated with disconnecting from others. Instead of the traditional phone call or face-to-face interaction between individuals, people are now starting to end relationships by simply changing their relationship status, knowing full well that their partner will soon see it. The problem with that is that you are left with no closure and the entire online world now knows you are no longer in a relationship. In a 2010 study conducted online, nearly one-quarter of the 1,000 individuals surveyed found out that their own relationship was over by seeing it on Facebook. New media websites have made our private lives much more public, especially when it comes to breaking up, since updates are able to be immediately viewed by everyone in our networks (which tend to be more people than we would normally tell personally); for example, having friends comment on your newly changed "single" relationship status, and having to explain what happened can be distressing.

This creates further problems, as it is even more crucial to 'save face' after one's relationship has been broken when one is connected to new media technologies. Erving Goffmanargues that all social life boils down to face-to-face interactions. These interpersonal interactions are mediated by what Goffman terms as "face-work", which are the actions undertaken to maintain consistency with one's face, and to uphold the expressive order of social situations. Individuals attempt to keep a positive image of the self when interacting with others, and in order to do so, they may have to alter their appearance or manner in some way. Such face-work can also be seen in new technologies, especially social media websites such as Facebook. If someone breaks up with you, you can actively choose what "face" you want to present to your friends, including your ex. You can choose to either post sad updates, which is the most natural thing you would want to do, or you can "save face" by posting happy updates and pictures of you going out with your friends. Even though you may be absolutely heartbroken within, Facebook allows you to hide your true feelings from the online world, and from your ex, by manipulating your profile. New media is being utilized as a tool for helping users present a desirable image of themselves, enabling them to save face in difficult situations. Nearly 35% of respondents in a study admitted to using their Facebook status to make someone think that they had plans, even if they did not.

Many people find that the only way to really move on from a past relationship is to cut the person out of their life completely. Social media has made this process much more complicated and difficult. In a 2012 study, 48% of the participants stated they had remained friends with their ex on Facebook, and of these people, 88% stated they 'creeped' their ex after the breakup. Many digital social networking sites leave behind a trail of a user's interactions, so deleting content may be an arduous process, more difficult than simply burning or throwing away an entire box of letters, photos, and mementos. Additionally, this content can still remain online.

Social overload

The increasing number of messages and social relationships embedded in SNS also increases the amount of social information demanding a reaction from SNS users. Consequently, SNS users perceive they are giving too much social support to other SNS friends. This dark side of SNS usage is called 'social overload'. It is caused by the extent of usage, number of friends, subjective social support norms, and type of relationship (online-only vs offline friends) while age has only an indirect effect. The psychological and behavioral consequences of social overload include perceptions of SNS exhaustion, low user satisfaction, and high intentions to reduce or stop using SNS.

Social anxiety

Smart phones and social networking services enable us to stay connected continuously with people around us or far away from us, which however is sometimes the root of our anxiety in social life. The eager to know what everyone was saying and the tendency to see if anyone shared new things are typical "symptoms" of this anxiety called FoMO. There is a study that examined possible connections between FOMO and social media engagement indicating that FoMO was associated with lower need satisfaction, mood and life satisfaction.

Another type of social anxiety is the FoBM (fear of being missed). It comes from the situation that we can't produce share-content for people to consume. The FoBM is a counterpart of FoMO; however, compared to FoMO it may have a more serious impact since the exclusion from the conversation can result in continuous exclusion later.

Effects on personal relationships and social capital

The number of contacts on a social platform is sometimes considered an indicator of social capital. However, studies show it is rather an indicator of low self-esteem and of a form of social compensation. Indeed, people tend to add friends to compensate low self-esteem and there is a high correlation between the number of "friends" on social media platforms and feeling social anxiety, leading to symptoms of major depression and dysthymia. If we consider this aspect with regards to the relationships maintained through social media platforms, we can easily point out a change in our understanding of friendship. As a matter of fact, online platforms and social media services altered the old definition of friendship. Indeed, friendship "redoubleth joys, and cutteth griefs in halves" as stated by Francis Bacon. However, nowadays we see that Facebook friends for instance encourage negative feelings, such as envy, revenge and sadness.

When it comes to friendship, we can wonder whether friendship on online platforms is a real form of friendship, or it is just a sort of metaphor to compensate for social communication problems. Actually, a lot of changes can be spotted in its old definition compared to the one in the era of social media. Friendship used to relate to the public sphere as explained in Nicomachean Ethics, however nowadays friendship is rather exposed publicly on different social media platforms.

Moreover, a study shows that Facebook users know only a bit more than two thirds of their "friends" on the platform, meaning that they did not know one third of the individuals in their friend-lists. This raises security and privacy issues and the project researchers alerted participants that they would better unfriend people they did not recognize.

Investigations

Social networking services are increasingly being used in legal and criminal investigations. Information posted on sites such as MySpace and Facebook has been used by police (forensic profiling), probation, and university officials to prosecute users of said sites. In some situations, content posted on MySpace has been used in court.

Facebook is increasingly being used by school administrations and law enforcement agencies as a source of evidence against student users. This site being the number one online destination for college students, allows users to create profile pages with personal details. These pages can be viewed by other registered users from the same school, which often include resident assistants and campus police who have signed up for the service. One UK police force has sifted pictures from Facebook and arrested some people who had been photographed in a public place holding a weapon such as a knife (having a weapon in a public place is illegal).

Application domains

Government applications

Banner in Bangkok, observed on June 30, 2014 during the 2014 Thai coup d'état, informing the Thaipublic that 'like' or 'share' activity on social media could land them in prison.

Social networking is more recently being used by various government agencies. Social networking tools serve as a quick and easy way for the government to get the suggestion of the public and to keep the public updated on their activity, however this comes with a significant risk of abuse, for example to cultivate a culture of fear such as that outlined in Nineteen Eighty-Four or THX-1138.

The Centers for Disease Control demonstrated the importance of vaccinations on the popular children's site Whyville and the National Oceanic and Atmospheric Administration has a virtual island on Second Life where people can explore caves or explore the effects of global warming. Likewise, NASA has taken advantage of a few social networking tools, including Twitter and Flickr. The NSA is taking advantage of them all. NASA is using such tools to aid the Review of U.S. Human Space Flight Plans Committee, whose goal it is to ensure that the nation is on a vigorous and sustainable path to achieving its boldest aspirations in space.

Business applications

The use of social networking services in an enterprise context presents the potential of having a major impact on the world of business and work (Fraser & Dutta 2008). Social networks connect people at low cost; this can be beneficial for entrepreneursand small businesses looking to expand their contact bases. These networks often act as a customer relationship management tool for companies selling products and services. Companies can also use social networks for advertising in the form of banners and text ads. Since businesses operate globally, social networks can make it easier to keep in touch with contacts around the world. Applications for social networking sites have extended toward businesses and brands are creating their own, high functioning sites, a sector known as brand networking. It is the idea that a brand can build its consumer relationship by connecting their consumers to the brand image on a platform that provides them relative content, elements of participation, and a ranking or score system. Brand networking is a new way to capitalize on social trends as a marketing tool. The power of social networks it beginning to permeate into internal culture of businesses where they are finding uses for collaboration, file sharing and knowledge transfer. The term "enterprise social software" is becoming increasingly popular for these types of applications.

Dating applications

Many social networks provide an online environment for people to communicate and exchange personal information for dating purposes.

Intentions can vary from looking for a one time date, short-term relationships, and long-term relationships. Most of these social networks, just like online dating services, require users to give out certain pieces of information. This usually includes a user's age, gender, location, interests, and perhaps a picture. Releasing very personal information is usually discouraged for safety reasons. This allows other users to search or be searched by some sort of criteria, but at the same time people can maintain a degree of anonymity similar to most online dating services. Online dating sites are similar to social networks in the sense that users create profiles to meet and communicate with others, but their activities on such sites are for the sole purpose of finding a person of interest to date. Social networks do not necessarily have to be for dating; many users simply use it for keeping in touch with friends, and colleagues.

However, an important difference between social networks and online dating services is the fact that online dating sites usually require a fee, where social networks are free. This difference is one of the reasons the online dating industry is seeing a massive decrease in revenue due to many users opting to use social networking services instead. Many popular online dating services such as Match.com, Yahoo Personals, and eHarmony.com are seeing a decrease in users, where social networks like MySpace and Facebook are experiencing an increase in users. The number of Internet users in the United States that visit online dating sites has fallen from a peak of 21% in 2003 to 10% in 2006.Whether it is the cost of the services, the variety of users with different intentions, or any other reason, it is undeniable that social networking sites are quickly becoming the new way to find dates online.

Educational applications

The National School Boards Association reports that almost 60% of students who use social networking talk about education topics online, and more than 50% talk specifically about schoolwork. Yet the vast majority of school districts have stringent rules against nearly all forms of social networking during the school day—even though students and parents report few problem behaviors online. Social networks focused on supporting relationships between teachers and their students are now used for learning, educator professional development, and content sharing. HASTAC is a collaborative social network space for new modes of learning and research in higher education, K-12, and lifelong learning; Ningsupports teachers; TermWiki, TeachStreet and other sites are being built to foster relationships that include educational blogs, eportfolios, formal and ad hoc communities, as well as communication such as chats, discussion threads, and synchronous forums. These sites also have content sharing and rating features. Social networks are also emerging as online yearbooks, both public and private. One such service is MyYearbook, which allows anyone from the general public to register and connect. A new trend emerging is private label yearbooks accessible only by students, parents, and teachers of a particular school, similar to Facebook's beginning within Harvard.

Finance applications

The use of virtual currency systems inside social networks create new opportunities for global finance. Hub Culture operates a virtual currency Ven used for global transactions among members, product sales and financial trades in commodities and carbon credits. In May 2010, carbon pricing contracts were introduced to the weighted basket of currencies and commodities that determine the floating exchange value of Ven. The introduction of carbon to the calculation price of the currency made Ven the first and only currency that is linked to the environment.

Medical and health applications

Social networks are beginning to be adopted by healthcare professionals as a means to manage institutional knowledge, disseminate peer to peer knowledge and to highlight individual physicians and institutions. The advantage of using a dedicated medical social networking site is that all the members are screened against the state licensing board list of practitioners. A new trend is emerging with social networks created to help its members with various physical and mental ailments. For people suffering from life altering diseases or chronic health conditions, companies such as HealthUnlocked and PatientsLikeMe offers their members the chance to connect with others dealing with similar issues and share experiences. For alcoholics and addicts, SoberCircle gives people in recovery the ability to communicate with one another and strengthen their recovery through the encouragement of others who can relate to their situation. DailyStrength is also a website that offers support groups for a wide array of topics and conditions, including the support topics offered by PatientsLikeMe and SoberCircle. Some social networks aim to encourage healthy lifestyles in their users. SparkPeople and HealthUnlocked offer community and social networking tools for peer support during weight loss. Fitocracy and QUENTIQ are focused on exercise, enabling users to share their own workouts and comment on those of other users. Other aspects of social network usage include the analysis of data coming from existing social networks (such as Twitter) to discover large crowd concentration events (based on tweets location statistical analysis) and disseminate the information to e.g. mobility-challenged individuals for e.g. avoiding the specific areas and optimizing their journey in an urban environment.

Social and political applications

Social networking sites have recently showed a value in social and political movements. In the Egyptian revolution, Facebook and Twitter both played an allegedly pivotal role in keeping people connected to the revolt.

Egyptian activists have credited social networking sites with providing a platform for planning protest and sharing news from Tahrir Square in real time. By presenting a platform for thousands of people to instantaneously share videos of mainly events featuring brutality, social networking can be a vital tool in revolutions.On the flip side, social networks enable government authorities to easily identify, and repress, protestors and dissidents. Another thing that social media helps with in political applications is getting the younger generations involved in politics and ongoing political issues.

Perhaps the most significant political application of social media is Barack Obama's election campaign in 2008. It was the first of its kind, as it successfully incorporated social media into its campaign winning strategy, evolving the way of political campaigns forever more in the ever-changing technological world we find ourselves in today. His campaign won by engaging everyday people and empowering volunteers, donors and advocates, through social networks, text messaging, email messaging and online videos. Obama's social media campaign was vast, with his campaign boasting 5 million 'friends' on over 15 social networking sites, with over 3 million friends just on Facebook. Another significant success of the campaign was online videos, with nearly 2,000 YouTube videos being put online, receiving over 80 million views.

In 2007, when Obama first announced his candidacy, there was no such thing as an iPhone or Twitter. However, a year later, Obama was sending out voting reminders to thousands of people through Twitter, showing just how fast social media moves. Obama's campaign was current and needed to be successful incorporating social media, as social media acts best and is most effective in real time.

Building up to the 2012 presidential election, it was interesting to see how strong the influence of social media would be following the 2008 campaigns, where Obama's winning campaign had been social media-heavy, whereas McCain's campaign did not really grasp social media. JFK was the first president who really understood television, and similarly, Obama is the first president to fully understand the power of social media. Obama has recognized social media is about creating relationships and connections and therefore used social media to the advantage of presidential election campaigns, in which Obama has dominated his opponents in terms of social media space.

Other political campaigns have followed on from Obama's successful social media campaigns, recognizing the power of social media and incorporating it as a key factor embedded within their political campaigns, for example Donald Trump's presidential electoral campaign, 2016. Dan Pfeiffer, Obama's former digital and social media guru, commented that Donald Trump is "way better at the internet than anyone else in the GOP which is partly why he is winning".

Research has shown that 66% of social media users actively engage in political activity online, and like many other behaviors, online activities translate into offline ones. With research from the 'MacArthur Research Network on Youth and Participatory Politics' stating that young people who are politically active online are double as likely to vote than those who are not politically active online. Therefore, political applications of social networking sites are crucial, particularly to engage with the youth, who perhaps are the least educated in politics and the most in social networking sites. Social media is therefore a very effective way in which politicians can connect with a younger audience through their political campaigns.

Online Business or e-business is any kind of business or commercial transaction that includes sharing information across the internet. Commerce constitutes the exchange of products and services between businesses, groups and individuals and can be seen as one of the essential activities of any business. Electronic commerce focuses on the use of ICT to enable the external activities and relationships of the business with individuals, groups and other businesses, while e-business refers to business with help of the internet. The term "e-business" was coined by IBM's marketing and Internet team in 1996.

In 1994, IBM, with its agency Ogilvy & Mather, began to use its foundation in IT solutions and expertise to market itself as a leader of conducting business on the Internet through the term "e-business." Then CEO Louis V. Gerstner, Jr. was prepared to invest $1 billion to market this new brand.

After conducting worldwide market research in October 1997, IBM began with an eight-page piece in the Wall Street Journal that would introduce the concept of "e-business" and advertise IBM's expertise in the new field. IBM decided not to trademark the term "e-business" in the hopes that other companies would use the term and create an entire new industry. However, this proved to be too successful and by 2000, to differentiate itself, IBM launched a $300 million campaign about its "e-business infrastructure" capabilities. Since that time, the terms, "e-business" and "e-commerce" have been loosely interchangeable and have become a part of the common vernacular.

Business model

When organizations go online, they have to decide which e-business models best suit their goals. A business model is defined as the organization of product, service and information flows, and the source of revenues and benefits for suppliers and customers. The concept of e-business model is the same but used in the online presence.

Revenue model

A key component of the business model is the revenue model or profit model, which is a framework for generating revenues. It identifies which revenue source to pursue, what value to offer, how to price the value, and who pays for the value. It is a key component of a company's business model. It primarily identifies what product or service will be created in order to generate revenues and the ways in which the product or service will be sold.

Without a well defined revenue model, that is, a clear plan of how to generate revenues, new businesses will more likely struggle due to costs which they will not be able to sustain. By having a clear revenue model, a business can focus on a target audience, fund development plans for a product or service, establish marketing plans, begin a line of credit and raise capital.

E-commerce

E-commerce (short for "electronic commerce") is trading in products or services using computer networks, such as the Internet. Electronic commerce draws on technologies such as mobile commerce, electronic funds transfer, supply chain management, Internet marketing, online transaction processing, electronic data interchange (EDI), inventory management systems, and automated data collection. Modern electronic commerce typically uses the World Wide Web for at least one part of the transaction's life cycle, although it may also use other technologies such as e-mail.

While much has been written of the economic advantages of Internet-enabled commerce, there is also evidence that some aspects of the internet such as maps and location-aware services may serve to reinforce economic inequality and the digital divide. Electronic commerce may be responsible for consolidation and the decline of mom-and-pop, brick and mortar businesses resulting in increases in income inequality. Author Andrew Keen, a long-time critic of the social transformations caused by the Internet, has recently focused on the economic effects of consolidation from Internet businesses, since these businesses employ much fewer people per dollar of sales than traditional retailers.

Security

E-business systems naturally have greater security risks than traditional business systems, therefore it is important for e-business systems to be fully protected against these risks. A far greater number of people have access to e-businesses through the internet than would have access to a traditional business. Customers, suppliers, employees, and numerous other people use any particular e-business system daily and expect their confidential information to stay secure. Hackers are one of the great threats to the security of e-businesses. Some common security concerns for e-Businesses include keeping business and customer information private and confidential, authenticity of data, and data integrity. Some of the methods of protecting e-business security and keeping information secure include physical security measures as well as data storage, data transmission, anti-virus software, firewalls, and encryption to list a few.

Privacy and confidentiality

Confidentiality is the extent to which businesses makes personal information available to other businesses and individuals. With any business, confidential information must remain secure and only be accessible to the intended recipient. However, this becomes even more difficult when dealing with e-businesses specifically. To keep such information secure means protecting any electronic records and files from unauthorized access, as well as ensuring safe transmission and data storage of such information. Tools such as encryption and firewalls manage this specific concern within e-business.

Authenticity

E-business transactions pose greater challenges for establishing authenticity due to the ease with which electronic information may be altered and copied. Both parties in an e-business transaction want to have the assurance that the other party is who they claim to be, especially when a customer places an order and then submits a payment electronically. One common way to ensure this is to limit access to a network or trusted parties by using a virtual private network (VPN) technology. The establishment of authenticity is even greater when a combination of techniques are used, and such techniques involve checking "something you know" (i.e. password or PIN), "something you need" (i.e. credit card), or "something you are" (i.e. digital signatures or voice recognition methods). Many times in e-business, however, "something you are" is pretty strongly verified by checking the purchaser's "something you have" (i.e. credit card) and "something you know" (i.e. card number).

Data integrity

Data integrity answers the question "Can the information be changed or corrupted in any way?" This leads to the assurance that the message received is identical to the message sent. A business needs to be confident that data is not changed in transit, whether deliberately or by accident. To help with data integrity, firewalls protect stored data against unauthorized access, while simply backing up data allows recovery should the data or equipment be damaged.

Non-repudiation

This concern deals with the existence of proof in a transaction. A business must have assurance that the receiving party or purchaser cannot deny that a transaction has occurred, and this means having sufficient evidence to prove the transaction. One way to address non-repudiation is using digital signatures. A digital signature not only ensures that a message or document has been electronically signed by the person, but since a digital signature can only be created by one person, it also ensures that this person cannot later deny that they provided their signature.

When certain electronic resources and information is limited to only a few authorized individuals, a business and its customers must have the assurance that no one else can access the systems or information. There are a variety of techniques to address this concern including firewalls, access privileges, user identification and authentication techniques (such as passwords and digital certificates), Virtual Private Networks (VPN), and much more.

Availability

This concern is specifically pertinent to a business' customers as certain information must be available when customers need it. Messages must be delivered in a reliable and timely fashion, and information must be stored and retrieved as required. Because availability of service is important for all e-business websites, steps must be taken to prevent disruption of service by events such as power outages and damage to physical infrastructure. Examples to address this include data backup, fire-suppression systems, Uninterrupted Power Supply (UPS) systems, virus protection, as well as making sure that there is sufficient capacity to handle the demands posed by heavy network traffic.

Cost

The business internet which supports e-business has a cost to maintain of about $2 trillion in outsourced IT dollars just in the United States alone. With each website custom crafted and maintained in code, the maintenance burden is enormous. In the twenty-first century, look for new businesses that will help standardize the look and feel of the internet presence of a business to be more uniform in nature to help reduce the cost of maintenance.

Security solutions

When it comes to security solutions, sustainable electronic business requires support for data integrity, strong authentication, and privacy.

Access and data integrity

There are several different ways to prevent access to the data that is kept online. One way is to use anti-virus software. This is something that most people use to protect their networks regardless of the data they have. E-businesses should use this because they can then be sure that the information sent and received to their system is clean. A second way to protect the data is to use firewalls and network protection. A firewall is used to restrict access to private networks, as well as public networks that a company may use. The firewall also has the ability to log attempts into the network and provide warnings as it is happening. They are very beneficial to keep third-parties out of the network. Businesses that use Wi-Fi need to consider different forms of protection because these networks are easier for someone to access. They should look into protected access, virtual private networks, or internet protocol security. Another option they have is an intrusion detection system. This system alerts when there are possible intrusions. Some companies set up traps or "hot spots" to attract people and are then able to know when someone is trying to hack into that area.

Encryption

Encryption, which is actually a part of cryptography, involves transforming texts or messages into a code which is unreadable. These messages have to be decrypted in order to be understandable or usable for someone. There is a key that identifies the data to a certain person or company. With public key encryption, there are actually two keys used. One is public and one is private. The public one is used for encryption, and the private for decryption. The level of the actual encryption can be adjusted and should be based on the information. The key can be just a simple slide of letters or a completely random mix-up of letters. This is relatively easy to implement because there is software that a company can purchase. A company needs to be sure that their keys are registered with a certificate authority.

Digital certificates

The point of a digital certificate is to identify the owner of a document. This way the receiver knows that it is an authentic document. Companies can use these certificates in several different ways. They can be used as a replacement for user names and passwords. Each employee can be given these to access the documents that they need from wherever they are. These certificates also use encryption. They are a little more complicated than normal encryption however. They actually used important information within the code. They do this in order to assure authenticity of the documents as well as confidentiality and data integrity which always accompany encryption. Digital certificates are not commonly used because they are confusing for people to implement. There can be complications when using different browsers, which means they need to use multiple certificates. The process is being adjusted so that it is easier to use.

Digital signatures

A final way to secure information online would be to use a digital signature. If a document has a digital signature on it, no one else is able to edit the information without being detected. That way if it is edited, it may be adjusted for reliability after the fact. In order to use a digital signature, one must use a combination of cryptography and a message digest. A message digest is used to give the document a unique value. That value is then encrypted with the sender's private key.

4

Basic Laws of Digital and Electronic Signature in India

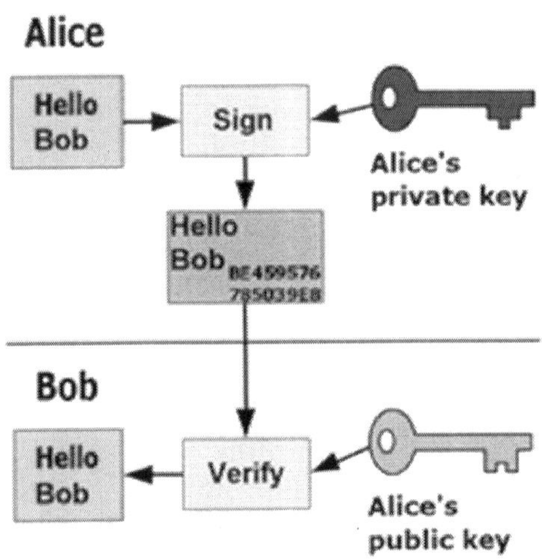

In this example the message is only signed and not encrypted. 1) Alice signs a message with her private key. 2) Bob can verify that Alice sent the message and that the message has not been modified.

A digital signature is a mathematical scheme for verifying the authenticity of digital messages or documents. A valid digital signature gives a recipient reason to believe that the message was created by a known sender (authentication), that the sender cannot deny having sent the message (non-repudiation), and that the message was not altered in transit (integrity).

Digital signatures are a standard element of most cryptographic protocol suites, and are commonly used for software distribution, financial transactions, contract management software, and in other cases where it is important to detect forgery or tampering.

Digital signatures are often used to implement electronic signatures, a broader term that refers to any electronic data that carries the intent of a signature, but not all electronic signatures use digital signatures. In some countries, including the United States, Algeria, Turkey, India, Brazil, Indonesia, Mexico, Saudi Arabia,, Uruguay, Switzerland and the countries of the European Union, electronic signatures have legal significance.

Digital signatures employ asymmetric cryptography. In many instances they provide a layer of validation and security to messages sent through a non-secure channel: Properly implemented, a digital signature gives the receiver reason to believe the message was sent by the claimed sender. Digital seals and signatures are equivalent to handwritten signatures and stamped seals. Digital signatures are equivalent to traditional handwritten signatures in many respects, but properly implemented digital signatures are more difficult to forge than the handwritten type. Digital signature schemes, in the sense used here, are cryptographically based, and must be implemented properly to be effective. Digital signatures can also provide non-repudiation, meaning that the signer cannot successfully claim they did not sign a message, while also claiming their private key remains secret. Further, some non-repudiation schemes offer a time stamp for the digital signature, so that even if the private key is exposed, the signature is valid. Digitally signed messages may be anything representable as a bitstring: examples include electronic mail, contracts, or a message sent via some other cryptographic protocol.

An electronic signature, or e-signature, refers to data in electronic form, which is logically associated with other data in electronic form and which is used by the signatory to sign. This type of signature provides the same legal standing as a handwritten signature as long as it adheres to the requirements of the specific regulation it was created under (e.g., eIDAS in the European Union, NIST-DSS in the USA or ZertES in Switzerland).

Electronic signatures are a legal concept distinct from digital signatures, a cryptographic mechanism often used to implement electronic signatures. While an electronic signature can be as simple as a name entered in an electronic document, digital signatures are increasingly used in e-commerce and in regulatory filings to implement electronic signatures in a cryptographically protected way. Standardization agencies like NIST or ETSI provide standards for their implementation (e.g., NIST-DSS, XAdES or PAdES). The concept itself is not new, with common law jurisdictions having recognized telegraph signatures as far back as the mid-19th century and faxed signatures since the 1980s.

In 1976, Whitfield Diffie and Martin Hellman first described the notion of a digital signature scheme, although they only conjectured that such schemes existed based on functions that are trapdoor one-way permutations. Soon afterwards, Ronald Rivest, Adi Shamir, and Len Adleman invented the RSA algorithm, which could be used to produce primitive digital signatures (although only as a proof-of-concept – "plain" RSA signatures are not secure). The first widely marketed software package to offer digital signature was Lotus Notes 1.0, released in 1989, which used the RSA algorithm.

Other digital signature schemes were soon developed after RSA, the earliest being Lamport signatures, Merkle signatures (also known as "Merkle trees" or simply "Hash trees"), and Rabin signatures.

In 1984, Shafi Goldwasser, Silvio Micali, and Ronald Rivest became the first to rigorously define the security requirements of digital signature schemes. They described a hierarchy of attack models for signature schemes, and also presented the GMR signature scheme, the first that could be proved to prevent even an existential forgery against a chosen message attack which is the currently accepted security definition for signature schemes. The first such scheme which is not built on trapdoor functions but rather on a family of function with a much weaker required property of one-way permutation was presented by Moni Naor and Moti Yung.

Method

One digital signature scheme (of many) is based on RSA. To create signature keys, generate a RSA key pair containing a modulus, N, that is the product of two random secret distinct large primes, along with integers, e and d, such that e d □ 1 (mod □(N)), where □ is the Euler phi-function. The signer's public key consists of N and e, and the signer's secret key contains d.

To sign a message, m, the signer computes a signature, □, such that □ □ m (mod N). To verify, the receiver checks that □ □ m (mod N).

Several early signature schemes were of a similar type: they involve the use of a trapdoor permutation, such as the RSA function, or in the case of the Rabin signature scheme, computing square modulo composite, N. A trapdoor permutation family is a family of permutations, specified by a parameter, that is easy to compute in the forward direction, but is difficult to compute in the reverse direction without already knowing the private key ("trapdoor"). Trapdoor permutations can be used for digital signature schemes, where computing the reverse direction with the secret key is required for signing, and computing the forward direction is used to verify signatures.

Used directly, this type of signature scheme is vulnerable to key-only existential forgery attack. To create a forgery, the attacker picks a random signature □ and uses the verification procedure to determine the message, m, corresponding to that signature. In practice, however, this type of signature is not used directly, but rather, the message to be signed is first hashed to produce a short digest, that is then padded to larger width comparable to N, then signed with the reverse trapdoor function. This forgery attack, then, only produces the padded hash function output that corresponds to , but not a message that leads to that value, which does not lead to an attack. In the random oracle model, hash-then-sign (an idealized version of that practice where hash and padding combined have close to N possible outputs), this form of signature is existentially unforgeable, even against a chosen-plaintext attack.

There are several reasons to sign such a hash (or message digest) instead of the whole document.

For efficiency

The signature will be much shorter and thus save time since hashing is generally much faster than signing in practice.

For compatibility

Messages are typically bit strings, but some signature schemes operate on other domains (such as, in the case of RSA, numbers modulo a composite number N). A hash function can be used to convert an arbitrary input into the proper format.

For integrity

Without the hash function, the text "to be signed" may have to be split (separated) in blocks small enough for the signature scheme to act on them directly. However, the receiver of the signed blocks is not able to recognize if all the blocks are present and in the appropriate order.

Notions of security

In their foundational paper, Goldwasser, Micali, and Rivest lay out a hierarchy of attack models against digital signatures:

1. In a key-only attack, the attacker is only given the public verification key.

2. In a known message attack, the attacker is given valid signatures for a variety of messages known by the attacker but not chosen by the attacker.

3. In an adaptive chosen message attack, the attacker first learns signatures on arbitrary messages of the attacker's choice.

They also describe a hierarchy of attack results:

1. A total break results in the recovery of the signing key.

2. A universal forgery attack results in the ability to forge signatures for any message.

3. A selective forgery attack results in a signature on a message of the adversary's choice.

4. An existential forgery merely results in some valid message/signature pair not already known to the adversary.

The strongest notion of security, therefore, is security against existential forgery under an adaptive chosen message attack.

Applications of digital signatures

As organizations move away from paper documents with ink signatures or authenticity stamps, digital signatures can provide added assurances of the evidence to provenance, identity, and status of an electronic document as well as acknowledging informed consent and approval by a signatory. The United States Government Printing Office (GPO) publishes electronic versions of the budget, public and private laws, and congressional bills with digital signatures. Universities including Penn State, University of Chicago, and Stanford are publishing electronic student transcripts with digital signatures.

Below are some common reasons for applying a digital signature to communications:

Authentication

Although messages may often include information about the entity sending a message, that information may not be accurate. Digital signatures can be used to authenticate the source of messages. When ownership of a digital signature secret key is bound to a specific user, a valid signature shows that the message was sent by that user. The importance of high confidence in sender authenticity is especially obvious in a financial context. For example, suppose a bank's branch office sends instructions to the central office requesting a change in the balance of an account. If the central office is not convinced that such a message is truly sent from an authorized source, acting on such a request could be a grave mistake.

Integrity

In many scenarios, the sender and receiver of a message may have a need for confidence that the message has not been altered during transmission. Although encryption hides the contents of a message, it may be possible to change an encrypted message without understanding it. (Some encryption algorithms, known as nonmalleable ones, prevent this, but others do not.) However, if a message is digitally signed, any change in the message after signature invalidates the signature. Furthermore, there is no efficient way to modify a message and its signature to produce a new message with a valid signature, because this is still considered to be computationally infeasible by most cryptographic hash functions (see collision resistance).

Non-repudiation

Non-repudiation, or more specifically non-repudiation of origin, is an important aspect of digital signatures. By this property, an entity that has signed some information cannot at a later time deny having signed it. Similarly, access to the public key only does not enable a fraudulent party to fake a valid signature.

Note that these authentication, non-repudiation etc. properties rely on the secret key not having been revoked prior to its usage. Public revocation of a key-pair is a required ability, else leaked secret keys would continue to implicate the claimed owner of the key-pair. Checking revocation status requires an "online" check; e.g., checking a certificate revocation list or via the Online Certificate Status Protocol. Very roughly this is analogous to a vendor who receives credit-cards first checking online with the credit-card issuer to find if a given card has been reported lost or stolen. Of course, with stolen key pairs, the theft is often discovered only after the secret key's use, e.g., to sign a bogus certificate for espionage purpose.

Additional security precautions

All public key / private key cryptosystems depend entirely on keeping the private key secret. A private key can be stored on a user's computer, and protected by a local password, but this has two disadvantages:

- the user can only sign documents on that particular computer
- the security of the private key depends entirely on the security of the computer

A more secure alternative is to store the private key on a smart card. Many smart cards are designed to be tamper-resistant (although some designs have been broken, notably by Ross Anderson and his students). In a typical digital signature implementation, the hash calculated from the document is sent to the smart card, whose CPU signs the hash using the stored private key of the user, and then returns the signed hash. Typically, a user must activate his smart card by entering a personal identification number or PIN code (thus providing two-factor authentication). It can be arranged that the private key never leaves the smart card, although this is not always implemented. If the smart card is stolen, the thief will still need the PIN code to generate a digital signature. This reduces the security of the scheme to that of the PIN system, although it still requires an attacker to possess the card. A mitigating factor is that private keys, if generated and stored on smart cards, are usually regarded as difficult to copy, and are assumed to exist in exactly one copy. Thus, the loss of the smart card may be detected by the owner and the corresponding certificate can be immediately revoked. Private keys that are protected by software only may be easier to copy, and such compromises are far more difficult to detect.

Using smart card readers with a separate keyboard

Entering a PIN code to activate the smart card commonly requires a numeric keypad. Some card readers have their own numeric keypad. This is safer than using a card reader integrated into a PC, and then entering the PIN using that computer's keyboard. Readers with a numeric keypad are meant to circumvent the eavesdropping threat where the computer might be running a keystroke logger, potentially compromising the PIN code. Specialized card readers are also less vulnerable to tampering with their software or hardware and are often EAL3 certified.

Other smart card designs

Smart card design is an active field, and there are smart card schemes which are intended to avoid these particular problems, though so far with little security proofs.

Using digital signatures only with trusted applications

One of the main differences between a digital signature and a written signature is that the user does not "see" what he signs. The user application presents a hash code to be signed by the digital signing algorithm using the private key. An attacker who gains control of the user's PC can possibly replace the user application with a foreign substitute, in effect replacing the user's own communications with those of the attacker. This could allow a malicious application to trick a user into signing any document by displaying the user's original on-screen, but presenting the attacker's own documents to the signing application.

To protect against this scenario, an authentication system can be set up between the user's application (word processor, email client, etc.) and the signing application. The general idea is to provide some means for both the user application and signing application to verify each other's integrity. For example, the signing application may require all requests to come from digitally signed binaries.

Using a network attached hardware security module

One of the main differences between a cloud based digital signature service and a locally provided one is risk. Many risk averse companies, including governments, financial and medical institutions, and payment processors require more secure standards, like FIPS 140-2 level 3 and FIPS 201 certification, to ensure the signature is validated and secure.

WYSIWYS

Technically speaking, a digital signature applies to a string of bits, whereas humans and applications "believe" that they sign the semantic interpretation of those bits. In order to be semantically interpreted, the bit string must be transformed into a form that is meaningful for humans and applications, and this is done through a combination of hardware and software based processes on a computer system. The problem is that the semantic interpretation of bits can change as a function of the processes used to transform the bits into semantic content. It is relatively easy to change the interpretation of a digital document by implementing changes on the computer system where the document is being processed. From a semantic perspective this creates uncertainty about what exactly has been signed. WYSIWYS (What You See Is What You Sign) means that the semantic interpretation of a signed message cannot be changed. In particular this also means that a message cannot contain hidden information that the signer is unaware of, and that can be revealed after the signature has been applied. WYSIWYS is a requirement for the validity of digital signatures, but this requirement is difficult to guarantee because of the increasing complexity of modern computer systems. The term WYSIWYS was coined by Peter Landrock and Torben Pedersen to describe some of the principles in delivering secure and legally binding digital signatures for Pan-European projects.

Digital signatures versus ink on paper signatures

An ink signature could be replicated from one document to another by copying the image manually or digitally, but to have credible signature copies that can resist some scrutiny is a significant manual or technical skill, and to produce ink signature copies that resist professional scrutiny is very difficult.

Digital signatures cryptographically bind an electronic identity to an electronic document and the digital signature cannot be copied to another document. Paper contracts sometimes have the ink signature block on the last page, and the previous pages may be replaced after a signature is applied. Digital signatures can be applied to an entire document, such that the digital signature on the last page will indicate tampering if any data on any of the pages have been altered, but this can also be achieved by signing with ink and numbering all pages of the contract.

Some digital signature algorithms

- RSA-based signature schemes, such as RSA-PSS
- DSA and its elliptic curve variant ECDSA
- Edwards-curve Digital Signature Algorithm and its Ed25519 variant.
- ElGamal signature scheme as the predecessor to DSA, and variants Schnorr signature and Pointcheval–Stern signature algorithm
- Rabin signature algorithm
- Pairing-based schemes such as BLS
- Undeniable signatures

• Aggregate signatureru - a signature scheme that supports aggregation: Given n signatures on n messages from n users, it is possible to aggregate all these signatures into a single signature whose size is constant in the number of users. This single signature will convince the verifier that the n users did indeed sign the n original messages. A scheme by Mihir Bellare and Gregory Neven may be used with Bitcoin.

• Signatures with efficient protocols - are signature schemes that facilitate efficient cryptographic protocols such as zero-knowledge proofs or secure computation.

The current state of use – legal and practical

All digital signature schemes share the following basic prerequisites regardless of cryptographic theory or legal provision:

1. Quality algorithms

Some public-key algorithms are known to be insecure, as practical attacks against them having been discovered.

2. Quality implementations

An implementation of a good algorithm (or protocol) with mistake(s) will not work.

3. Users (and their software) must carry out the signature protocol properly.

4. The private key must remain private

If the private key becomes known to any other party, that party can produce perfect digital signatures of anything whatsoever.

5. The public key owner must be verifiable

A public key associated with Bob actually came from Bob. This is commonly done using a public key infrastructure (PKI) and the public key󠀠user association is attested by the operator of the PKI (called a certificate authority). For 'open' PKIs in which anyone can request such an attestation (universally embodied in a cryptographically protected identity certificate), the possibility of mistaken attestation is non-trivial. Commercial PKI operators have suffered several publicly known problems. Such mistakes could lead to falsely signed, and thus wrongly attributed, documents. 'Closed' PKI systems are more expensive, but less easily subverted in this way.

Only if all of these conditions are met will a digital signature actually be any evidence of who sent the message, and therefore of their assent to its contents. Legal enactment cannot change this reality of the existing engineering possibilities, though some such have not reflected this actuality.

Legislatures, being importuned by businesses expecting to profit from operating a PKI, or by the technological avant-garde advocating new solutions to old problems, have enacted statutes and/or regulations in many jurisdictions authorizing, endorsing, encouraging, or permitting digital signatures and providing for (or limiting) their legal effect. The first appears to have been in Utah in the United States, followed closely by the states Massachusetts and California. Other countries have also passed statutes or issued regulations in this area as well and the UN has had an active model law project for some time. These enactments (or proposed enactments) vary from place to place, have typically embodied expectations at variance (optimistically or pessimistically) with the state of the underlying cryptographic engineering, and have had the net effect of confusing potential users and specifiers, nearly all of whom are not cryptographically knowledgeable. Adoption of technical standards for digital signatures have lagged behind much of the legislation, delaying a more or less unified engineering position on interoperability, algorithm choice, key lengths, and so on what the engineering is attempting to provide.

Industry standards

Some industries have established common interoperability standards for the use of digital signatures between members of the industry and with regulators. These include the Automotive Network Exchange for the automobile industry and the SAFE-BioPharma Association for the healthcare industry.

Using separate key pairs for signing and encryption

In several countries, a digital signature has a status somewhat like that of a traditional pen and paper signature, as in the 1999 EU digital signature directive and 2014 EU follow-on legislation. Generally, these provisions mean that anything digitally signed legally binds the signer of the document to the terms therein. For that reason, it is often thought best to use separate key pairs for encrypting and signing. Using the encryption key pair, a person can engage in an encrypted conversation (e.g., regarding a real estate transaction), but the encryption does not legally sign every message she or he sends. Only when both parties come to an agreement do they sign a contract with their signing keys, and only then are they legally bound by the terms of a specific document. After signing, the document can be sent over the encrypted link. If a signing key is lost or compromised, it can be revoked to mitigate any future transactions. If an encryption key is lost, a backup or key escrow should be utilized to continue viewing encrypted content. Signing keys should never be backed up or escrowed unless the backup destination is securely encrypted.

In contract law

Since well before the American Civil War began in 1861, morse code was used to send messages electrically by telegraphy. Some of these messages were agreements to terms that were intended as enforceable contracts. An early acceptance of the enforceability of telegraphic messages as electronic signatures came from the New Hampshire Supreme Court in 1869.

In the 1980s, many companies and even some individuals began using fax machines for high-priority or time-sensitive delivery of documents. Although the original signature on the original document was on paper, the image of the signature and its transmission was electronic.

Courts in various jurisdictions have decided that enforceable electronic signatures can include agreements made by email, entering a personal identification number (PIN) into a bank ATM, signing a credit or debit slip with a digital pen pad device (an application of graphics tablet technology) at a point of sale, installing software with a clickwrap software license agreement on the package, and signing electronic documents online.

The first agreement signed electronically by two sovereign nations was a Joint Communiqué recognizing the growing importance of the promotion of electronic commerce, signed by the United States and Ireland in 1998.

Enforceability

In 1996 the United Nations published the UNCITRAL Model Law on Electronic Commerce. Article 7 of the UNCITRAL Model Law on Electronic Commerce was highly influential in the development of electronic signature laws around the world, including in the US. In 2001, UNCITRAL concluded work on a dedicated text, the UNCITRAL Model Law on Electronic Signatures, which has been adopted in some 30 jurisdictions. The latest UNCITRAL text dealing with electronic signatures is article 9, paragraph 3 of the United Nations Convention on the Use of Electronic Communications in International Contracts, 2005, which establishes a mechanism for functional equivalence between electronic and handwritten signatures at the international level as well as for the cross-border recognition.

Canadian law (PIPEDA) attempts to clarify the situation by first defining a generic electronic signature as "a signature that consists of one or more letters, characters, numbers or other symbols in digital form incorporated in, attached to or associated with an electronic document", then defining a secure electronic signature as an electronic signature with specific properties. PIPEDA's secure electronic signature regulations refine the definition as being a digital signature applied and verified in a specific manner.

In the European Union, EU Regulation No 910/2014 on electronic identification and trust services for electronic transactions in the European internal market (eIDAS) sets the legal frame for electronic signatures. It repeals Directive 1999/93/EC. The current and applicable version of eIDAS was published by the European Parliament and the European Councilon

July 23, 2014. Following Article 25 (1) of the eIDAS regulation, an advanced electronic signature shall "not be denied legal effect and admissibility as evidence in legal proceedings". However it will reach a higher probative value when enhanced to the level of a qualified electronic signature. By requiring the use of a qualified electronic signature creation device and being based on a certificate that has been issued by a qualified trust service provider, the upgraded advanced signature then carries according to Article 25 (2) of the eIDAS Regulation the same legal value as a handwritten signature. However, this is only regulated in the European Union and similarly through ZertES in Switzerland. A qualified electronic signature is not defined in the United States.

The U.S. Code defines an electronic signature for the purpose of US law as "an electronic sound, symbol, or process, attached to or logically associated with a contract or other record and executed or adopted by a person with the intent to sign the record." It may be an electronic transmission of the document which contains the signature, as in the case of facsimile transmissions, or it may be encoded message, such as telegraphy using Morse code.

In the United States, the definition of what qualifies as an electronic signature is wide and is set out in the Uniform Electronic Transactions Act ("UETA") released by the National Conference of Commissioners on Uniform State Laws (NCCUSL) in 1999. It was influenced by ABA committee white papers and the uniform law promulgated by NCCUSL. Under UETA, the term means "an electronic sound, symbol, or process, attached to or logically associated with a record and executed or adopted by a person with the intent to sign the record." This definition and many other core concepts of UETA are echoed in the U.S. ESign Act of 2000. 47 US states, the District of Columbia, and the US Virgin Islands have enacted UETA. Only New York, Washington State, and Illinois have not enacted UETA, but each of those states has adopted its own electronic signatures statute.

Legal definitions

Various laws have been passed internationally to facilitate commerce by the use of electronic records and signatures in interstate and foreign commerce. The intent is to ensure the validity and legal effect of contracts entered into electronically. For instance,

PIPEDA (Canadian federal law)

(1) An electronic signature is "a signature that consists of one or more letters, characters, numbers or other symbols in digital form incorporated in, attached to or associated with an electronic document";

(2) A secure electronic signature is as an electronic signature that

(a) is unique to the person making the signature;

(b) the technology or process used to make the signature is under the sole control of the person making the signature;

(c) the technology or process can be used to identify the person using the technology or process; and

(d) the electronic signature can be linked with an electronic document in such a way that it can be used to determine whether the electronic document has been changed since the electronic signature was incorporated in, attached to or associated with the electronic document.

ESIGN Act Sec 106 (US federal law)

(2) ELECTRONIC- The term 'electronic' means relating to technology having electrical, digital, magnetic, wireless, optical, electromagnetic, or similar capabilities.

(4) ELECTRONIC RECORD- The term 'electronic record' means a contract or other record created, generated, sent, communicated, received, or stored by electronic means.

(5) ELECTRONIC SIGNATURE- The term 'electronic signature' means an electronic sound, symbol, or process, attached to or logically associated with a contract or other record and executed or adopted by a person with the intent to sign the record.

GPEA Sec 1710 (US federal law)

(1) ELECTRONIC SIGNATURE.—the term "electronic signature" means a method of signing an electronic message that—

(A) identifies and authenticates a particular person as the source of the electronic message; and

(B) indicates such person's approval of the information contained in the electronic message.

UETA Sec 2 (US state law)

(5) "Electronic" means relating to technology having electrical, digital, magnetic, wireless, optical, electromagnetic, or similar capabilities.

(6) "Electronic agent" means a computer program or an electronic or other automated means used independently to initiate an action or respond to electronic records or performances in whole or in part, without review or action by an individual.

(7) "Electronic record" means a record created, generated, sent, communicated, received, or stored by electronic means.

(8) "Electronic signature" means an electronic sound, symbol, or process attached to or logically associated with a record and executed or adopted by a person with the intent to sign the record.

Biometric signature

Electronic signature may also refer to electronic forms of processing or verifying identity through use of biometric "signatures" or biologically identifying qualities of an individual. Such signatures use the approach of attaching some biometric measurement, or hash of said measurement, to a document as evidence. For instance, fingerprints, hand geometry (finger lengths and palm size), iris patterns, or even retinal patterns. All of these are collected using electronic sensors of some kind. Since each of these physical characteristics has claims to uniqueness among humans, each is to some extent useful as a signature.

Biometric measurements of this type are useless as passwords, as they can't be changed if compromised. However, they might be serviceable as electronic signatures of a kind, except that to date they have been so easily spoofable that they can carry little assurance that the person who purportedly signed a document was actually the person who did. Unfortunately, each is easily spoofable by a replay of the electronic signal produced and submitted to the computer system responsible for 'affixing' a signature to a document. Wiretapping techniques often suffice for this. In the particular case of fingerprints, a Japanese professor and some graduate students managed to spoof all of the commercially available fingerprint readers available to them with some ordinary kitchen chemistry (gummy bear candy gel) and a little ingenuity. No actual fingers were needed to successfully spoof every reading device. In another example, researchers in Vietnam successfully demonstrated in late 2017 how a specially crafted mask could beat Apple's Face ID program on iPhone X.

5

UNCITRAL: Model Law on Electronic Commerce, 1996

The Model Law on Electronic Commerce (MLEC) purports to enable and facilitate commerce conducted using electronic means by providing national legislators with a set of internationally acceptable rules aimed at removing legal obstacles and increasing legal predictability for electronic commerce. In particular, it is intended to overcome obstacles arising from statutory provisions that may not be varied contractually by providing equal treatment to paper-based and electronic information. Such equal treatment is essential for enabling the use of paperless communication, thus fostering efficiency in international trade.

Why is it relevant?

The MLEC was the first legislative text to adopt the fundamental principles of non-discrimination, technological neutrality and functional equivalence that are widely regarded as the founding elements of modern electronic commerce law. The principle of non-discrimination ensures that a document would not be denied legal effect, validity or enforceability solely on the grounds that it is in electronic form. The principle of technological neutrality mandates the adoption of provisions that are neutral with respect to technology used. In light of the rapid technological advances, neutral rules aim at accommodating any future development without further legislative work. The functional equivalence principle lays out criteria under which electronic communications may be considered equivalent to paper-based communications. In particular, it sets out the specific requirements that electronic communications need to meet in order to fulfil the same purposes and functions that certain notions in the traditional paper-based system - for example, "writing," "original," "signed," and "record"- seek to achieve.

Key provisions

Besides formulating the legal notions of non-discrimination, technological neutrality and functional equivalence, the MLEC establishes rules for the formation and validity of contracts concluded by electronic means, for the attribution of data messages, for the acknowledgement of receipt and for determining the time and place of dispatch and receipt of data messages.

It should be noted that certain provisions of the MLEC were amended by the Electronic Communications Convention in light of recent electronic commerce practice. Moreover, part II of the MLEC, dealing with electronic commerce in connection with carriage of goods, has been complemented by other legislative texts, including the United Nations Convention on Contracts for the International Carriage of Goods Wholly or Partly by Sea (the "Rotterdam Rules") and may be the object of additional work of UNCITRAL in the future.

The UNCITRAL Model Law on Electronic Commerce was adopted by the United Nations Commission on International Trade Law (UNCITRAL) in 1996 in furtherance of its mandate to promote the harmonization and unification of international trade law, so as to remove unnecessary obstacles to international trade caused by inadequacies and divergences in the law affecting trade. Over the past quarter of a century, UNCITRAL, whose membership consists of States from all regions and of all levels of economic development, has implemented its mandate by formulating international conventions (the United Nations Conventions on Contracts for the International Sale of Goods, on the Limitation Period in the International Sale of Goods, on the Carriage of Goods by Sea, 1978 ("Hamburg Rules"), on the Liability of Operators of Transport Terminals in International Trade, on International Bills of Exchange and International Promissory Notes, and on Independent Guarantees and Stand-by Letters of Credit), model laws (the UNCITRAL Model Laws on International Commercial Arbitration, on International Credit Transfers and on Procurement of Goods, Construction and Services), the UNCITRAL Arbitration Rules, the UNCITRAL Conciliation Rules, and legal guides (on construction contracts, countertrade transactions and electronic funds transfers). 493

The Model Law was prepared in response to a major change in the means by which communications are made between parties using computerized or other modern techniques in doing business (sometimes referred to as "trading partners"). The Model Law is intended to serve as a model to countries for the evaluation and modernization of certain aspects of their laws and practices in the field of commercial relationships involving the use of computerized or other modern communication techniques, and for the establishment of relevant legislation where none presently exists. The text of the Model Law, as reproduced above, is set forth in annex I to the report of UNCITRAL on the work of its twenty-ninth session. 494

. The Commission, at its seventeenth session (1984), considered a report of the Secretary-General entitled "Legal aspects of automatic data processing" (A/CN.9/254), which identified several legal issues relating to the legal value of computer records, the requirement of a "writing", authentication, general conditions, liability and bills of lading. The Commission took note of a report of the Working Party on Facilitation of International Trade Procedures (WP.4), which is jointly sponsored by the Economic Commission for Europe and the United Nations Conference on Trade and Development, and is responsible for the development of UN/EDIFACT standard messages. That report suggested that, since the legal problems arising in this field were essentially those of international trade law, the Commission as the core legal body in the field of international trade law appeared to be the appropriate central forum to undertake and coordinate the necessary action. The Commission decided to place the subject of the legal implications of automatic data processing to the flow of international trade on its programme of work as a priority item.
495

At its eighteenth session (1985), the Commission had before it a report by the Secretariat entitled "Legal value of computer records" (A/CN.9/265). That report came to the conclusion that, on a global level, there were fewer problems in the use of data stored in computers as evidence in litigation than might have been expected. It noted that a more serious legal obstacle to the use of computers and computer-to-computer telecommunications in international trade arose out of requirements that documents had to be signed or be in paper form. After discussion of the report, the Commission adopted the following recommendation, which expresses some of the principles on which the Model Law is based: 496

"The United Nations Commission on International Trade Law, 497

"Noting that the use of automatic data processing (ADP) is about to become firmly established throughout the world in many phases of domestic and international trade as well as in administrative services, 498

"Noting also that legal rules based upon pre-ADP paper-based means of documenting international trade may create an obstacle to such use of ADP in that they lead to legal insecuri 499

"Noting further with appreciation the efforts of the Council of Europe, the Customs Co-operation Council and the United Nations Economic Commission for Europe to overcome obstacles to the use of ADP in international trade arising out of these legal rules, 500

"Considering at the same time that there is no need for a unification of the rules of evidence regarding the use of computer records in international trade, in view of the experience showing that substantial differences in the rules of evidence as they apply to the paper-based system of documentation have caused so far no noticeable harm to the development of international trade, 501

"Considering also that the developments in the use of ADP are creating a desirability in a number of legal systems for an adaptation of existing legal rules to these developments, having due regard, however, to the need to encourage the employment of such ADP means that would provide the same or greater reliability as paper-based documentation, 502

" Recommends to Governments: 503

"(a) to review the legal rules affecting the use of computer records as evidence in litigation in order to eliminate unnecessary obstacles to their admission, to be assured that the rules are consistent with developments in technology, and to provide appropriate means for a court to evaluate the credibility of the data contained in those records; 504

"(b) to review legal requirements that certain trade transactions or trade related documents be in writing, whether the written form is a condition to the enforceability or to the validity of the transaction or document, with a view to permitting, where appropriate, the transaction or document to be recorded and transmitted in computer-readable form; 505

"(c) to review legal requirements of a handwritten signature or other paper-based method of authentication on trade related documents with a view to permitting, where appropriate, the use of electronic means of authentication; 506

"(d) to review legal requirements that documents for submission to governments be in writing and manually signed with a view to permitting, where appropriate, such documents to be submitted in computer-readable form to those administrative services which have acquired the necessary equipment and established the necessary procedures; 507

"2. Recommends to international organizations elaborating legal texts related to trade to take account of the present Recommendation in adopting such texts and, where appropriate, to consider modifying existing legal texts in line with the present Recommendation." 508

That recommendation (hereinafter referred to as the "1985 UNCITRAL Recommendation") was endorsed by the General Assembly in resolution 40/71, paragraph 5(b), of 11 December 1985 as follows: 509

"The General Assembly, 510

"... Calls upon Governments and international organizations to take action, where appropriate, in conformity with the Commission's recommendation so as to ensure legal security in the context of the widest possible use of automated data processing in international trade; ...". 511

As was pointed out in several documents and meetings involving the international electronic commerce community, e.g. in meetings of WP. 4, there was a general feeling that, in spite of the efforts made through the 1985 UNCITRAL Recommendation, little progress had been made to achieve the removal of the mandatory requirements in national legislation regarding the use of paper and handwritten signatures. It has been suggested by the Norwegian Committee on Trade Procedures (NORPRO) in a letter to the Secretariat that "one reason for this could be that the 1985 UNCITRAL Recommendation advises on the need for legal update, but does not give any indication of how it could be done". In this vein, the Commission considered what follow-up action to the 1985 UNCITRAL Recommendation could usefully be taken so as to enhance the needed modernization of legislation. The decision by UNCITRAL to formulate model legislation on legal issues of electronic data interchange and related means of communication may be regarded as a consequence of the process that led to the adoption by the Commission of the 1985 UNCITRAL Recommendation. 512

At its twenty-first session (1988), the Commission considered a proposal to examine the need to provide for the legal principles that would apply to the formation of international commercial contracts by electronic means. It was noted that there existed no refined legal structure for the important and rapidly growing field of formation of contracts by electronic means and that future work in that area could help to fill a legal vacuum and to reduce uncertainties and difficulties encountered in practice. The Commission requested the Secretariat to prepare a preliminary study on the topic. 513

At its twenty-third session (1990), the Commission had before it a report entitled "Preliminary study of legal issues related to the formation of contracts by electronic means" (A/CN.9/333). The report summarized work that had been undertaken in the European Communities and in the United States of America on the requirement of a "writing" as well as other issues that had been identified as arising in the formation of contracts by electronic means. The efforts to overcome some of those problems by the use of model communication agreements were also discussed. 514

At its twenty-fourth session (1991), the Commission had before it a report entitled "Electronic Data Interchange" (A/CN.9/350). The report described the current activities in the various organizations involved in the legal issues of electronic data interchange (EDI) and analysed the contents of a number of standard interchange agreements already developed or then being developed. It pointed out that such documents varied considerably according to the various needs of the different categories of users they were intended to serve and that the variety of contractual arrangements had sometimes been described as hindering the development of a satisfactory legal framework for the business use of electronic commerce. It suggested that there was a need for a general framework that would identify the issues and provide a set of legal principles and basic legal rules governing communication through electronic commerce. It concluded that such a basic framework could, to a certain extent, be created by contractual arrangements between parties to an electronic commerce relationship and that the existing contractual frameworks that were proposed to the community of users of electronic commerce were often incomplete, mutually incompatible, and inappropriate for international use since they relied to a large extent upon the structures of local law. 515

With a view to achieving the harmonization of basic rules for the promotion of electronic commerce in international trade, the report suggested that the Commission might wish to consider the desirability of preparing a standard communication agreement for use in international trade. It pointed out that work by the Commission in this field would be of particular importance since it would involve participation of all legal systems, including those of developing countries that were already or would soon be confronted with the issues of electronic commerce. 516

The Commission was agreed that the legal issues of electronic commerce would become increasingly important as the use of electronic commerce developed and that it should undertake work in that field. There was wide support for the suggestion that the Commission should undertake the preparation of a set of legal principles and basic legal rules governing communication through electronic commerce. The Commission came to the conclusion that it would be premature to engage immediately in the preparation of a standard communication agreement and that it might be preferable to monitor developments in other organizations, particularly the Commission of the European Communities and the Economic Commission for Europe. It was pointed out that high-speed electronic commerce required a new examination of basic contract issues such as offer and acceptance, and that consideration should be given to legal implications of the role of central data managers in international commercial law. 517

After deliberation, the Commission decided that a session of the Working Group on International Payments would be devoted to identifying the legal issues involved and to considering possible statutory provisions, and that the Working Group would report to the Commission on the desirability and feasibility of undertaking further work such as the preparation of a standard communication agreement. 518

The Working Group on International Payments, at its twenty-fourth session, recommended that the Commission should undertake work towards establishing uniform legal rules on electronic commerce. It was agreed that the goals of such work should be to facilitate the increased use of electronic commerce and to meet the need for statutory provisions to be developed in the field of electronic commerce, particularly with respect to such issues as formation of contracts; risk and liability of commercial partners and third-party service providers involved in electronic commerce relationships; extended definitions of "writing" and "original" to be used in an electronic commerce environment; and issues of negotiability and documents of title (A/CN.9/360). 519

While it was generally felt that it was desirable to seek the high degree of legal certainty and harmonization provided by the detailed provisions of a uniform law, it was also felt that care should be taken to preserve a flexible approach to some issues where legislative action might be premature or inappropriate. As an example of such an issue, it was stated that it might be fruitless to attempt to provide legislative unification of the rules on evidence that may apply to electronic commerce massaging (ibid., para. 130). It was agreed that no decision should be taken at that early stage as to the final form or the final content of the legal rules to be prepared. In line with the flexible approach to be taken, it was noted that situations might arise where the preparation of model contractual clauses would be regarded as an appropriate way of addressing specific issues (ibid., para. 132). 520

. The Commission, at its twenty-fifth session (1992), endorsed the recommendation contained in the report of the Working Group (ibid., paras. 129-133) and entrusted the preparation of legal rules on electronic commerce (which was then referred to as "electronic data interchange" or "EDI") to the Working Group on International Payments, which it renamed the Working Group on Electronic Data Interchange. 521

The Working Group devoted its twenty-fifth to twenty-eighth sessions to the preparation of legal rules applicable to "electronic data interchange (EDI) and other modern means of communication" (reports of those sessions are found in documents A/CN.9/373, 387, 390 and 406). 522

The Working Group carried out its task on the basis of background working papers prepared by the Secretariat on possible issues to be included in the Model Law. Those background papers included A/CN.9/WG.IV/WP.53 (Possible issues to be included in the programme of future work on the legal aspects of EDI) and A/CN.9/WG.IV/WP.55 (Outline of possible uniform rules on the legal aspects of electronic data interchange). The draft articles of the Model Law were submitted by the Secretariat in documents A/CN.9/WG.IV/WP.57, 60 and 62. The Working Group also had before it a proposal by the United Kingdom of Great Britain and Northern Ireland relating to the possible contents of the draft Model Law (A/CN.9/WG.IV/WP.58). 523

The Working Group noted that, while practical solutions to the legal difficulties raised by the use of electronic commerce were often sought within contracts (A/CN.9/WG.IV/WP.53, paras. 35-36), the contractual approach to electronic commerce was developed not only because of its intrinsic advantages such as its flexibility, but also for lack of specific provisions of statutory or case law. The contractual approach was found to be limited in that it could not overcome any of the legal obstacles to the use of electronic commerce that might result from mandatory provisions of applicable statutory or case law. In that respect, one difficulty inherent in the use of communication agreements resulted from uncertainty as to the weight that would be carried by some contractual stipulations in case of litigation. Another limitation to the contractual approach resulted from the fact that parties to a contract could not effectively regulate the rights and obligations of third parties. At least for those parties not participating in the contractual arrangement, statutory law based on a model law or an international convention seemed to be needed (see A/CN.9/350, para. 107). 524

The Working Group considered preparing uniform rules with the aim of eliminating the legal obstacles to, and uncertainties in, the use of modern communication techniques, where effective removal of such obstacles and uncertainties could only be achieved by statutory provisions. One purpose of the uniform rules was to enable potential electronic commerce users to establish a legally secure electronic commerce relationship by way of a communication agreement within a closed network. The second purpose of the uniform rules was to support the use of electronic commerce outside such a closed network, i.e., in an open environment. However, the aim of the uniform rules was to enable, and not to impose, the use of EDI and related means of communication. Moreover, the aim of the uniform rules was not to deal with electronic commerce relationships from a technical perspective but rather to create a legal environment that would be as secure as possible, so as to facilitate the use of electronic commerce between communicating parties. 525

As to the form of the uniform rules, the Working Group was agreed that it should proceed with its work on the assumption that the uniform rules should be prepared in the form of statutory provisions. While it was agreed that the form of the text should be that of a "model law", it was felt, at first, that, owing to the special nature of the legal text being prepared, a more flexible term than "model law" needed to be found. It was observed that the title should reflect that the text contained a variety of provisions relating to existing rules scattered throughout various parts of the national laws in an enacting State. It was thus a possibility that enacting States would not incorporate the text as a whole and that the provisions of such a "model law" might not appear together in any one particular place in the national law. The text could be described, in the parlance of one legal system, as a "miscellaneous statute amendment act". The Working Group agreed that this special nature of the text would be better reflected by the use of the term "model statutory provisions". The view was also expressed that the nature and purpose of the "model statutory provisions" could be explained in an introduction or guidelines accompanying the text. 526

At its twenty-eighth session, however, the Working Group reviewed its earlier decision to formulate a legal text in the form of "model statutory provisions" (A/CN.9/390, para. 16). It was widely felt that the use of the term "model statutory provisions" might raise uncertainties as to the legal nature of the instrument. While some support was expressed for the retention of the term "model statutory provisions", the widely prevailing view was that the term "model law" should be preferred. It was widely felt that, as a result of the course taken by the Working Group as its work progressed towards the completion of the text, the model statutory provisions could be regarded as a balanced and discrete set of rules, which could also be implemented as a whole in a single instrument (A/CN.9/406, para. 75). Depending on the situation in each enacting State, however, the Model Law could be implemented in various ways, either as a single statute or in various pieces of legislation. 527

The text of the draft Model Law as approved by the Working Group at its twenty-eighth session was sent to all Governments and to interested international organizations for comment. The comments received were reproduced in document A/CN.9/409 and Add.1-4. The text of the draft articles of the Model Law as presented to the Commission by the Working Group was contained in the annex to document A/CN.9/406. 528

At its twenty-eighth session (1995), the Commission adopted the text of articles 1 and 3 to 11 of the draft Model Law and, for lack of sufficient time, did not complete its review of the draft Model Law, which was placed on the agenda of the twenty-ninth session of the Commission. 529

The Commission, at its twenty-eighth session, recalled that, at its twenty-seventh session (1994), general support had been expressed in favour of a recommendation made by the Working Group that preliminary work should be undertaken on the issue of negotiability and transferability of rights in goods in a computer-based environment as soon as the preparation of the Model Law had been completed. It was noted that, on that basis, a preliminary debate with respect to future work to be undertaken in the field of electronic data interchange had been held in the context of the twenty-ninth session of the Working Group (for the report on that debate, see A/CN.9/407, paras. 106-118). At that session, the Working Group also considered proposals by the International Chamber of Commerce (A/CN.9/WG.IV/WP.65) and the United Kingdom of Great Britain and Northern Ireland (A/CN.9/WG.IV/WP.66) relating to the possible inclusion in the draft Model Law of additional provisions to the effect of ensuring that certain terms and conditions that might be incorporated in a data message by means of a mere reference would be recognized as having the same degree of legal effectiveness as if they had been fully stated in the text of the data message (for the report on the discussion, see A/CN.9/407, paras. 100-105). It was agreed that the issue of incorporation by reference might need to be considered in the context of future work on negotiability and transferability of rights in goods (A/CN.9/407, para. 103). The Commission endorsed the recommendation made by the Working Group that the Secretariat should be entrusted with the preparation of a background study on negotiability and transferability of EDI transport documents, with particular emphasis on EDI maritime transport documents, taking into account the views expressed and the suggestions made at the twenty-ninth session of the Working Group. 530

. On the basis of the study prepared by the Secretariat (A/CN.9/WG.IV/WP.69), the Working Group, at its thirtieth session, discussed the issues of transferability of rights in the context of transport documents and approved the text of draft statutory provisions dealing with the specific issues of contracts of carriage of goods involving the use of data messages (for the report on that session, see A/CN.9/421). The text of those draft provisions as presented to the Commission by the Working Group for final review and possible addition as part II of the Model Law was contained in the annex to document A/CN.9/421.

In preparing the Model Law, the Working Group noted that it would be useful to provide in a commentary additional information concerning the Model Law. In particular, at the twenty-eighth session of the Working Group, during which the text of the draft Model Law was finalized for submission to the Commission, there was general support for a suggestion that the draft Model Law should be accompanied by a guide to assist States in enacting and applying the draft Model Law. The guide, much of which could be drawn from the travaux pr□paratoires of the draft Model Law, would also be helpful to users of electronic means of communication as well as to scholars in that area. The Working Group noted that, during its deliberations at that session, it had proceeded on the assumption that the draft Model Law would be accompanied by a guide. For example, the Working Group had decided in respect of a number of issues not to settle them in the draft Model Law but to address them in the guide so as to provide guidance to States enacting the draft Model Law. The Secretariat was requested to prepare a draft and submit it to the Working Group for consideration at its twenty-ninth session (A/CN.9/406, para. 177).

. At its twenty-ninth session, the Working Group discussed the draft Guide to Enactment of the Model Law (hereinafter referred to as "the draft Guide") as set forth in a note prepared by the Secretariat (A/CN.9/WG.IV/WP.64). The Secretariat was requested to prepare a revised version of the draft Guide reflecting the decisions made by the Working Group and taking into account the various views, suggestions and concerns that had been expressed at that session. At its twenty-eighth session, the Commission placed the draft Guide to Enactment of the Model Law on the agenda of its twenty-ninth session. 533

150. At its twenty-ninth session (1996), the Commission, after consideration of the text of the draft Model Law as revised by the drafting group, adopted the following decision at its 605th meeting, on 12 June 1996: 534

"The United Nations Commission on International Trade Law,

535

"Recalling its mandate under General Assembly resolution 2205 (XXI) of 17 December 1966 to further the progressive harmonization and unification of the law of international trade, and in that respect to bear in mind the interests of all peoples, and in particular those of developing countries, in the extensive development of international trade,

"Noting that an increasing number of transactions in international trade are carried out by means of electronic data interchange and other means of communication commonly referred to as 'electronic commerce', which involve the use of alternatives to paper-based forms of communication and storage of information,

"Recalling the recommendation on the legal value of computer records adopted by the Commission at its eighteenth session, in 1985, and paragraph 5(b) of General Assembly resolution 40/71 of 11 December 1985 calling upon Governments and international organizations to take action, where appropriate, in conformity with the recommendation of the Commission so as to ensure legal security in the context of the widest possible use of automated data processing in international trade,

"Being of the opinion that the establishment of a model law facilitating the use of electronic commerce, and acceptable to States with different legal, social and economic systems, contributes to the development of harmonious international economic relations,

"Being convinced that the UNCITRAL Model Law on Electronic Commerce will significantly assist all States in enhancing their legislation governing the use of alternatives to paper-based forms of communication and storage of information, and in formulating such legislation where none currently exists,

"1. Adopts the UNCITRAL Model Law on Electronic Commerce as it appears in annex I to the report on the current session;

"2. Requests the Secretary-General to transmit the text of the UNCITRAL Model Law on Electronic Commerce, together with the Guide to Enactment of the Model Law prepared by the Secretariat, to Governments and other interested bodies;

"3. Recommends that all States give favourable consideration to the UNCITRAL Model Law on Electronic Commerce when they enact or revise their laws, in view of the need for uniformity of the law applicable to alternatives to paper-based forms of communication and storage of information."

The Concept of Hash

Function

A hash function is any function that can be used to map data of arbitrary size to data of a fixed size. The values returned by a hash function are called hash values, hash codes, digests, or simply hashes. Hash functions are often used in combination with a hash table, a common data structure used in computer software for rapid data lookup. Hash functions accelerate table or database lookup by detecting duplicated records in a large file. One such application is finding similar stretches in DNA sequences. They are also useful in cryptography. A cryptographic hash function allows one to easily verify that some input data maps to a given hash value, but if the input data is unknown, it is deliberately difficult to reconstruct it (or any equivalent alternatives) by knowing the stored hash value. This is used for assuring integrity of transmitted data, and is the building block for HMACs, which provide message authentication.

Hash functions are related to (and often confused with) checksums, check digits, fingerprints, lossy compression, randomization functions, error-correcting codes, and ciphers. Although the concepts overlap to some extent, each one has its own uses and requirements and is designed and optimized differently. The HashKeeper database maintained by the American National Drug Intelligence Center, for instance, is more aptly described as a catalogue of file fingerprints than of hash values.

Uses

Hash tables

Hash functions are used in hash tables, to quickly locate a data record (e.g., a dictionary definition) given its search key (the headword). Specifically, the hash function is used to map the search key to a list; the index gives the place in the hash table where the corresponding record should be stored. Hash tables are also used to implement associative arraysand dynamic sets.

Typically, the domain of a hash function (the set of possible keys) is larger than its range (the number of different table indices), and so it will map several different keys to the same index which could result in collisions. So then, each slot of a hash table is associated with (implicitly or explicitly) a set of records, rather than a single record. For this reason, each slot of a hash table is often called a bucket, and hash values are also called bucket listing or a bucket index.

Thus, the hash function only hints at the record's location. Still, in a half-full table, a good hash function will typically narrow the search down to only one or two entries.

People who write complete hash table implementations choose a specific hash function—such as a Jenkins hash or Zobrist hashing—and independently choose a hash-table collision resolution scheme—such as coalesced hashing, cuckoo hashing, or hopscotch hashing.

Caches

Hash functions are also used to build caches for large data sets stored in slow media. A cache is generally simpler than a hashed search table, since any collision can be resolved by discarding or writing back the older of the two colliding items. This is also used in file comparison.

Bloom filters

Hash functions are an essential ingredient of the Bloom filter, a space-efficient probabilistic data structure that is used to test whether an element is a member of a set.

Finding duplicate records

When storing records in a large unsorted file, one may use a hash function to map each record to an index into a table T, and to collect in each bucket T[i] a list of the numbers of all records with the same hash value i. Once the table is complete, any two duplicate records will end up in the same bucket. The duplicates can then be found by scanning every bucket T[i] which contains two or more members, fetching those records, and comparing them. With a table of appropriate size, this method is likely to be much faster than any alternative approach (such as sorting the file and comparing all consecutive pairs).

Protecting data

A hash value can be used to uniquely identify secret information. This requires that the hash function is collision-resistant, which means that it is very hard to find data that will generate the same hash value. These functions are categorized into cryptographic hash functions and provably secure hash functions. Functions in the second category are the most secure but also too slow for most practical purposes. Collision resistance is accomplished in part by generating very large hash values. For example, SHA-2, one of the most widely used cryptographic hash functions, generates 256-bit values.

Finding similar records

Hash functions can also be used to locate table records whose key is similar, but not identical, to a given key; or pairs of records in a large file which have similar keys. For that purpose, one needs a hash function that maps similar keys to hash values that differ by at most m, where m is a small integer (say, 1 or 2). If one builds a table T of all record numbers, using such a hash function, then similar records will end up in the same bucket, or in nearby buckets. Then one need only check the records in each bucket T[i] against those in buckets T[i+k] where k ranges between –m and m.

This class includes the so-called acoustic fingerprint algorithms, that are used to locate similar-sounding entries in large collection of audio files. For this application, the hash function must be as insensitive as possible to data capture or transmission errors, and to trivial changes such as timing and volume changes, compression, etc.

Finding similar substrings

The same techniques can be used to find equal or similar stretches in a large collection of strings, such as a document repository or a genomic database. In this case, the input strings are broken into many small pieces, and a hash function is used to detect potentially equal pieces, as above.

The Rabin–Karp algorithm is a relatively fast string searching algorithm that works in O(n) time on average. It is based on the use of hashing to compare strings.

Geometric hashing

This principle is widely used in computer graphics, computational geometry and many other disciplines, to solve many proximity problems in the plane or in three-dimensional space, such as finding closest pairs in a set of points, similar shapes in a list of shapes, similar images in an image database, and so on. In these applications, the set of all inputs is some sort of metric space, and the hashing function can be interpreted as a partition of that space into a grid of cells. The table is often an array with two or more indices (called a grid file, grid index, bucket grid, and similar names), and the hash function returns an index tuple. This special case of hashing is known as geometric hashing or the grid method. Geometric hashing is also used in telecommunications (usually under the name vector quantization) to encode and compress multi-dimensional signals.

Standard uses of hashing in cryptography

Some standard applications that employ hash functions include authentication, message integrity (using an HMAC (Hashed MAC)), message fingerprinting, data corruption detection, and digital signature efficiency.

Properties

Good hash functions, in the original sense of the term, are usually required to satisfy certain properties listed below. The exact requirements are dependent on the application. For example, a hash function well suited to indexing data will probably be a poor choice for a cryptographic hash function.

Determinism

A hash procedure must be deterministic—meaning that for a given input value it must always generate the same hash value. In other words, it must be a function of the data to be hashed, in the mathematical sense of the term. This requirement excludes hash functions that depend on external variable parameters, such as pseudo-random number generatorsor the time of day. It also excludes functions that depend on the memory address of the object being hashed in cases that the address may change during execution (as may happen on systems that use certain methods of garbage collection), although sometimes rehashing of the item is possible.

The determinism is in the context of the reuse of the function. For example, Python adds the feature that hash functions make use of a randomized seed that is generated once when the Python process starts in addition to the input to be hashed. The Python hash is still a valid hash function when used within a single run. But if the values are persisted (for example, written to disk) they can no longer be treated as valid hash values, since in the next run the random value might differ.

Uniformity

A good hash function should map the expected inputs as evenly as possible over its output range. That is, every hash value in the output range should be generated with roughly the same probability. The reason for this last requirement is that the cost of hashing-based methods goes up sharply as the number of collisions—pairs of inputs that are mapped to the same hash value—increases. If some hash values are more likely to occur than others, a larger fraction of the lookup operations will have to search through a larger set of colliding table entries.

Note that this criterion only requires the value to be uniformly distributed, not random in any sense. A good randomizing function is (barring computational efficiency concerns) generally a good choice as a hash function, but the converse need not be true.

Hash tables often contain only a small subset of the valid inputs. For instance, a club membership list may contain only a hundred or so member names, out of the very large set of all possible names. In these cases, the uniformity criterion should hold for almost all typical subsets of entries that may be found in the table, not just for the global set of all possible entries.

In other words, if a typical set of m records is hashed to n table slots, the probability of a bucket receiving many more than m/n records should be vanishingly small. In particular, if mis less than n, very few buckets should have more than one or two records. (In an ideal "perfect hash function", no bucket should have more than one record; but a small number of collisions is virtually inevitable, even if n is much larger than m – see the birthday problem).

When testing a hash function, the uniformity of the distribution of hash values can be evaluated by the chi-squared test.

Defined range

It is often desirable that the output of a hash function have fixed size (but see below). If, for example, the output is constrained to 32-bit integer values, the hash values can be used to index into an array. Such hashing is commonly used to accelerate data searches. On the other hand, cryptographic hash functions produce much larger hash values, in order to ensure the computational complexity of brute-force inversion. For example, SHA-1, one of the most widely used cryptographic hash functions, produces a 160-bit value.

Producing fixed-length output from variable length input can be accomplished by breaking the input data into chunks of specific size. Hash functions used for data searches use some arithmetic expression which iteratively processes chunks of the input (such as the characters in a string) to produce the hash value. In cryptographic hash functions, these chunks are processed by a one-way compression function, with the last chunk being padded if necessary. In this case, their size, which is called block size, is much bigger than the size of the hash value. For example, in SHA-1, the hash value is 160 bits and the block size 512 bits.

Variable range

In many applications, the range of hash values may be different for each run of the program, or may change along the same run (for instance, when a hash table needs to be expanded). In those situations, one needs a hash function which takes two parameters—the input data z, and the number n of allowed hash values.

A common solution is to compute a fixed hash function with a very large range (say, 0 to 2 – 1), divide the result by n, and use the division's remainder. If n is itself a power of 2, this can be done by bit masking and bit shifting. When this approach is used, the hash function must be chosen so that the result has fairly uniform distribution between 0 and n – 1, for any value of n that may occur in the application. Depending on the function, the remainder may be uniform only for certain values of n, e.g. odd or prime numbers.

We can allow the table size n to not be a power of 2 and still not have to perform any remainder or division operation, as these computations are sometimes costly. For example, let nbe significantly less than 2. Consider a pseudorandom number generator (PRNG) function P(key) that is uniform on the interval [0, 2 – 1]. A hash function uniform on the interval [0, n-1] is n P(key)/2. We can replace the division by a (possibly faster) right bit shift: nP(key) >> b.

Variable range with minimal movement (dynamic hash function)

When the hash function is used to store values in a hash table that outlives the run of the program, and the hash table needs to be expanded or shrunk, the hash table is referred to as a dynamic hash table.

A hash function that will relocate the minimum number of records when the table is – where z is the key being hashed and n is the number of allowed hash values – such that H(z,n + 1) = H(z,n) with probability close to n/(n + 1).

Linear hashing and spiral storage are examples of dynamic hash functions that execute in constant time but relax the property of uniformity to achieve the minimal movement property.

Extendible hashing uses a dynamic hash function that requires space proportional to n to compute the hash function, and it becomes a function of the previous keys that have been inserted.

Several algorithms that preserve the uniformity property but require time proportional to n to compute the value of H(z,n) have been invented.

A hash function with minimal movement is especially useful in distributed hash tables.

Data normalization

In some applications, the input data may contain features that are irrelevant for comparison purposes. For example, when looking up a personal name, it may be desirable to ignore the distinction between upper and lower case letters. For such data, one must use a hash function that is compatible with the data equivalence criterion being used: that is, any two inputs that are considered equivalent must yield the same hash value. This can be accomplished by normalizing the input before hashing it, as by upper-casing all letters.

Continuity

"A hash function that is used to search for similar (as opposed to equivalent) data must be as continuous as possible; two inputs that differ by a little should be mapped to equal or nearly equal hash values."

Note that continuity is usually considered a fatal flaw for checksums, cryptographic hash functions, and other related concepts. Continuity is desirable for hash functions only in some applications, such as hash tables used in Nearest neighbor search.

Non-invertible

In cryptographic applications, hash functions are typically expected to be practically non-invertible, meaning that it is not realistic to reconstruct the input datum x from its hash value h(x) alone without spending great amounts of computing time (see also One-way function).

Hash function algorithms

For most types of hashing functions, the choice of the function depends strongly on the nature of the input data, and their probability distribution in the intended application.

Trivial hash function

If the data to be hashed is small enough, one can use the data itself (reinterpreted as an integer) as the hashed value. The cost of computing this "trivial" (identity) hash function is effectively zero. This hash function is perfect, as it maps each input to a distinct hash value.

The meaning of "small enough" depends on the size of the type that is used as the hashed value. For example, in Java, the hash code is a 32-bit integer. Thus the 32-bit integer Integer and 32-bit floating-point Float objects can simply use the value directly; whereas the 64-bit integer Long and 64-bit floating-point Double cannot use this method.

Other types of data can also use this perfect hashing scheme. For example, when mapping character strings between upper and lower case, one can use the binary encoding of each character, interpreted as an integer, to index a table that gives the alternative form of that character ("A" for "a", "8" for "8", etc.). If each character is stored in 8 bits (as in extended ASCII or ISO Latin 1), the table has only 2 = 256 entries; in the case of Unicode characters, the table would have 17×2 = 1114112 entries.

The same technique can be used to map two-letter country codes like "us" or "za" to country names (26 = 676 table entries), 5-digit zip codes like 13083 to city names (100000entries), etc. Invalid data values (such as the country code "xx" or the zip code 00000) may be left undefined in the table or mapped to some appropriate "null" value.

Perfect hashing

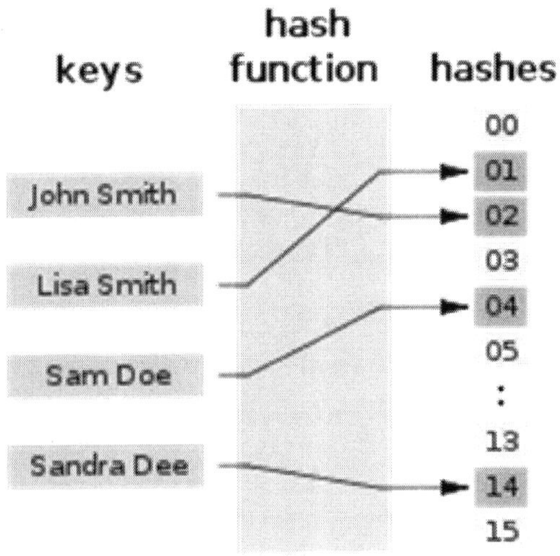

A perfect hash function for the four names shown

A hash function that is injective—that is, maps each valid input to a different hash value—is said to be perfect. With such a function one can directly locate the desired entry in a hash table, without any additional searching.

Minimal perfect hashing

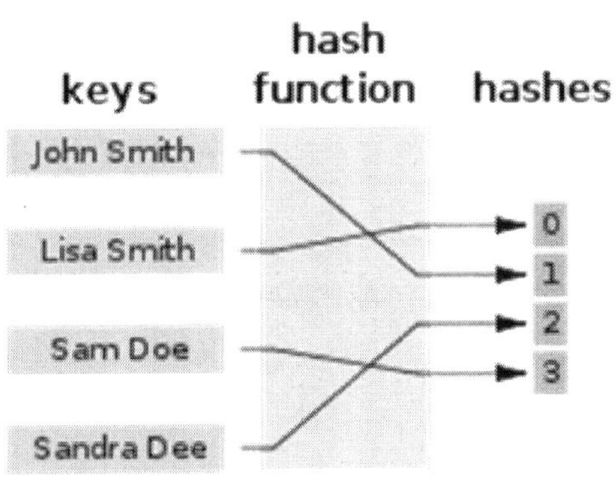

A minimal perfect hash function for the four names shown

A perfect hash function for n keys is said to be minimal if its range consists of n consecutive integers, usually from 0 to n–1. Besides providing single-step lookup, a minimal perfect hash function also yields a compact hash table, without any vacant slots. Minimal perfect hash functions are much harder to find than perfect ones with a wider range.

Hashing uniformly distributed data

If the inputs are bounded-length strings and each input may independently occur with uniform probability (such as telephone numbers, car license plates, invoice numbers, etc.), then a hash function needs to map roughly the same number of inputs to each hash value. For instance, suppose that each input is an integer z in the range 0 to N−1, and the output must be an integer h in the range 0 to n−1, where N is much larger than n. Then the hash function could be h = z mod n (the remainder of z divided by n), or h = (z × n) ÷ N (the value zscaled down by n/N and truncated to an integer), or many other formulas.

Hashing data with other distributions

These simple formulas will not do if the input values are not equally likely, or are not independent. For instance, most patrons of a supermarket will live in the same geographic area, so their telephone numbers are likely to begin with the same 3 to 4 digits. In that case, if m is 10000 or so, the division formula (z × m) ÷ M, which depends mainly on the leading digits, will generate a lot of collisions; whereas the remainder formula z mod m, which is quite sensitive to the trailing digits, may still yield a fairly even distribution.

Hashing variable-length data

When the data values are long (or variable-length) character strings—such as personal names, web page addresses, or mail messages—their distribution is usually very uneven, with complicated dependencies. For example, text in any natural language has highly non-uniform distributions of characters, and character pairs, vary characteristic of the language. For such data, it is prudent to use a hash function that depends on all characters of the string—and depends on each character in a different way.

This schema is also used in many text checksum and fingerprint algorithms. The state variable S may be a 32- or 64-bit unsigned integer; in that case, S0 can be 0, and F(S,n) can be just S mod n. The best choice of F is a complex issue and depends on the nature of the data. If the units b[k] are single bits, then F(S,b) could be, for instance

Here highbit(S) denotes the most significant bit of S; the '*' operator denotes unsigned integer multiplication with lost overflow; '^' is the bitwise exclusive or operation applied to words; and P is a suitable fixed word.

Special-purpose hash functions

In many cases, one can design a special-purpose (heuristic) hash function that yields many fewer collisions than a good general-purpose hash function. For example, suppose that the input data are file names such as FILE0000.CHK, FILE0001.CHK, FILE0002.CHK, etc., with mostly sequential numbers. For such data, a function that extracts the numeric part kof the file name and returns k mod n would be nearly optimal. Needless to say, a function that is exceptionally good for a specific kind of data may have dismal performance on data with different distribution.

Rolling hash

In some applications, such as substring search, one must compute a hash function h for every k-character substring of a given n-character string t; where k is a fixed integer, and n is greater than k. The straightforward solution, which is to extract every such substring s of t and compute h(s) separately, requires a number of operations proportional to k•n. However, with the proper choice of h, one can use the technique of rolling hash to compute all those hashes with an effort proportional to k + n.

Universal hashing

A universal hashing scheme is a randomized algorithm that selects a hashing function h among a family of such functions, in such a way that the probability of a collision of any two distinct keys is 1/n, where n is the number of distinct hash values desired—independently of the two keys. Universal hashing ensures (in a probabilistic sense) that the hash function application will behave as well as if it were using a random function, for any distribution of the input data. It will, however, have more collisions than perfect hashing and may require more operations than a special-purpose hash function. See also unique permutation hashing.

Hashing with checksum functions

One can adapt certain checksum or fingerprinting algorithms for use as hash functions. Some of those algorithms will map arbitrarily long string data z, with any typical real-world distribution—no matter how non-uniform and dependent—to a 32-bit or 64-bit string, from which one can extract a hash value in 0 through n – 1.

This method may produce a sufficiently uniform distribution of hash values, as long as the hash range size n is small compared to the range of the checksum or fingerprint function. However, some checksums fare poorly in the avalanche test, which may be a concern in some applications. In particular, the popular CRC32 checksum provides only 16 bits (the higher half of the result) that are usable for hashing. Moreover, each bit of the input has a deterministic effect on each bit of the CRC32 output; that is, one can tell without looking at the rest of the input which bits of the output will flip if the input bit is flipped, so care must be taken to use all 32 bits when computing the hash from the checksum.

Multiplicative hashing

Multiplicative hashing is a simple type of hash function often used by teachers introducing students to hash tables. Standard multiplicative hashing uses the formula which produces a hash value in . The value is an appropriately chosen value that should be relatively prime to . An important practical special case occurs when and are powers of 2 and is the machine word size. In this case this formula becomes . This is special because arithmetic modulo is done by default in low-level programming languages and integer division by a power of 2 is simply a right-shift, so, in C, for example, this function becomes

and for fixed and this translates into a single integer multiplication and right-shift making it one of the fastest hash functions to compute. Furthermore, if is a uniformly random odd integer in then this hash function is nearly universal in the sense that, for any , .

In many applications, such as hash tables, collisions make the system a little slower but are otherwise harmless. In such systems, it is often better to use hash functions based on multiplication—such as MurmurHash and the SBoxHash—or even simpler hash functions such as CRC32—and tolerate more collisions; rather than use a more complex hash function that avoids many of those collisions but takes longer to compute. Multiplicative hashing is susceptible to a "common mistake" that leads to poor diffusion—higher-value input bits do not affect lower-value output bits.

Hashing with cryptographic hash functions

Some cryptographic hash functions, such as SHA-1, have even stronger uniformity guarantees than checksums or fingerprints, and thus can provide very good general-purpose hashing functions.

In ordinary applications, this advantage may be too small to offset their much higher cost. However, this method can provide uniformly distributed hashes even when the keys are chosen by a malicious agent. This feature may help to protect services against denial of service attacks.

Hashing by nonlinear table lookup

Tables of random numbers (such as 256 random 32-bit integers) can provide high-quality nonlinear functions to be used as hash functions or for other purposes such as cryptography. The key to be hashed is split into 8-bit (one-byte) parts, and each part is used as an index for the nonlinear table. The table values are then added by arithmetic or XOR addition to the hash output value. Because the table is just 1024 bytes in size, it fits into the cache of modern microprocessors and allows very fast execution of the hashing algorithm. As the table value is on average much longer than 8 bits, one bit of input affects nearly all output bits.

This algorithm has proven to be very fast and of high quality for hashing purposes (especially hashing of integer-number keys).

Efficient hashing of strings

Modern microprocessors will allow for much faster processing, if 8-bit character strings are not hashed by processing one character at a time, but by interpreting the string as an array of 32 bit or 64 bit integers and hashing/ accumulating these "wide word" integer values by means of arithmetic operations (e.g. multiplication by constant and bit-shifting). The remaining characters of the string which are smaller than the word length of the CPU must be handled differently (e.g. being processed one character at a time).

This approach has proven to speed up hash code generation by a factor of five or more on modern microprocessors of a word size of 64 bit.

Another approach is to convert strings to a 32 or 64 bit numeric value and then apply a hash function. One method that avoids the problem of strings having great similarity ("Aaaaaaaaaa" and "Aaaaaaaaab") is to use a Cyclic redundancy check (CRC) of the string to compute a 32- or 64-bit value. While it is possible that two different strings will have the same CRC, the likelihood is very small and only requires that one check the actual string found to determine whether one has an exact match. CRCs will be different for strings such as "Aaaaaaaaaa" and "Aaaaaaaaab". Although CRC codes can be used as hash values, they are not cryptographically secure, because they are not collision-resistant.

Locality-sensitive hashing

Locality-sensitive hashing (LSH) is a method of performing probabilistic dimension reduction of high-dimensional data. The basic idea is to hash the input items so that similar items are mapped to the same buckets with high probability (the number of buckets being much smaller than the universe of possible input items). This is different from the conventional hash functions, such as those used in cryptography, as in this case the goal is to minimize the probability of "collision" of every item.

One example of LSH is MinHash algorithm used for finding similar documents (such as web-pages):

Let h be a hash function that maps the members of A and B to distinct integers, and for any set S define h(S) to be the member x of S with the minimum value of h(x). Then h(A) = h(B) exactly when the minimum hash value of the union A ▯ B lies in the intersection A ▯ B. Therefore,

Pr[h(A) = h(B)] = J(A,B). where J is Jaccard index.

In other words, if r is a random variable that is one when h(A) = h(B) and zero otherwise, then r is an unbiased estimator of J(A,B), although it has too high a variance to be useful on its own. The idea of the MinHash scheme is to reduce the variance by averaging together several variables constructed in the same way.

O

6

Certifying Authority

A robot certificate authority is a certificate authority (CA) which automatically signs public keys which match some requirement.

Typically Robot CAs are set up to validate that the public key belonging to an e-mail address does actually belong to the e-mail address. This is achieved by the Robot CA signing each uid on the public key and sending the signed copy to the e-mail address, encrypted with the public key. If the public key belongs to whoever reads the e-mail address, they receive the signed copy, can decrypt it and then publish it to the public key servers. If the public key does not belong to whoever reads the e-mail address, they are unable to decrypt the encrypted key, but the accompanying message gives them sufficient information to let them know that someone is attempting to impersonate them.

Robot CAs are considered significantly less secure than other CAs, which typically require multiple forms of photograph identification. In particular most robot CAs are only as strong as the underlying e-mail infrastructure: anyone who can read another person's mail can impersonate them and anyone who can read and delete another person's e-mail can get the signature without the person knowing if they don't read their e-mail at exactly the right time or the impostor prevents the signature e-mail from being seen. Robot CAs also offer no evidence as to the real identity of an OpenPGP user, merely their e-mail address. All well behaved Robot CAs use a signature policy URL, which is the URL of the policy under which the keys are signed.

A Robot CA also has the side effect of serving as a time stamp server for keys because a time stamp is included in the signature added to the key. The signature is evidence that the key existed and was in use at a certain point in time.

Certifying Authority

CA is an entity that issues digital certificates. A digital certificate certifies the ownership of a public key by the named subject of the certificate. This allows others (relying parties) to rely upon signatures or on assertions made about the private key that corresponds to the certified public key. A CA acts as a trusted third party—trusted both by the subject (owner) of the certificate and by the party relying upon the certificate. The format of these certificates is specified by the X.509 standard.

One particularly common use for certificate authorities is to sign certificates used in HTTPS, the secure browsing protocol for the World Wide Web. Another common use is in issuing identity cards by national governments for use in electronically signing documents.

Trusted certificates can be used to create secure connections to a server via the Internet. A certificate is essential in order to circumvent a malicious party which happens to be on the route to a target server which acts as if it were the target. Such a scenario is commonly referred to as a man-in-the-middle attack. The client uses the CA certificate to authenticate the CA signature on the server certificate, as part of the authorizations before launching a secure connection. Usually, client software—for example, browsers—include a set of trusted CA certificates. This makes sense, as many users need to trust their client software. A malicious or compromised client can skip any security check and still fool its users into believing otherwise.

The clients of a CA are server supervisors who call for a certificate that their servers will bestow to users. Commercial CAs charge to issue certificates, and their customers anticipate the CA's certificate to be contained within the majority of web browsers, so that safe connections to the certified servers work efficiently out-of-the-box. The quantity of internet browsers, other devices and applications which trust a particular certificate authority is referred to as ubiquity. Mozilla, which is a non-profit business, issues several commercial CA certificates with its products. While Mozilla developed their own policy, the CA/Browser Forum developed similar guidelines for CA trust. A single CA certificate may be shared among multiple CAs or their resellers. A root CA certificate may be the base to issue multiple intermediate CA certificates with varying validation requirements.

In addition to commercial CAs, some non-profits issue digital certificates to the public without charge; notable examples are CAcert and Let's Encrypt.

Large organizations or government bodies may have their own PKIs (public key infrastructure), each containing their own CAs. Any site using self-signed certificates acts as its own CA.

Browsers and other clients of sorts characteristically allow users to add or do away with CA certificates at will. While server certificates regularly last for a relatively short period, CA certificates are further extended, so, for repeatedly visited servers, it is less error-prone importing and trusting the CA issued, rather than confirm a security exemption each time the server's certificate is renewed.

Less often, trustworthy certificates are used for encrypting or signing messages. CAs dispense end-user certificates too, which can be used with S/MIME. However, encryption entails the receiver's public key and, since authors and receivers of encrypted messages, apparently, know one another, the usefulness of a trusted third party remains confined to the signature verification of messages sent to public mailing lists.

Providers

Worldwide, the certificate authority business is fragmented, with national or regional providers dominating their home market. This is because many uses of digital certificates, such as for legally binding digital signatures, are linked to local law, regulations, and accreditation schemes for certificate authorities.

However, the market for globally trusted TLS/SSL server certificates is largely held by a small number of multinational companies. This market has significant barriers to entry due to the technical requirements. While not legally required, new providers may choose to undergo annual security audits (such as WebTrust for certificate authorities in North America and ETSI in Europe) to be included as a trusted root by a web browser or operating system. More than 180 root certificates are trusted in the Mozilla Firefox web browser, representing approximately eighty organizations. Over 200 root certificates are trusted by macOS. As of Android 4.2 (Jelly Bean), Android currently contains over 100 CAs that are updated with each release.

On November 18, 2014, a group of companies and nonprofit organizations, including the Electronic Frontier Foundation, Mozilla, Cisco, and Akamai, announced Let's Encrypt, a nonprofit certificate authority that provides free domain validated X.509 certificates as well as software to enable installation and maintenance of certificates. Let's Encrypt is operated by the newly formed Internet Security Research Group, a California nonprofit recognized as tax-exempt under Section 501(c)(3).

According to NetCraft in May 2015, the industry standard for monitoring active TLS certificates, states that "Although the global [TLS] ecosystem is competitive, it is dominated by a handful of major CAs — three certificate authorities (Symantec, Comodo, GoDaddy) account for three-quarters of all issued [TLS] certificates on public-facing web servers. The top spot has been held by Symantec (or VeriSign before it was purchased by Symantec) ever since [our] survey began, with it currently accounting for just under a third of all certificates. To illustrate the effect of differing methodologies, amongst the million busiest sites Symantec issued 44% of the valid, trusted certificates in use — significantly more than its overall market share."

Validation standards

The commercial CAs that issue the bulk of certificates for HTTPS servers typically use a technique called "domain validation" to authenticate the recipient of the certificate. The techniques used for domain validation vary between CAs, but in general domain validation techniques are meant to prove that the certificate applicant controls a given domain name, not any information about the applicant's identity.

Many Certificate Authorities also offer Extended Validation (EV) certificates as a more rigorous alternative to domain validated certificates. Extended validation is intended to verify not only control of a domain name, but additional identity information to be included in the certificate. Some browsers display this additional identity information in a green box in the URL bar. One limitation of EV as a solution to the weaknesses of domain validation is that attackers could still obtain a domain validated certificate for the victim domain, and deploy it during an attack; if that occurred, the difference observable to the victim user would be the absence of a green bar with the company name. There is some question as to whether users would be likely to recognise this absence as indicative of an attack being in progress: a test using Internet Explorer 7 in 2009 showed that the absence of IE7's EV warnings were not noticed by users, however Microsoft's current browser, Edge, shows a significantly greater difference between EV and domain validated certificates, with domain validated certificates having a hollow, grey lock.

Validation weaknesses

Domain validation suffers from certain structural security limitations. In particular, it is always vulnerable to attacks that allow an adversary to observe the domain validation probes that CAs send. These can include attacks against the DNS, TCP, or BGP protocols (which lack the cryptographic protections of TLS/SSL), or the compromise of routers. Such attacks are possible either on the network near a CA, or near the victim domain itself.

One of the most common domain validation techniques involves sending an email containing an authentication token or link to an email address that is likely to be administratively responsible for the domain. This could be the technical contact email address listed in the domain's WHOIS entry, or an administrative email like admin@, administrator@, webmaster@, hostmaster@ or postmaster@ the domain. Some Certificate Authorities may accept confirmation using root@, info@, or support@ in the domain. The theory behind domain validation is that only the legitimate owner of a domain would be able to read emails sent to these administrative addresses.

Domain validation implementations have sometimes been a source of security vulnerabilities. In one instance, security researchers showed that attackers could obtain certificates for webmail sites because a CA was willing to use an email address like ssladmin@domain.com for domain.com, but not all webmail systems had reserved the "ssladmin" username to prevent attackers from registering it.

Prior to 2011, there was no standard list of email addresses that could be used for domain validation, so it was not clear to email administrators which addresses needed to be reserved. The first version of the CA/Browser Forum Baseline Requirements, adopted November 2011, specified a list of such addresses. This allowed mail hosts to reserve those addresses for administrative use, though such precautions are still not universal. In January 2015, a Finnish man registered the username "hostmaster" at the Finnish version of Microsoft Live and was able to obtain a domain-validated certificate for live.fi, despite not being the owner of the domain name.

Issuing a certificate

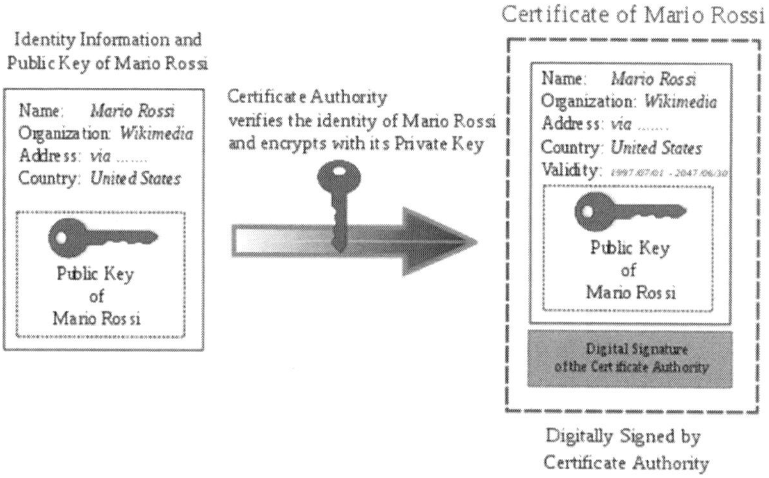

The procedure of obtaining a Public key certificate

A CA issues digital certificates that contain a public key and the identity of the owner. The matching private key is not made available publicly, but kept secret by the end user who generated the key pair. The certificate is also a confirmation or validation by the CA that the public key contained in the certificate belongs to the person, organization, server or other entity noted in the certificate. A CA's obligation in such schemes is to verify an applicant's credentials, so that users and relying parties can trust the information in the CA's certificates. CAs use a variety of standards and tests to do so. In essence, the certificate authority is responsible for saying "yes, this person is who they say they are, and we, the CA, certify that".

If the user trusts the CA and can verify the CA's signature, then they can also assume that a certain public key does indeed belong to whoever is identified in the certificate.

Example

Public-key cryptography can be used to encrypt data communicated between two parties. This can typically happen when a user logs on to any site that implements the HTTP Secure protocol. In this example let us suppose that the user logs on to their bank's homepage www.bank.example to do online banking. When the user opens www.bank.example homepage, they receive a public key along with all the data that their web-browser displays. The public key could be used to encrypt data from the client to the server but the safe procedure is to use it in a protocol that determines a temporary shared symmetric encryption key; messages in such a key exchange protocol can be enciphered with the bank's public key in such a way that only the bank server has the private key to read them.

The rest of the communication then proceeds using the new (disposable) symmetric key, so when the user enters some information to the bank's page and submits the page (sends the information back to the bank) then the data the user has entered to the page will be encrypted by their web browser. Therefore, even if someone can access the (encrypted) data that was communicated from the user to www.bank.example, such eavesdropper cannot read or decipher it.

This mechanism is only safe if the user can be sure that it is the bank that they see in their web browser. If the user types in www.bank.example, but their communication is hijacked and a fake website (that pretends to be the bank website) sends the page information back to the user's browser, the fake web-page can send a fake public key to the user (for which the fake site owns a matching private key). The user will fill the form with their personal data and will submit the page. The fake web-page will then get access to the user's data.

This is what the certificate authority mechanism is intended to prevent. A certificate authority (CA) is an organization that stores public keys and their owners, and every party in a communication trusts this organization (and knows its public key). When the user's web browser receives the public key from www.bank.example it also receives a digital signature of the key (with some more information, in a so-called X.509 certificate). The browser already possesses the public key of the CA and consequently can verify the signature, trust the certificate and the public key in it: since www.bank.example uses a public key that the certification authority certifies, a fake www.bank.example can only use the same public key. Since the fake www.bank.example does not know the corresponding private key, it cannot create the signature needed to verify its authenticity.

Security

It is difficult to assure correctness of match between data and entity when the data are presented to the CA (perhaps over an electronic network), and when the credentials of the person/company/program asking for a certificate are likewise presented. This is why commercial CAs often use a combination of authentication techniques including leveraging government bureaus, the payment infrastructure, third parties' databases and services, and custom heuristics. In some enterprise systems, local forms of authentication such as Kerberos can be used to obtain a certificate which can in turn be used by external relying parties. Notaries are required in some cases to personally know the party whose signature is being notarized; this is a higher standard than is reached by many CAs. According to the American Bar Association outline on Online Transaction Management the primary points of US Federal and State statutes enacted regarding digital signatures has been to "prevent conflicting and overly burdensome local regulation and to establish that electronic writings satisfy the traditional requirements associated with paper documents." Further the US E-Sign statute and the suggested UETA code help ensure that:

1. a signature, contract or other record relating to such transaction may not be denied legal effect, validity, or enforceability solely because it is in electronic form; and

2. a contract relating to such transaction may not be denied legal effect, validity or enforceability solely because an electronic signature or electronic record was used in its formation.

Despite the security measures undertaken to correctly verify the identities of people and companies, there is a risk of a single CA issuing a bogus certificate to an imposter. It is also possible to register individuals and companies with the same or very similar names, which may lead to confusion. To minimize this hazard, the certificate transparency initiativeproposes auditing all certificates in a public unforgeable log, which could help in the prevention of phishing.

In large-scale deployments, Alice may not be familiar with Bob's certificate authority (perhaps they each have a different CA server), so Bob's certificate may also include his CA's public key signed by a different CA, which is presumably recognizable by Alice. This process typically leads to a hierarchy or mesh of CAs and CA certificates.

Authority revocation lists

An authority revocation list (ARL) is a form of certificate revocation list (CRL) containing certificates issued to certificate authorities, contrary to CRLs which contain revoked end-entity certificates.

Industry organizations

- Certificate Authority Security Council (CASC) – In February 2013, the CASC was founded as an industry advocacy organization dedicated to addressing industry issues and educating the public on internet security. The founding members are the seven largest Certificate Authorities.

- Common Computing Security Standards Forum (CCSF) – In 2009 the CCSF was founded to promote industry standards that protect end users. Comodo Group CEO Melih Abdulhayoğlu is considered the founder of the CCSF.

- CA/Browser Forum – In 2005, a new consortium of Certificate Authorities and web browser vendors was formed to promote industry standards and baseline requirements for internet security. Comodo Group CEO Melih Abdulhayoğlu organized the first meeting and is considered the founder of the CA/Browser Forum.

Baseline requirements

The CA/Browser Forum publishes the Baseline Requirements, a list of policies and technical requirements for CAs to follow. These are a requirement for inclusion in the certificate stores of Firefox and Safari.

CA compromise

If the CA can be subverted, then the security of the entire system is lost, potentially subverting all the entities that trust the compromised CA.

For example, suppose an attacker, Eve, manages to get a CA to issue to her a certificate that claims to represent Alice. That is, the certificate would publicly state that it represents Alice, and might include other information about Alice. Some of the information about Alice, such as her employer name, might be true, increasing the certificate's credibility. Eve, however, would have the all-important private key associated with the certificate. Eve could then use the certificate to send digitally signed email to Bob, tricking Bob into believing that the email was from Alice. Bob might even respond with encrypted email, believing that it could only be read by Alice, when Eve is actually able to decrypt it using the private key.

A notable case of CA subversion like this occurred in 2001, when the certificate authority VeriSign issued two certificates to a person claiming to represent Microsoft. The certificates have the name "Microsoft Corporation", so they could be used to spoof someone into believing that updates to Microsoft software came from Microsoft when they actually did not. The fraud was detected in early 2001. Microsoft and VeriSign took steps to limit the impact of the problem.

In 2011 fraudulent certificates were obtained from Comodo and DigiNotar, allegedly by Iranian hackers. There is evidence that the fraudulent DigiNotar certificates were used in a man-in-the-middle attack in Iran.

In 2012, it became known that Trustwave issued a subordinate root certificate that was used for transparent traffic management (man-in-the-middle) which effectively permitted an enterprise to sniff SSL internal network traffic using the subordinate certificate.

Key storage

An attacker who steals a certificate authority's private keys is able to forge certificates as if they were CA, without needed ongoing access to the CA's systems. Key theft is therefore one of the main risks certificate authorities defend against. Publicly trusted CAs almost always store their keys on a hardware security module (HSM), which allows them to sign certificates with a key, but generally prevent extraction of that key with both physical and software controls. CAs typically take the further precaution of keeping the key for their long-term root certificates in an HSM that is kept offline, except when it is needed to sign shorter-lived intermediate certificates. The intermediate certificates, stored in an online HSM, can do the day-to-day work of signing end-entity certificates and keeping revocation information up to date.

CAs sometimes use a key ceremony when generating signing keys, in order to ensure that the keys are not tampered with or copied.

Implementation weakness of the trusted third party scheme

The critical weakness in the way that the current X.509 scheme is implemented is that any CA trusted by a particular party can then issue certificates for any domain they choose. Such certificates will be accepted as valid by the trusting party whether they are legitimate and authorized or not. This is a serious shortcoming given that the most commonly encountered technology employing X.509 and trusted third parties is the https protocol. As all major web browsers are distributed to their end-users pre-configured with a list of trusted CAs that numbers in the dozens this means that any one of these pre-approved trusted CAs can issue a valid certificate for any domain whatsoever. The industry response to this has been muted. Given that the contents of a browser's pre-configured trusted CA list is determined independently by the party that is distributing or causing to be installed the browser application there is really nothing that the CAs themselves can do.

This issue is the driving impetus behind the development of the DNS-based Authentication of Named Entities (DANE) protocol. If adopted in conjunction with Domain Name System Security Extensions (DNSSEC) DANE will greatly reduce if not completely eliminate the role of trusted third parties in a domain's PKI.

Software

Various software is available to operate a certificate authority. Generally such software is required to sign certificates, maintain revocation information, and operate OCSP or CRLservices. Some examples are:

- DogTag
- EJBCA
- gnoMint
- OpenCA
- OpenSSL, an SSL/TLS library that comes with tools allowing its use as a simple certificate authority
- EasyRSA, OpenVPN's command line CA utilities using OpenSSL.
- r509
- TinyCA, which is a perl gui on top of some CPAN modules.
- XCA
- XiPKI, CA and OCSP responder. With SHA3 support, OSGi-based (Java).
- Boulder is an automated server that uses the Automated Certificate Management Environment (ACME) protocol.
- Windows Server contains a CA as part of Certificate Services for the creation of digital certificates. In Windows Server 2008 and later the CA may be installed as part of Active Directory Certificate Services.
- OpenXPKI

Information Technology Act, 2000

The Information Technology Act, 2000 (also known as ITA-2000, or the IT Act) is an Act of the Indian Parliament (No 21 of 2000) notified on 17 October 2000. It is the primary law in India dealing with cybercrime and electronic commerce. It is based on the United Nations Model Law on Electronic Commerce 1996 (UNCITRAL Model) recommended by the General Assembly of United Nations by a resolution dated 30 January 1997.

The bill was passed in the budget session of 2000 and signed by President K. R. Narayanan on 9 May 2000. The bill was finalised by group of officials headed by then Minister of Information Technology Pramod Mahajan.

The original Act contained 94 sections, divided in 13 chapters and 4 schedules. The laws apply to the whole of India. Persons of other nationalities can also be indicted under the law, if the crime involves a computer or network located in India.

The Act provides legal framework for electronic governance by giving recognition to electronic records and digital signatures. The formations of Controller of Certifying Authorities was directed by the Act, to regulate issuing of digital signatures. It also defines cyber crimes and prescribed penalties for them. It also established a Cyber Appellate Tribunal to resolve disputes rising from this new law.The Act also amended various sections of Indian Penal Code, 1860, Indian Evidence Act, 1872, Banker's Book Evidence Act, 1891, and Reserve Bank of India Act, 1934 to make them compliant with new technologies.

Amendments

A major amendment was made in 2008. It introduced the Section 66A which penalized sending of "offensive messages". It also introduced the Section 69, which gave authorities the power of "interception or monitoring or decryption of any information through any computer resource". It also introduced for child porn, cyber terrorism and voyeurism. It was passed on 22 December 2008 without any debate in Lok Sabha. The next day it was passed by the Rajya Sabha. It was signed into law by President Pratibha Patil, on 5 February 2009.

Offences

List of offences and the corresponding penalties:

Notable cases

- In February 2001, in one of the first cases, the Delhi police arrested two men running a web-hosting company. The company had shut down a website over non-payment of dues. The owner of the site had claimed that he had already paid and complained to the police. The Delhi police had charged the men for hacking under Section 66 of the IT Act and breach of trust under Section 408 of the Indian Penal Code. The two men had to spend 6 days in Tihar jail waiting for bail. Bhavin Turakhia, chief executive officer of directi.com, a webhosting firm said that this interpretation of the law would be problematic for web-hosting companies.

- In February 2017, M/s Voucha Gram India Pvt.Ltd, owner of Delhi based Ecommerce Portal www.gyftr.com made a Complaint with Hauz Khas Police Station against some hackers from different cities accusing them for IT Act / Theft / Cheating / Misappropriation / Criminal Conspiracy / Criminal Breach of Trust / Cyber Crime of Hacking / Snooping / Tampering with Computer source documents and the Web Site and extending the threats of dire consequences to employees, as a result four hackers were arrested by South Delhi Police for Digital Shoplifting.

Section 66A

- In September 2012, a freelance cartoonist Aseem Trivedi was arrested under the Section 66A of the IT Act, Section 2 of Prevention of Insults to National Honour Act, 1971 and for sedition under the Section 124 of the Indian Penal Code. His cartoons depicting widespread corruption in India were considered offensive.

• On 12 April 2012, a Chemistry professor from Jadavpur University, Ambikesh Mahapatra, was arrested for sharing a cartoon of West Bengal Chief Minister Mamata Banerjee and then Railway Minister Mukul Roy. The email was sent from the email address of a housing society. Subrata Sengupta, the secretary of the housing society, was also arrested. They were charged under Section 66A and B of the IT Act, for defamation under Sections 500, for obscene gesture to a woman under Section 509, and abetting a crime under Section 114 of the Indian Penal Code.

• On 30 October 2012, a Puducherry businessman Ravi Srinivasan was arrested under Section 66A. He had sent tweet accusing Karti Chidambaram, son of then Finance MinisterP. Chidambaram, of corruption. Karti Chidambaram had complained to the police.

• On 19 November 2012, a 21-year-old girl was arrested from Palghar for posting a message on Facebook criticising the shutdown in Mumbai for the funeral of Bal Thackeray. Another 20-year-old girl was arrested for "liking" the post. They were initially charged under Section 295A of the Indian Penal Code (hurting religious sentiments) and Section 66A of the IT Act. Later, Section 295A was replaced by Section 505(2) (promoting enmity between classes). A group of Shiv Sena workers vandalised a hospital run by the uncle of one of girls. On 31 January 2013, a local court dropped all charges against the girls.

• On 18 March 2015, a teenaged boy was arrested from Bareilly, Uttar Pradesh, for making a post on Facebook insulting politician Azam Khan. The post allegedly contained hate speech against a community and was falsely attributed to Azam Khan by the boy. He was charged under Section 66A of the IT Act, and Sections 153A (promoting enmity between different religions), 504 (intentional insult with intent to provoke breach of peace) and 505 (public mischief) of Indian Penal Code. After the Section 66A was repealed on 24 March, the state government said that they would continue the prosecution under the remaining charges.

Criticisms

Publishing offensive, false or threatening information Any person who sends by any means of a computer resource any information that is grossly offensive or has a menacing character; or any information which he knows to be false, but for the purpose of causing annoyance, inconvenience, danger, obstruction, insult shall be punishable with imprisonment for a term which may extend to three years and with fine. Imprisonment up to three years, with fine.

In December 2012, P Rajeev, a Rajya Sabha member from Kerala, tried to pass a resolution seeking to amend the Section 66A. He was supported by D. Bandyopadhyay, Gyan Prakash Pilania, Basavaraj Patil Sedam, Narendra

Kumar Kashyap, Rama Chandra Khuntia and Baishnab Charan Parida. P Rajeev pointed that cartoons and editorials allowed in traditional media, were being censored in the new media. He also said that law was barely debated before being passed in December 2008.

Rajeev Chandrasekhar suggested the 66A should only apply to person to person communication pointing to a similar section under the Indian Post Office Act, 1898. Shantaram Naikopposed any changes, saying that the misuse of law was sufficient to warrant changes. Then Minister for Communications and Information Technology Kapil Sibal defended the existing law, saying that similar laws existed in US and UK. He also said that a similar provision existed under Indian Post Office Act, 1898. However, P Rajeev said that the UK dealt only with communication from person to person.

Petitions challenging constitutionality

In November 2012, IPS officer Amitabh Thakur and his wife social activist Nutan Thakur, filed a petition in the Lucknow bench of the Allahabad High Court claiming that the Section 66A violated the freedom of speech guaranteed in the Article 19(1)(a) of the Constitution of India. They said that the section was vague and frequently misused.

Also in November 2012, a Delhi-based law student, Shreya Singhal, filed a Public Interest Litigation (PIL) in the Supreme Court of India. She argued that the Section 66A was vaguely phrased, as result it violated Article 14, 19 (1) (a) and Article 21 of the Constitution. The PIL was accepted on 29 November 2012. A similar petition was also filed by the founder of MouthShut.com, Faisal Farooqui, and NGO Common Cause represented by Prashant Bhushan In August 2014, the Supreme Court asked the central government to respond to petitions filed by Mouthshut.com and later petition filed by the Internet and Mobile Association of India (IAMAI) which claimed that the IT Act gave the government power to arbitrarily remove user-generated content.

Revocation by the Supreme Court

On 24 March 2015, the Supreme Court of India, gave the verdict that Section 66A is unconstitutional in entirety. The court said that Section 66A of IT Act 2000 is "arbitrarily, excessively and disproportionately invades the right of free speech" provided under Article 19(1) of the Constitution of India. But the Court turned down a plea to strike down sections 69A and 79 of the Act, which deal with the procedure and safeguards for blocking certain websites.

Strict data privacy rules

The data privacy rules introduced in the Act in 2011 have been described as too strict by some Indian and US firms. The rules require firms to obtain written permission from customers before collecting and using their personal data. This has affected US firms which outsource to Indian companies.

However, some companies have welcomed the strict rules, saying it will remove fears of outsourcing to Indian companies.

Section 69 and mandatory decryption

The Section 69 allows intercepting any information and ask for information decryption. To refuse decryption is an offence. The Indian Telegraph Act, 1885 allows the government to tap phones. But, according to a 1996 Supreme Court verdict the government can tap phones only in case of a "public emergency". But, there is no such restriction on Section 69.On 20 December 2018, the Ministry of Home Affairs cited Section 69 in the issue of an order authorising ten central agencies to intercept, monitor, and decrypt "any information generated, transmitted, received or stored in any computer." While some claim this to be a violation of the fundamental right to privacy, the Ministry of Home Affairs has claimed its validity on the grounds of national security.

Future changes

On 2 April 2015, the Chief Minister of Maharashtra, Devendra Fadnavis revealed to the state assembly that a new law was being framed to replace the repealed Section 66A. Fadnavis was replying to a query Shiv Sena leader Neelam Gorhe. Gorhe had said that repeal of the law would encourage online miscreants and asked whether the state government would frame a law to this regard. Fadnavis said that the previous law had resulted in no convictions, so the law would be framed such that it would be strong and result in convictions.

On 13 April 2015, it announced that the Ministry of Home Affairs would form a committee of officials from the Intelligence Bureau, Central Bureau of Investigation, National Investigation Agency, Delhi Police and ministry itself to produce a new legal framework. This step was reportedly taken after complaints from intelligence agencies that, they were no longer able to counter online posts that involved national security matter or incite people to commit an offence, such as online recruitment for ISIS. Former Minister of State with the Ministry of Information Technology, Milind Deora has supported a new "unambiguous section to replace 66A".

Controller

Appointment of Controller and other officers. –

(1) The Central Government may, by notification in the Official Gazette, appoint a Controller of Certifying Authorities for the purposes of this Act and may, also by the same or subsequent notification, appoint such number of Deputy Controllers and Assistant Controllers as it deems fit.

(2) The Controller shall discharge his functions under this Act subject to the general control and directions of the Central Government.

(3) The Deputy Controllers and Assistant Controllers shall perform functions assigned to them by the Controller under the general superintendence and control of the Controller.

(4) The qualifications, experience and terms and conditions of service of Controller, Deputy Controllers and Assistant Controller shall be such as may be prescribed by the Central Government.

(5) The Head Office and Branch Officer of the officer of the Controller shall be at such places as the Central Government may specify, and these may be established at such places as the Central Government may think fit.

(6) There shall be a seal of the Office of the Controller.

Functions of Controller. –

The Controller may perform all or any of the following function, namely:

(a) exercising supervision over the activities of Certifying Authorities;

(b) certifying public keys of the Certifying Authorities;

(c) laying down the standards to be maintained by Certifying Authorities;

(d) specifying the qualifications and experience which employees of the Certifying Authorities should possess;

(e) specifying the conditions subject to which the Certifying Authority shall conduct their business;

(f) specifying the contents of written, printed or visual materials and advertisements that may be distributed or used in respect of a Digital Signature Certificate and the public key;

(g) specifying the form and content of a Digital Signature Certificate and the key;

(h) specifying the form the manner in which accounts shall be maintained by the Certifying Authorities;

(i) specifying the terms and conditions subject to which auditors may be appointed and the remuneration to be paid to them;

(j) facilitating the establishment of any electronic system by a Certifying Authority either solely or jointly with other Certifying Authorities and regulation of such system;

(k) specifying the manner in which the Certifying Authorities shall conduct their dealings with the subscribers;

(l) resolving any conflict of interests between the Certifying Authorities and the subscribers;

(m) laying down the duties of the Certifying Authorities;

(n) maintaining a data-base containing the disclosure record of ever Certifying Authority containing such particulars as may be specified by regulations which shall be accessible to public.

License issue Digital Signature Certificates

As per Section 18 of The Information Technology Act, 2000 provides the required legal sanctity to the digital signatures based on asymmetric cryptosystems. The digital signatures are now accepted at par with handwritten signatures and the electronic documents that have been digitally signed are treated at par with paper documents.

The IT Act provides for the Controller of Certifying Authorities(CCA) to license and regulate the working of Certifying Authorities. The Certifying Authorities (CAs) issue digital signature certificates for electronic authentication of users.

The Controller of Certifying Authorities (CCA) has been appointed by the Central Government under section 17 of the Act for purposes of the IT Act. The Office of the CCA came into existence on November 1, 2000. It aims at promoting the growth of E-Commerce and E- Governance through the wide use of digital signatures.

The Controller of Certifying Authorities (CCA) has established the Root Certifying Authority (RCAI) of India under section 18(b) of the IT Act to digitally sign the public keys of Certifying Authorities (CA) in the country. The RCAI is operated as per the standards laid down under the Act.

The CCA certifies the public keys of CAs using its own private key, which enables users in the cyberspace to verify that a given certificate is issued by a licensed CA. For this purpose it operates, the Root Certifying Authority of India(RCAI). The CCA also maintains the Repository of Digital Certificates, which contains all the certificates issued to the CAs in the country.

(1) Subject to the provisions of sub-section (2), any person may make an application to the Controller for a license to issue Digital Signature Certificates.

(2) No license shall be issued under sub-section (1), unless the applicant fulfills such requirements with respect to qualification, expertise, manpower, financial resources and other infrastructure facilities, which are necessary to issue Digital Signature Certificates as may be prescribed by the Central Government.

(3) A license granted under this section shall-

(a) be valid for such period as may be prescribed by the Central Government;

(b) not be transferable or heritable;

(c) be subject to such terms and conditions as may be specified by the regulations.

Certifying Authority to issue Digital Signature Certificate.

1. Any person may make an application to the Certifying Authority for the issue of a Digital Signature Certificate in such form as may be prescribed by the Central Government

2. Every such application shall be accompanied by such fee not exceeding twenty-five thousand rupees as may be prescribed by the Central Government, to be paid to the Certifying Authority:

Provided that while prescribing fees under sub-section (2) different fees may be prescribed for different classes of applicants'.

3. Every such application shall be accompanied by a certification practice statement or where there is no such statement, a statement containing such particulars, as may be specified by regulations.

4. On receipt of an application under sub-section (1), the Certifying Authority may, after consideration of the certification practice statement or the other statement under sub-section (3) and after making such enquiries as it may deem fit, grant the Digital Signature Certificate or for reasons to be recorded in writing, reject the application:

Provided that no Digital Signature Certificate shall be granted unless the Certifying Authority is satisfied that -

1. the applicant holds the private key corresponding to the public key to be listed in the Digital Signature Certificate.

2. the applicant holds a private key, which is capable of creating a digital signature.

3. the public key to be listed in the certificate can be used to verify a digital signature affixed by the private key held by the applicant:

Provided further that no application shall be rejected unless the applicant has been given a reasonable opportunity of showing cause against the proposed rejection.

Representations upon issuance of Digital Signature Certificate.

A Certifying Authority while issuing a Digital Signature Certificate shall certify that--

1. it has complied with the provisions of this Act and the rules and regulations made thereunder.

2. it has published the Digital Signature Certificate or otherwise made it available to such person relying on it and the subscriber has accepted it.

3. the subscriber holds the private key corresponding to the public key, listed in the Digital Signature Certificate.

4. the subscriber's public key and private key constitute a functioning key pair.

5. the information contained in the Digital Signature Certificate is accurate, and

6. it has no knowledge of any material fact, which if it had been included in the Digital Signature Certificate would adversely affect the reliability of the representations made in clauses (a) to (d).

Suspension of Digital Signature Certificate.

1. Subject to the provisions of sub-section (2), the Certifying Authority which has issued a Digital Signature Certificate may suspend such Digital Signature Certificate -

1. on receipt of a request to that effect from -

1. the subscriber listed in toe Digital Signature Certificate, or

2. any person duly authorised to act on behalf of that subscriber

2. if it is of opinion that the Digital Signature Certificate should be suspended in public interest

2. A Digital Signature Certificate shall not be suspended for a period exceeding fifteen days unless the subscriber has been given an opportunity of being heard in the matter.

3. On suspension of a Digital Signature Certificate under this section, the Certifying Authority shall communicate the same to the subscriber.

Revocation of Digital Signature Certificate.

1. A Certifying Authority may revoke a Digital Signature Certificate issued by it -

1. where the subscriber or any other person authorised by him makes a request to that effect, or

2. upon the death of the subscriber, or

3. upon the dissolution of the firm or winding up of the company where the subscriber is a firm or a company.

2. Subject to the provisions of sub-section (3) and without prejudice to the provisions of sub-section (1), a CertifyingAuthority may revoke a Digital Signature Certificate which has been issued by it at any time, if it is of opinion that -

3. a material fact represented in the Digital Signature Certificate is false or has been concealed.

4. a requirement for issuance of the Digital Signature Certificate was not satisfied.

5. the Certifying Authority's private key or security system was compromised in a manner materially affecting the Digital Signature Certificate's reliability.

6. the subscriber has been declared insolvent or dead or where a subscriber is a firm or a company, which has been dissolved, wound-up or otherwise ceased to exist.

7. A Digital Signature Certificate shall not be revoked unless the subscriber has been given an opportunity of being heard in the matter.

8. On revocation of a Digital Signature Certificate under this section, the Certifying Authority shall communicate the same to the subscriber.

39. Notice of suspension or revocation.

1. Where a Digital Signature Certificate is suspended or revoked under section 37 or section 38, the Certifying Authority shall publish a notice of such suspension or revocation, as the case may be, in the repository specified in the Digital Signature Certificate for publication of such notice.

2. Where one or more repositories are specified, the Certifying Authority shall publish notices of such suspension or revocation, as the case may he. in all such repositories.

Information Technology Act, 2000

The Information Technology Act, 2000 (also known as ITA-2000, or the IT Act) is an Act of the Indian Parliament (No 21 of 2000) notified on 17 October 2000. It is the primary law in India dealing with cybercrime and electronic commerce. It is based on the United Nations Model Law on Electronic Commerce 1996 (UNCITRAL Model) recommended by the General Assembly of United Nations by a resolution dated 30 January 1997.

The bill was passed in the budget session of 2000 and signed by President K. R. Narayanan on 9 May 2000. The bill was finalised by group of officials headed by then Minister of Information Technology Pramod Mahajan.

Summary

The original Act contained 94 sections, divided in 13 chapters and 4 schedules. The laws apply to the whole of India. Persons of other nationalities can also be indicted under the law, if the crime involves a computer or network located in India.

The Act provides legal framework for electronic governance by giving recognition to electronic records and digital signatures. The formations of Controller of Certifying Authorities was directed by the Act, to regulate issuing of digital signatures. It also defines cyber crimes and prescribed penalties for them. It also established a Cyber Appellate Tribunal to resolve disputes rising from this new law.The Act also amended various sections of Indian Penal Code, 1860, Indian Evidence Act, 1872, Banker's Book Evidence Act, 1891, and Reserve Bank of India Act, 1934 to make them compliant with new technologies.

Amendments

A major amendment was made in 2008. It introduced the Section 66A which penalized sending of "offensive messages". It also introduced the Section 69, which gave authorities the power of "interception or monitoring or decryption of any information through any computer resource". It also introduced for child porn, cyber terrorism and voyeurism. It was passed on 22 December 2008 without any debate in Lok Sabha. The next day it was passed by the Rajya Sabha. It was signed into law by President Pratibha Patil, on 5 February 2009.

Petitions challenging constitutionality

In November 2012, IPS officer Amitabh Thakur and his wife social activist Nutan Thakur, filed a petition in the Lucknow bench of the Allahabad High Court claiming that the Section 66A violated the freedom of speech guaranteed in the Article 19(1)(a) of the Constitution of India. They said that the section was vague and frequently misused.

Also in November 2012, a Delhi-based law student, Shreya Singhal, filed a Public Interest Litigation (PIL) in the Supreme Court of India. She argued that the Section 66A was vaguely phrased, as result it violated Article 14, 19 (1) (a) and Article 21 of the Constitution. The PIL was accepted on 29 November 2012. A similar petition was also filed by the founder of MouthShut.com, Faisal Farooqui, and NGO Common Cause represented by Prashant Bhushan In August 2014, the Supreme Court asked the central government to respond to petitions filed by Mouthshut.com and later petition filed by the Internet and Mobile Association of India (IAMAI) which claimed that the IT Act gave the government power to arbitrarily remove user-generated content.

Revocation by the Supreme Court

On 24 March 2015, the Supreme Court of India, gave the verdict that Section 66A is unconstitutional in entirety. The court said that Section 66A of IT Act 2000 is "arbitrarily, excessively and disproportionately invades the right of free speech" provided under Article 19(1) of the Constitution of India. But the Court turned down a plea to strike down sections 69A and 79 of the Act, which deal with the procedure and safeguards for blocking certain websites.

Strict data privacy rules

The data privacy rules introduced in the Act in 2011 have been described as too strict by some Indian and US firms. The rules require firms to obtain written permission from customers before collecting and using their personal data. This has affected US firms which outsource to Indian companies. However, some companies have welcomed the strict rules, saying it will remove fears of outsourcing to Indian companies.

Section 69 and mandatory decryption

The Section 69 allows intercepting any information and ask for information decryption. To refuse decryption is an offence. The Indian Telegraph Act, 1885 allows the government to tap phones. But, according to a 1996 Supreme Court verdict the government can tap phones only in case of a "public emergency". But, there is no such restriction on Section 69.On 20 December 2018, the Ministry of Home Affairs cited Section 69 in the issue of an order authorising ten central agencies to intercept, monitor, and decrypt "any information generated, transmitted, received or stored in any computer." While some claim this to be a violation of the fundamental right to privacy, the Ministry of Home Affairs has claimed its validity on the grounds of national security.

Future changes

On 2 April 2015, the Chief Minister of Maharashtra, Devendra Fadnavis revealed to the state assembly that a new law was being framed to replace the repealed Section 66A. Fadnavis was replying to a query Shiv Sena leader Neelam Gorhe. Gorhe had said that repeal of the law would encourage online miscreants and asked whether the state government would frame a law to this regard. Fadnavis said that the previous law had resulted in no convictions, so the law would be framed such that it would be strong and result in convictions.

On 13 April 2015, it announced that the Ministry of Home Affairs would form a committee of officials from the Intelligence Bureau, Central Bureau of Investigation, National Investigation Agency, Delhi Police and ministry itself to produce a new legal framework. This step was reportedly taken after complaints from intelligence agencies that, they were no longer able to counter online posts that involved national security matter or incite people to commit an offence, such as online recruitment for ISIS. Former Minister of State with the Ministry of Information Technology, Milind Deora has supported a new "unambiguous section to replace 66A".

7

Conceptual Framework of E-commerce

E-commerce is the activity of buying or selling of products on online services or over the Internet. Electronic commerce draws on technologies such as mobile commerce, electronic funds transfer, supply chain management, Internet marketing, online transaction processing, electronic data interchange (EDI), inventory management systems, and automated data collection systems.

Modern electronic commerce typically uses the World Wide Web for at least one part of the transaction's life cycle although it may also use other technologies such as e-mail. Typical e-commerce transactions include the purchase of online books (such as Amazon) and music purchases (music download in the form of digital distribution such as iTunes Store), and to a less extent, customized/personalized online liquor store inventory services. There are three areas of e-commerce: online retailing, electric markets, and online auctions. E-commerce is supported by electronic business.

E-commerce businesses may also employ some or all of the followings:

- Online shopping for retail sales direct to consumers via Web sites and mobile apps, and conversational commerce via live chat, chatbots, and voice assistants
- Providing or participating in online marketplaces, which process third-party business-to-consumer or consumer-to-consumer sales
- Business-to-business buying and selling;
- Gathering and using demographic data through web contacts and social media

- Business-to-business (B2B) electronic data interchange
- Marketing to prospective and established customers by e-mail or fax (for example, with newsletters)
- Engaging in pretail for launching new products and services
- Online financial exchanges for currency exchanges or trading purposes.

A timeline for the development of e-commerce:

- 1971 or 1972: The ARPANET is used to arrange a cannabis sale between students at the Stanford Artificial Intelligence Laboratory and the Massachusetts Institute of Technology, later described as "the seminal act of e-commerce" in John Markoff's book What the Dormouse Said.
- 1979: Michael Aldrich demonstrates the first online shopping system.
- 1981: Thomson Holidays UK is the first business-to-business online shopping system to be installed.
- 1982: Minitel was introduced nationwide in France by France Télécom and used for online ordering.
- 1983: California State Assembly holds first hearing on "electronic commerce" in Volcano, California. Testifying are CPUC, MCI Mail, Prodigy, CompuServe, Volcano Telephone, and Pacific Telesis. (Not permitted to testify is Quantum Technology, later to become AOL.)
- 1984: Gateshead SIS/Tesco is first B2C online shopping system and Mrs Snowball, 72, is the first online home shopper
- 1984: In April 1984, CompuServe launches the Electronic Mall in the USA and Canada. It is the first comprehensive electronic commerce service.
- 1989: In May 1989, Sequoia Data Corp. Introduced Compumarket, the first internet based system for e-commerce. Sellers and buyers could post items for sale and buyers could search the database and make purchases with a credit card.
- 1990: Tim Berners-Lee writes the first web browser, WorldWideWeb, using a NeXT computer.
- 1992: Book Stacks Unlimited in Cleveland opens a commercial sales website (www.books.com) selling books online with credit card processing.
- 1993: Paget Press releases edition No. 3 of the first app store, The Electronic AppWrapper
- 1994: Netscape releases the Navigator browser in October under the code name Mozilla. Netscape 1.0 is introduced in late 1994 with SSL encryption that made transactions secure.

- 1994: Ipswitch IMail Server becomes the first software available online for sale and immediate download via a partnership between Ipswitch, Inc. and OpenMarket.
- 1994: "Ten Summoner's Tales" by Sting becomes the first secure online purchase through NetMarket.
- 1995: The US National Science Foundation lifts its former strict prohibition of commercial enterprise on the Internet.
- 1995: Thursday 27 April 1995, the purchase of a book by Paul Stanfield, Product Manager for CompuServe UK, from W H Smith's shop within CompuServe's UK Shopping Centre is the UK's first national online shopping service secure transaction. The shopping service at launch featured W H Smith, Tesco, Virgin Megastores/Our Price, Great Universal Stores (GUS), Interflora, Dixons Retail, Past Times, PC World (retailer) and Innovations.
- 1995: Jeff Bezos launches Amazon.com and the first commercial-free 24-hour, internet-only radio stations, Radio HK and NetRadio start broadcasting. eBay is founded by computer programmer Pierre Omidyar as AuctionWeb.
- 1996: The use of Excalibur BBS with replicated "Storefronts" was an early implementation of electronic commerce started by a group of SysOps in Australia and replicated to global partner sites.
- 1998: Electronic postal stamps can be purchased and downloaded for printing from the Web.
- 1999: Alibaba Group is established in China. Business.com sold for US $7.5 million to eCompanies, which was purchased in 1997 for US $149,000. The peer-to-peer filesharing software Napster launches. ATG Stores launches to sell decorative items for the home online.
- 1999: Global e-commerce reaches $150 billion
- 2000: The dot-com bust.
- 2001: Alibaba.com achieved profitability in December 2001.
- 2002: eBay acquires PayPal for $1.5 billion. Niche retail companies Wayfair and NetShops are founded with the concept of selling products through several targeted domains, rather than a central portal.
- 2003: Amazon.com posts first yearly profit.
- 2004: DHgate.com, China's first online b2b transaction platform, is established, forcing other b2b sites to move away from the "yellow pages" model.
- 2007: Business.com acquired by R.H. Donnelley for $345 million.
- 2014: US e-commerce and Online Retail sales projected to reach $294

billion, an increase of 12 percent over 2013 and 9% of all retail sales. Alibaba Group has the largest Initial public offering ever, worth $25 billion.

- 2015: Amazon.com accounts for more than half of all e-commerce growth, selling almost 500 Million SKU's in the US.

- 2017: Retail ecommerce sales across the world reached $2.304 trillion, which was a 24.8 percent increase than previous year

Business application

An example of an older generation of avatar-style automated online assistant on a merchandising website.

Some common applications related to electronic commerce are:

- Conversational commerce: e-commerce via chat
- Digital Wallet
- Document automation in supply chain and logistics
- Electronic tickets
- Enterprise content management
- Group buying
- Instant messaging
- Newsgroups
- Online banking
- Online office suites
- Online shopping and order tracking
- Pretail
- Print on demand
- Shopping cart software
- Social networking
- Teleconferencing
- Virtual assistant (artificial intelligence)
- Domestic and international payment systems

Governmental regulation

In the United States, certain electronic commerce activities are regulated by the Federal Trade Commission (FTC). These activities include the use of commercial e-mails, online advertising and consumer privacy. The CAN-SPAM Act of 2003 establishes national standards for direct marketing over e-mail. The Federal Trade Commission Act regulates all forms of advertising, including online advertising, and states that advertising must be truthful and non-deceptive. Using its authority under Section 5 of the FTC Act, which prohibits unfair or deceptive practices, the FTC has brought a number of cases to enforce the promises in corporate privacy statements, including promises about the security of consumers' personal information. As a result, any corporate privacy policy related to e-commerce activity may be subject to enforcement by the FTC.

The Ryan Haight Online Pharmacy Consumer Protection Act of 2008, which came into law in 2008, amends the Controlled Substances Act to address online pharmacies.

Conflict of laws in cyberspace is a major hurdle for harmonization of legal framework for e-commerce around the world. In order to give a uniformity to e-commerce law around the world, many countries adopted the UNCITRAL Model Law on Electronic Commerce (1996).

Internationally there is the International Consumer Protection and Enforcement Network (ICPEN), which was formed in 1991 from an informal network of government customer fair trade organisations. The purpose was stated as being to find ways of co-operating on tackling consumer problems connected with cross-border transactions in both goods and services, and to help ensure exchanges of information among the participants for mutual benefit and understanding. From this came Econsumer.gov, an ICPEN initiative since April 2001. It is a portal to report complaints about online and related transactions with foreign companies.

There is also Asia Pacific Economic Cooperation (APEC) was established in 1989 with the vision of achieving stability, security and prosperity for the region through free and open trade and investment. APEC has an Electronic Commerce Steering Group as well as working on common privacy regulations throughout the APEC region.

In Australia, Trade is covered under Australian Treasury Guidelines for electronic commerce and the Australian Competition and Consumer Commission regulates and offers advice on how to deal with businesses online, and offers specific advice on what happens if things go wrong.

In the United Kingdom, The Financial Services Authority (FSA) was formerly the regulating authority for most aspects of the EU's Payment Services Directive (PSD), until its replacement in 2013 by the Prudential Regulation Authority and the Financial Conduct Authority. The UK implemented the PSD through the Payment Services Regulations 2009 (PSRs), which came into effect on 1 November 2009. The PSR affects firms providing payment services and their customers. These firms include banks, non-bank credit card issuers and non-bank merchant acquirers, e-money issuers, etc. The PSRs created a new class of regulated firms known as payment institutions (PIs), who are subject to prudential requirements. Article 87 of the PSD requires the European Commission to report on the implementation and impact of the PSD by 1 November 2012.

In India, the Information Technology Act 2000 governs the basic applicability of e-commerce.

In China, the Telecommunications Regulations of the People's Republic of China (promulgated on 25 September 2000), stipulated the Ministry of Industry and Information Technology (MIIT) as the government department regulating all telecommunications related activities, including electronic commerce. On the same day, The Administrative Measures on Internet Information Services released, is the first administrative regulation to address profit-generating activities conducted through the Internet, and lay the foundation for future regulations governing e-commerce in China. On 28 August 2004, the eleventh session of the tenth NPC Standing Committee adopted The Electronic Signature Law, which regulates data message, electronic signature authentication and legal liability issues. It is considered the first law in China's e-commerce legislation. It was a milestone in the course of improving China's electronic commerce legislation, and also marks the entering of China's rapid development stage for electronic commerce legislation.

Forms

Contemporary electronic commerce can be classified into two categories. The first category is business based on types of goods sold (involves everything from ordering "digital" content for immediate online consumption, to ordering conventional goods and services, to "meta" services to facilitate other types of electronic commerce). The second category is based on the nature of the participant (B2B, B2C, C2B and C2C);

On the institutional level, big corporations and financial institutions use the internet to exchange financial data to facilitate domestic and international business. Data integrity and security are pressing issues for electronic commerce.

Aside from traditional e-commerce, the terms m-Commerce (mobile commerce) as well (around 2013) t-Commerce have also been used.

Global trends

In 2010, the United Kingdom had the highest per capita e-commerce spending in the world. As of 2013, the Czech Republic was the European country where e-commerce delivers the biggest contribution to the enterprises´ total revenue. Almost a quarter (24%) of the country's total turnover is generated via the online channel.

Among emerging economies, China's e-commerce presence continues to expand every year. With 668 million Internet users, China's online shopping sales reached $253 billion in the first half of 2015, accounting for 10% of total Chinese consumer retail sales in that period. The Chinese retailers have been able to help consumers feel more comfortable shopping online. e-commerce transactions between China and other countries increased 32% to 2.3 trillion yuan ($375.8 billion) in 2012 and accounted for 9.6% of China's total international trade. In 2013, Alibaba had an e-commerce market share of 80% in China. In 2014, there were 600 million Internet users in China (twice as many as in the US), making it the world's biggest online market. China is also the largest e-commerce market in the world by value of sales, with an estimated US$899 billion in 2016.

Recent research clearly indicates that electronic commerce, commonly referred to as e-commerce, presently shapes the manner in which people shop for products. The GCC countries have a rapidly growing market and are characterized by a population that becomes wealthier (Yuldashev). As such, retailers have launched Arabic-language websites as a means to target this population. Secondly, there are predictions of increased mobile purchases and an expanding internet audience (Yuldashev). The growth and development of the two aspects make the GCC countries to become larger players in the electronic commerce market with time progress. Specifically, research shows that e-commerce market is expected to grow to over $20 billion by the year 2020 among these GCC countries (Yuldashev). The e-commerce market has also gained much popularity among the western countries, and in particular Europe and the U.S. These countries have been highly characterized with consumer-packaged-goods (CPG) (Geisler, 34). However, trends show that there are future signs of a reverse. Similar to the GCC countries, there has been increased purchase of goods and services in online channels rather than offline channels. Activist investors are trying hard to consolidate and slash their overall cost and the governments in western countries continue to impose more regulation on CPG manufacturers (Geisler, 36). In these senses, CPG investors are being forced to adapt e-commerce as it is effective as a well as a means for them to thrive.

In 2013, Brazil's e-commerce was growing quickly with retail e-commerce sales expected to grow at a double-digit pace through 2014. By 2016, eMarketer expected retail e-commerce sales in Brazil to reach $17.3 billion. India has an Internet user base of about 460 million as of December 2017. Despite being third largest user base in world, the penetration of Internet is low compared to markets like the United States, United Kingdom or France but is growing at a much faster rate, adding around 6 million new entrants every month. In India, cash on delivery is the most preferred payment method, accumulating 75% of the e-retail activities. The India retail market is expected to rise from 2.5% in 2016 to 5% in 2020.

The future trends in the GCC countries will be similar with that of the western countries. Despite the forces that push business to adapt e-commerce as a means to sell goods and products, the manner in which customers make purchases is similar in countries from these two regions. For instance, there has been an increased usage of smartphones which comes in conjunction with an increase in the overall internet audience from the regions. Yuldashev writes that consumers are scaling up to more modern technology that allows for mobile marketing. However, the percentage of smartphone and internet users who make online purchases is expected to vary in the first few years. It will be independent on the willingness of the people to adopt this new trend (The Statistics Portal). For example, UAE has the greatest smartphone penetration of 73.8 percent and has 91.9 percent of its population has access to the internet. On the other hand, smartphone penetration in Europe has been reported to be at 64.7 percent (The Statistics Portal). Regardless, the disparity in percentage between these regions is expected to level out in future because e-commerce technology is expected to grow allowing for more users. The e-commerce business within these two regions will result in a competition. Government bodies at country level will enhance their measures and strategies to ensure sustainability and consumer protection (Krings, et al.). These increased measures will raise the environmental and social standards in the countries, factors that will determine the success of e-commerce market in these countries. For example, an adoption of tough sanctions will make it difficult for companies to enter the e-commerce market while lenient sanctions will allow ease of companies. As such, the future trends between GCC countries and the Western countries will be independent of these sanctions (Krings, et al.). These countries need to make rational conclusions in coming up with effective sanctions.

The rate of growth of the number of internet users in the Arab countries has been rapid – 13.1% in 2015. A significant portion of the e-commerce market in the Middle East comprises people in the 30–34 year age group. Egypt has the largest number of internet users in the region, followed by Saudi Arabia and Morocco; these constitute 3/4th of the region's share. Yet, internet penetration is low: 35% in Egypt and 65% in Saudi Arabia.

E-commerce has become an important tool for small and large businesses worldwide, not only to sell to customers, but also to engage them.

In 2012, e-commerce sales topped $1 trillion for the first time in history.

Mobile devices are playing an increasing role in the mix of e-commerce, this is also commonly called mobile commerce, or m-commerce. In 2014, one estimate saw purchases made on mobile devices making up 25% of the market by 2017.

For traditional businesses, one research stated that information technology and cross-border e-commerce is a good opportunity for the rapid development and growth of enterprises. Many companies have invested enormous volume of investment in mobile applications. The DeLone and McLean Model stated that three perspectives contribute to a successful e-business: information system quality, service quality and users' satisfaction. There is no limit of time and space, there are more opportunities to reach out to customers around the world, and to cut down unnecessary intermediate links, thereby reducing the cost price, and can benefit from one on one large customer data analysis, to achieve a high degree of personal customization strategic plan, in order to fully enhance the core competitiveness of the products in company.

Modern 3D graphics technologies, such as Facebook 3D Posts, are considered by some social media marketers and advertisers as a more preferable way to promote consumer goods than static photos, and some brands like Sony are already paving the way for augmented reality commerce. Wayfair now lets you inspect a 3D version of its furniture in a home setting before buying.

Logistics

Logistics in e-commerce mainly concerns fulfillment. Online markets and retailers have to find the best possible way to fill orders and deliver products. Small companies usually control their own logistic operation because they do not have the ability to hire an outside company. Most large companies hire a fulfillment service that takes care of a company's logistic needs.

Contrary to common misconception, there are significant barriers to entry in e-commerce.

Impact on markets and retailers

Store closing flags outside a Toys R Us in New Jersey. Despite investments, the chain struggled to win market share in the age of digital commerce.

E-commerce markets are growing at noticeable rates. The online market is expected to grow by 56% in 2015–2020. In 2017, retail e-commerce sales worldwide amounted to 2.3 trillion US dollars and e-retail revenues are projected to grow to 4.88 trillion US dollars in 2021. Traditional markets are only expected 2% growth during the same time. Brick and mortarretailers are struggling because of online retailer's ability to offer lower prices and higher efficiency. Many larger retailers are able to maintain a presence offline and online by linking physical and online offerings.

E-commerce allows customers to overcome geographical barriers and allows them to purchase products anytime and from anywhere. Online and traditional markets have different strategies for conducting business. Traditional retailers offer fewer assortment of products because of shelf space where, online retailers often hold no inventory but send customer orders directly to the manufacture. The pricing strategies are also different for traditional and online retailers. Traditional retailers base their prices on store traffic and the cost to keep inventory. Online retailers base prices on the speed of delivery.

There are two ways for marketers to conduct business through e-commerce: fully online or online along with a brick and mortar store. Online marketers can offer lower prices, greater product selection, and high efficiency rates. Many customers prefer online markets if the products can be delivered quickly at relatively low price. However, online retailers cannot offer the physical experience that traditional retailers can. It can be difficult to judge the quality of a product without the physical experience, which may cause customers to experience product or seller uncertainty. Another issue regarding the online market is concerns about the security of online transactions. Many customers remain loyal to well-known retailers because of this issue.

Security is a primary problem for e-commerce in developed and developing countries. E-commerce security is protecting business' websites and costumers from unauthorized access, use, alteration, or destruction. The type of threats include: malicious codes, unwanted programs (ad ware, spyware), phishing, hacking, and cyber vandalism. E-commerce websites use different tools to avert security threats. These tools include firewalls, encryption software, digital certificates, and passwords.

Impact on supply chain management

For a long time, companies had been troubled by the gap between the benefits which supply chain technology has and the solutions to deliver those benefits. However, the emergence of e-commerce has provided a more practical and effective way of delivering the benefits of the new supply chain technologies.

E-commerce has the capability to integrate all inter-company and intra-company functions, meaning that the three flows (physical flow, financial flow and information flow) of the supply chain could be also affected by e-commerce. The affections on physical flows improved the way of product and inventory movement level for companies. For the information flows, e-commerce optimised the capacity of information processing than companies used to have, and for the financial flows, e-commerce allows companies to have more efficient payment and settlement solutions.

In addition, e-commerce has a more sophisticated level of impact on supply chains: Firstly, the performance gap will be eliminated since companies can identify gaps between different levels of supply chains by electronic means of solutions; Secondly, as a result of e-commerce emergence, new capabilities such implementing ERP systems, like SAP ERP, Xero, or Megaventory, have helped companies to manage operations with customers and suppliers. Yet these new capabilities are still not fully exploited. Thirdly, technology companies would keep investing on new e-commerce software solutions as they are expecting investment return. Fourthly, e-commerce would help to solve many aspects of issues that companies may feel difficult to cope with, such as political barriers or cross-country changes. Finally, e-commerce provides companies a more efficient and effective way to collaborate with each other within the supply chain.

Impact on employment

E-commerce helps create new job opportunities due to information related services, software app and digital products. It also causes job losses. The areas with the greatest predicted job-loss are retail, postal, and travel agencies. The development of e-commerce will create jobs that require highly skilled workers to manage large amounts of information, customer demands, and production processes. In contrast, people with poor technical skills cannot enjoy the wages welfare. On the other hand, because e-commerce requires sufficient stocks that could be delivered to customers in time, the warehouse becomes an important element. Warehouse needs more staff to manage, supervise and organize, thus the condition of warehouse environment will be concerned by employees.

Impact on customers

E-commerce brings convenience for customers as they do not have to leave home and only need to browse website online, especially for buying the products which are not sold in nearby shops. It could help customers buy wider range of products and save customers' time. Consumers also gain power through online shopping. They are able to research products and compare prices among retailers. Also, online shopping often provides sales promotion or discounts code, thus it is more price effective for customers. Moreover, e-commerce provides products' detailed information; even the in-store staff cannot offer such detailed explanation. Customers can also review and track the order history online.

E-commerce technologies cut transaction costs by allowing both manufactures and consumers to skip through the intermediaries. This is achieved through by extending the search area best price deals and by group purchase. The success of e-commerce in urban and regional levels depend on how the local firms and consumers have adopted to e-commerce.

However, e-commerce lacks human interaction for customers, especially who prefer face-to-face connection. Customers are also concerned with the security of online transactions and tend to remain loyal to well-known retailers. In recent years, clothing retailers such as Tommy Hilfiger have started adding Virtual Fit platforms to their e-commerce sites to reduce the risk of customers buying the wrong sized clothes, although these vary greatly in their fit for purpose. When the customer regret the purchase of a product, it involves returning goods and refunding process. This process is inconvenient as customers need to pack and post the goods. If the products are expensive, large or fragile, it refers to safety issues.

Distribution channels

E-commerce has grown in importance as companies have adopted pure-click and brick-and-click channel systems. We can distinguish pure-click and brick-and-click channel system adopted by companies.

- Pure-click or pure-play companies are those that have launched a website without any previous existence as a firm.
- Bricks-and-clicks companies are those existing companies that have added an online site for e-commerce.
- Click to-brick online retailers that later open physical locations to supplement their online efforts.

Types of digital channels

E-commerce may take place on retailers' Web sites or mobile apps, or those of e-commerce marketplaces such as on Amazon, or Tmall from AliBaba. Those channels may also be supported by conversational commerce, e.g. live chat or chatbots on Web sites. Conversational commerce may also be standalone such as live chat or chatbots on messaging apps and via voice assistants.

Recommendation

The contemporary e-commerce trend recommends companies to shift the traditional business model where focus on "standardized products, homogeneous market and long product life cycle" to the new business model where focus on "varied and customized products". E-commerce requires the company to have the ability to satisfy multiple needs of different customers and provide them with wider range of products.

With more choices of products, the information of products for customers to select and meet their needs become crucial. In order to address the mass customization principle to the company, the use of recommender system is suggested. This system helps recommend the proper products to the customers and helps customers make the decision during the purchasing process. The recommender system could be operated through the top sellers on the website, the demographics of customers or the consumers' buying behavior. However, there are 3 main ways of recommendations: recommending products to customers directly, providing detailed products' information and showing other buyers' opinions or critiques. It is benefit for consumer experience without physical shopping. In general, recommender system is used to contact customers online and assist finding the right products they want effectively and directly.

8

Conversational Commerce

Conversational commerce is e-commerce via various means of conversation:

- live chat on e-commerce Web sites,
- live chat on messaging apps
- chatbots on messaging apps or Web sites
- via voice assistants

Is an asynchronous real-time discussion between two or more parties as it relates to products, services, or needs where a direct relationship between the parties is established and a value based transaction likely results.

Web chat

Companies like [24]7 and LivePerson have powered live conversations between customers and human agents as far back as the 2000s, before retailers provided service on messaging apps.

WeChat in China

During this time, in China, e-commerce via WeChat – at its core a messaging app, but also letting merchants display their goods in mobile Web pages and via social feeds – grew strongly. By 2013 e-commerce in China had overtaken that of the U.S.

Facebook Messenger

In 2016, Facebook announced its Facebook Messenger chatbot platform, heralding the arrival of conversational commerce via the most widely used messaging app in the world outside China. More than 34,000 businesses had opened shop on Messenger by August 2017.

Early cited examples of conversational commerce chatbots on Facebook Messenger include 1-800-FLOWERS with an IBM Watson artificial intelligence-powered chatbot/assistant, and Mexican airline Aeroméxico, whose chat platform running on Yalochat lets customers search, book, track, or check in for flights; ask any question, using A.I. and NLP to provide answers; or pull the chatbot into a group chat.

WhatsApp

In September 2017 WhatsApp announced the pilot of its new Enterprise solution, the first time large companies would be able to attend to large groups of customers in an approved WhatsApp solution, after WhatsApp banned earlier unofficial solutions. Companies who piloted the solution included airlines Aeromexico, KLM, Latin American online travel agency Despegar and online retailer Linio.

Enterprise solutions for Whatsapp have been available since 2015 from a variety of third party vendors, and though unofficial, they have been used by major companies and Governments including the Governments of Colombia and Costa Rica.

Website

The usap.gov website

A website is a collection of related web pages, including multimedia content, typically identified with a common domain name, and published on at least one web server. Notable examples are wikipedia.org, google.com, and amazon.com.

A website may be accessible via a public Internet Protocol (IP) network, such as the Internet, or a private local area network (LAN), by referencing a uniform resource locator (URL) that identifies the site.

Websites can have many functions and can be used in various fashions; a website can be a personal website, a corporate website for a company, a government website, an organization website, etc. Websites are typically dedicated to a particular topic or purpose, ranging from entertainment and social networking to providing news and education. All publicly accessible websites collectively constitute the World Wide Web, while private websites, such as a company's website for its employees, are typically a part of an intranet.

Web pages, which are the building blocks of websites, are documents, typically composed in plain text interspersed with formatting instructions of Hypertext Markup Language (HTML, XHTML). They may incorporate elements from other websites with suitable markup anchors. Web pages are accessed and transported with the Hypertext Transfer Protocol (HTTP), which may optionally employ encryption (HTTP Secure, HTTPS) to provide security and privacy for the user. The user's application, often a web browser, renders the page content according to its HTML markup instructions onto a display terminal.

Hyperlinking between web pages conveys to the reader the site structure and guides the navigation of the site, which often starts with a home page containing a directory of the site web content. Some websites require user registration or subscription to access content. Examples of subscription websites include many business sites, news websites, academic journal websites, gaming websites, file-sharing websites, message boards, web-based email, social networking websites, websites providing real-time stock market data, as well as sites providing various other services. End users can access websites on a range of devices, including desktop and laptop computers, tablet computers, smartphones and smart TVs.

NASA.gov homepage as it appeared in April 2015

The World Wide Web (WWW) was created in 1990 by the British CERN physicist Tim Berners-Lee. On 30 April 1993, CERN announced that the World Wide Web would be free to use for anyone. Before the introduction of HTML and HTTP, other protocols such as File Transfer Protocol and the gopher protocol were used to retrieve individual files from a server. These protocols offer a simple directory structure which the user navigates and where they choose files to download. Documents were most often presented as plain text files without formatting, or were encoded in word processor formats.

Websites have many functions and can be used in various fashions; a website can be a personal website, a commercial website, a government website or a non-profit organization website. Websites can be the work of an individual, a business or other organization, and are typically dedicated to a particular topic or purpose. Any website can contain a hyperlink to any other website, so the distinction between individual sites, as perceived by the user, can be blurred. Websites are written in, or converted to, HTML (Hyper Text Markup Language) and are accessed using a software interface classified as a user agent. Web pages can be viewed or otherwise accessed from a range of computer-based and Internet-enabled devices of various sizes, including desktop computers, laptops, tablet computers and smartphones. A website is hosted on a computer system known as a web server, also called an HTTP (Hyper Text Transfer Protocol) server. These terms can also refer to the software that runs on these systems which retrieves and delivers the web pages in response to requests from the website's users. Apache is the most commonly used web server software (according to Netcraft statistics) and Microsoft's IIS is also commonly used. Some alternatives, such as Nginx, Lighttpd, Hiawatha or Cherokee, are fully functional and lightweight.

Static website

A static website is one that has web pages stored on the server in the format that is sent to a client web browser. It is primarily coded in Hypertext Markup Language (HTML); Cascading Style Sheets (CSS) are used to control appearance beyond basic HTML. Images are commonly used to effect the desired appearance and as part of the main content. Audio or video might also be considered "static" content if it plays automatically or is generally non-interactive. This type of website usually displays the same information to all visitors. Similar to handing out a printed brochure to customers or clients, a static website will generally provide consistent, standard information for an extended period of time. Although the website owner may make updates periodically, it is a manual process to edit the text, photos and other content and may require basic website design skills and software. Simple forms or marketing examples of websites, such as classic website, a five-page website or a brochure website are often static websites, because they present pre-defined, static information to the user. This may include information about a company and its products and services through text, photos, animations, audio/video, and navigation menus.

Static websites can be edited using four broad categories of software:

- Text editors, such as Notepad or TextEdit, where content and HTML markup are manipulated directly within the editor program

- WYSIWYG offline editors, such as Microsoft FrontPage and Adobe Dreamweaver (previously Macromedia Dreamweaver), with which the site is edited using a GUI and the final HTML markup is generated automatically by the editor software

- WYSIWYG online editors which create media rich online presentation like web pages, widgets, intro, blogs, and other documents.

- Template-based editors such as iWeb allow users to create and upload web pages to a web server without detailed HTML knowledge, as they pick a suitable template from a palette and add pictures and text to it in a desktop publishing fashion without direct manipulation of HTML code.

Static websites may still use server side includes (SSI) as an editing convenience, such as sharing a common menu bar across many pages. As the site's behaviour to the reader is still static, this is not considered a dynamic site.

Dynamic website

Server-side programming languages repartition on 28 April 2016.

A dynamic website is one that changes or customizes itself frequently and automatically. Server-side dynamic pages are generated "on the fly" by computer code that produces the HTML (CSS are responsible for appearance and thus, are static files). There are a wide range of software systems, such as CGI, Java Servlets and Java Server Pages (JSP), Active Server Pages and ColdFusion (CFML) that are available to generate dynamic web systems and dynamic sites. Various web application frameworks and web template systems are available for general-use programming languages like Perl, PHP, Python and Ruby to make it faster and easier to create complex dynamic websites.

A site can display the current state of a dialogue between users, monitor a changing situation, or provide information in some way personalized to the requirements of the individual user. For example, when the front page of a news site is requested, the code running on the web server might combine stored HTML fragments with news stories retrieved from a database or another website via RSS to produce a page that includes the latest information. Dynamic sites can be interactive by using HTML forms, storing and reading back browser cookies, or by creating a series of pages that reflect the previous history of clicks. Another example of dynamic content is when a retail website with a database of media products allows a user to input a search request, e.g. for the keyword Beatles. In response, the content of the web page will spontaneously change the way it looked before, and will then display a list of Beatles products like CDs, DVDs and books. Dynamic HTML uses JavaScript code to instruct the web browser how to interactively modify the page contents. One way to simulate a certain type of dynamic website while avoiding the performance loss of initiating the dynamic engine on a per-user or per-connection basis, is to periodically automatically regenerate a large series of static pages.

Multimedia and interactive content

Early websites had only text, and soon after, images. Web browser plug ins were then used to add audio, video, and interactivity (such as for a rich Internet application that mirrors the complexity of a desktop application like a word processor). Examples of such plug-ins are Microsoft Silverlight, Adobe Flash, Adobe Shockwave, and applets written in Java.HTML 5 includes provisions for audio and video without plugins. JavaScript is also built into most modern web browsers, and allows for website creators to send code to the web browser that instructs it how to interactively modify page content and communicate with the web server if needed. The browser's internal representation of the content is known as the Document Object Model (DOM) and the technique is known as Dynamic HTML. A 2010-era trend in websites called "responsive design" has given the best of viewing experience as it provides with a device based layout for users. These websites change their layout according to the device or mobile platform thus giving a rich user experience.

Spelling

While "web site" was the original spelling (sometimes capitalized "Web site", since "Web" is a proper noun when referring to the World Wide Web), this variant has become rarely used, and "website" has become the standard spelling. All major style guides, such as The Chicago Manual of Style and the AP Stylebook, have reflected this change.

Types

Websites can be divided into two broad categories—static and interactive. Interactive sites are part of the Web 2.0 community of sites, and allow for interactivity between the site owner and site visitors or users. Static sites serve or capture information but do not allow engagement with the audience or users directly. Some websites are informational or produced by enthusiasts or for personal use or entertainment. Many websites do aim to make money, using one or more business models, including:

- Posting interesting content and selling contextual advertising either through direct sales or through an advertising network.
- E-commerce: products or services are purchased directly through the website
- Advertising products or services available at a brick and mortar business

• Freemium: basic content is available for free but premium content requires a payment (e.g., WordPress website, it is an open source platform to build a blog or website.)

There are many varieties of websites, each specializing in a particular type of content or use, and they may be arbitrarily classified in any number of ways. A few such classifications might include:

Some websites may be included in one or more of these categories. For example, a business website may promote the business's products, but may also host informative documents, such as white papers. There are also numerous sub-categories to the ones listed above. For example, a porn site is a specific type of e-commerce site or business site (that is, it is trying to sell memberships for access to its site) or have social networking capabilities. A fansite may be a dedication from the owner to a particular celebrity. Websites are constrained by architectural limits (e.g., the computing power dedicated to the website). Very large websites, such as Facebook, Yahoo!, Microsoft, and Google employ many servers and load balancing equipment such as Cisco Content Services Switches to distribute visitor loads over multiple computers at multiple locations. As of early 2011, Facebook utilized 9 data centers with approximately 63,000 servers.

In February 2009, Netcraft, an Internet monitoring company that has tracked Web growth since 1995, reported that there were 215,675,903 websites with domain names and content on them in 2009, compared to just 19,732 websites in August 1995. After reaching 1 billion websites in September 2014, a milestone confirmed by NetCraft in its October 2014 Web Server Survey and that Internet Live Stats was the first to announce—as attested by this tweet from the inventor of the World Wide Web himself, Tim Berners-Lee—the number of websites in the world has subsequently declined, reverting to a level below 1 billion. This is due to the monthly fluctuations in the count of inactive websites. The number of websites continued growing to over 1 billion by March 2016, and has continued growing since.

Internet & Jurisdiciary

The Internet & Jurisdiction Policy Network, also known as "I&J Policy Network", "Internet & Jurisdiction, or simply "I&J", is a multistakeholder organization addressing the tension between the cross-border Internet and national jurisdictions. It's Secretariat facilitates a global policy process between key stakeholders to enable transnational cooperation and policy coherence. Participants in the Policy Network work together to preserve the cross-border nature of the Internet, protect human rights, fight abuses, and enable the global digital economy. Since 2012, the Internet & Jurisdiction Policy Network has engaged more than 200 key entities from different stakeholder groups around the world, including governments, the world's largest Internet companies, the technical community, civil society groups, leading universities and international organizations.

The Secretariat of the Internet & Jurisdiction Policy Network is based in Paris, France. It was founded in 2012 by Executive Director Bertrand de La Chapelle and Deputy Director Paul Fehlinger.

Enabling Multistakeholder Cooperation

The Internet & Jurisdiction Policy Network bridges relevant stakeholder groups and policy silos in order to enable transnational cooperation. It strives to fill the institutional gap in Internet governance at the intersection of digital economy, human rights, and cybersecurity. Through global, regional, and thematic meetings, its Secretariat facilitates a neutral dialogue process with the mission of building trust among the different actors and help them develop the operational solutions necessary for the coexistence of diverse laws on the cross-border Internet.

The Internet & Jurisdiction Secretariat reports every year on progress at the Internet Governance Forum (IGF) organized by the United Nations. At the IGF 2016, The Internet & Jurisdiction Policy Network was granted for the first time an "Open Forum", a format traditionally reserved to treaty-based organizations. In June 2016 at the OECD Ministerial Meeting on the Digital Economy in Cancún, Mexico, the Background Report Economic and Social Benefits of Internet Openness, cited the Internet & Jurisdiction multistakeholder process as being exemplary: "The [Principles for Internet Policy Making of the 2011 OECD Council Recommendation] endorse the development of voluntary codes of conduct through multi-stakeholder processes, such as the Internet & Jurisdiction [Policy Network]." In April 2018, the G7 Cyber Group expressed its support for the ongoing work of the Internet & Jurisdiction Policy Network. The organization was selected as one of 40 worldwide initiatives to be showcased with a dedicated session to the inaugural Paris Peace Forum on November 11-13, 2018, which was attended by over 70 heads of state.

Programs of the Internet & Jurisdiction Policy Network

As of 2018, the work of the Internet & Jurisdiction Policy Network is structured around three programs, which structure the ongoing multistakeholder development of policy standards and operational frameworks:

- Data & Jurisdiction: How can transnational data flows and the protection of privacy be reconciled with lawful access requirements to address crime?
- Content & Jurisdiction: How can we manage globally available content in light of the diversity of local laws and norms applicable on the internet?

• Domains & Jurisdiction: How can the neutrality of the internet's technical layer be preserved when national laws are applied on the Domain Name System?

Global Conferences of the Internet & Jurisdiction Policy Network

The Global Conferences of the Internet & Jurisdiction Policy Network are milestone meetings in which stakeholders take stock of the intersessional work and decide on common objectives and next steps for the policy development work. Stakeholder Plenary Sessions are held in the innovative heptagon seating format invented by the Secretariat of the Policy Network.

1st Global Conference of the Internet & Jurisdiction Policy Network in Paris

The 1st Global Conference of the Internet & Jurisdiction Policy Network took place on November 14 16, 2016 in Paris, France. It was organized in partnership with the Government of France and institutionally supported by the OECD, the European Commission, UNESCO, the Council of Europe, the Slovak Presidency of the Council of the European Union, and ICANN. The French Ministry of Foreign Affairs provided its Ministerial Conference Center as the venue. It was the first time that more than 200 senior representatives from more than 40 countries from states, Internet companies, technical operators, civil society, academia and international organizations gathered to specifically address the issue of jurisdiction on the Internet. As The Economist reported: "If nothing is done, many who met [at the Global Conference of the Internet & Jurisdiction Policy Network] in Paris worried, the open internet could be a thing of the past within a decade or two. What is needed, they said, is more international co-operation—but not of the old kind." As an outcome, stakeholders identified concrete "areas for cooperation" to help the development of shared policy standards and frameworks for legal interoperability and due process across borders. The Global Internet and Jurisdiction Conference firmly placed the topic of jurisdiction on the Internet governance agenda, as recommended in the 2014 NETmundial Roadmap for the Future Evolution of Internet Governance Ecosystem. The 1st Global Conference of the Internet & Jurisdiction Policy Network was recognized by the 2017 United Nations Secretary-General's Report "Progress Made in the Implementation of and Follow-up to the Outcomes of the World Summit on the Information Society", and the I&J Secretariat was invited to present outcomes to the G7 Cyber Group in March 2017 and the G20 Multistakeholder Conference on the Digital Future in April 2017.

2nd Global Conference of the Internet & Jurisdiction Policy Network in Ottawa

The 2nd Global Conference of the Internet & Jurisdiction Policy Network took place on February 26–28, 2018 in Ottawa, Canada. It was organized in partnership with the Government of Canada and institutionally supported by the OECD, the European Commission, UNESCO, the Council of Europe, and ICANN. Three multistakeholder Contact Groups were formed as an outcome of the first Global Conference in Paris for each of the three Programs of the Policy Network. They elaborated in 2017 so-called "Policy Options Documents". Based on these, the over 200 senior-level stakeholder from more than 40 countries defined common objectives to develop concrete solutions to pressing jurisdictional challenges on the internet and adopted the Ottawa Roadmap. The Ottawa Roadmap established for the first time agreed Work Plans with structuring components for each Program of the Policy Network to advance towards policy coherence and joint action. Ahead of the 2nd Global Conference, co-founder of the internet Vint Cerf called in a Financial Times Op-Ed upon stakeholders that "the future of the cross-border internet depends on [its outcomes]". Politico asked "The internet is broken. Can this group fix it?". In April 2018, the Group of Seven (G7) Cyber Group expressed its support for the "continued multi-stakeholder work under the auspices of the Internet and Jurisdiction Policy Network, including most recently the Ottawa Road Map that came out of the 2nd Global Conference on Internet and Jurisdiction held in Ottawa in February 2018". To implement the Ottawa Roadmap, 120 representatives from five continents, composed of Members from governments, companies, civil society and international organizations, work together in three Contact Groups (Data & Jurisdiction, Content & Jurisdiction, Domains & Jurisdiction) to develop proposals for policy standards and operational solutions.

3rd Global Conference of the Internet & Jurisdiction Policy Network in Berlin

The 3rd Global Conference of the Internet & Jurisdiction Policy Network will take place on June 3–5, 2019 in Berlin, Germany. It is organized in partnership with the Government of Germany, and institutionally supported by the Council of Europe, European Commission, ICANN, OECD, UN ECLAC, and UNESCO.

To enable evidence-based policy innovation, Internet & Jurisdiction created the open access, indexed and searchable I&J Retrospect Database. By early 2018, it contains over 1500 cases from more than 120 countries dating back to 2012 that document the increasing tension between the cross-border Internet and national jurisdictions. It is a resource that allows stakeholders to better understand global trends. Every month, the members of the I&J Observatory crowd-rank the top 20 cases that are added to the I&J Retrospect Database. The I&J Observatory is an international network of 31 leading experts from 29 universities and research centers in 17 countries that supports the Internet & Jurisdiction Policy Network. Members come from institutions such as Harvard University, Humboldt Institute for Internet and Society,

Institute for Technology & Society Rio, National Law University Delhi, Oxford University, and Stanford University.

E-governance

Electronic governance or e-governance is the application of information and communication technology (ICT) for delivering government services, exchange of information, communication transactions, integration of various stand-alone systems and services between government-to-citizen (G2C), government-to-business (G2B), government-to-government (G2G), government-to-employees (G2E) as well as back-office processes and interactions within the entire government framework. Through e-governance, government services are made available to citizens in a convenient, efficient, and transparent manner. The three main target groups that can be distinguished in governance concepts are government, citizens, and businesses/interest groups. In e-governance, there are no distinct boundaries.

Although the two terms are often used interchangeably, there is a difference between e-governance and e-government. E-government refers to the use of the ICTs in public administration which, when combined with organizational change and new skills, are intended to improve public services and democratic processes and to strengthen support to the public. However, e-government has no provision for governance of ICTs. The governance of ICTs typically requires a substantial increase in regulation and policy-making capabilities, as well as additional expertise and opinion-shaping processes among various social stakeholders. The perspective of e-governance is "the use of the technologies that both help to govern and have to be governed". The central goal of e-governance is to reach the beneficiary and to ensure that their service needs are met. Ideally, the government will automatically recognize the importance of achieving this goal in order to maximize its efficiency.

Furthermore, e-government uses one-way communication protocol whereas e-governance uses two-way communication protocol. Establishing the identity of the end beneficiary is a challenge in all citizen-centric services. Statistical information published by governments and global bodies do not always reveal the facts. The best form of e-governance cuts down on the unwanted interference of too many layers while delivering governmental services. It depends on good infrastructural setup with the support of local processes and parameters for governments to reach their citizens or end beneficiaries. A budget for planning, development, and growth can be derived from well laid out e-governance systems.

The relevance of BI Analytics has brought forth a paradigm shift in assimilating and visualizing huge chunks of data in near real-time manner. The pivot of all good decision-making systems is correct, up-to-date and compliant data. Governments not only want the transformation of their own country and countrymen but also expect improved relations and healthy trade across the world. Development should be transformative and continuously evolving. Internal as well as external IT systems should work in tandem with government policies and procedures. Data Analytics has the ability to change the color and complexion of the world. E-governance should induce up-to-date information, initiate effective interaction, and engage with transparent transactions in compliance with rule of law, thus enabling a sustainable transformation model.

The public–private partnership (PPP)-based e-governance projects are hugely successful in India. Many countries implement e-government policy in an attempt to build a corruption-free government.

Government to citizen

The goal of government-to-citizen (G2C) e-governance is to offer a variety of ICT services to citizens in an efficient and economical manner and to strengthen the relationship between government and citizens using technology.

There are several methods of government-to-customer e-governance. Two-way communication allows citizens to instant message directly with public administrators, and cast remote electronic votes (electronic voting) and instant opinion voting. Transactions such as payment of services, such as city utilities, can be completed online or over the phone. Mundane services such as name or address changes, applying for services or grants, or transferring existing services are more convenient and no longer have to be completed face to face.

By country

G2C e-governance is unbalanced across the globe as not everyone has Internet access and computing skills, but the United States, European Union, and Asia are ranked the top three in development.

The Federal Government of the United States has a broad framework of G2C technology to enhance citizen access to Government information and services. benefits.gov is an official US government website that informs citizens of benefits they are eligible for and provides information on how to apply for assistance. US State Governments also engage in G2C interaction through the Department of Transportation, Department of Public Safety, United States Department of Health and Human Services, United States Department of Education, and others. As with e-governance on the global level, G2C services vary from state to state. The Digital States Survey ranks states on social measures, digital democracy, e-commerce, taxation, and revenue. The 2012 report shows Michigan and Utah in the lead and Florida and Idaho with the lowest scores. Municipal governments in the United States also use government-to-customer technology to complete transactions and inform the public. Much like states, cities are awarded for innovative technology. Government Technology's "Best of the Web 2012" named Louisville, KY, Arvada, CO, Raleigh, NC, Riverside, CA, and Austin, TX the top five G2C city portals.

European countries were ranked second among all geographic regions. The Single Point of Access for Citizens of Europe supports travel within Europe and Europe is a 1999 initiative supporting an online government. Main focuses are to provide public information, allow customers to have access to basic public services, simplify online procedures, and promote electronic signatures. Estonia is the first and the only country in the world with e-residency which enables anyone in the world outside Estonia to access Estonian online services.

Asia is ranked third in comparison, and there are diverse G2C programs between countries. Singapore's eCitizen Portal is an organized single access point to government information and services. South Korea's Home Tax Service (HTS) provides citizens with 24/7 online services such as tax declaration. Taiwan has top ranking G2C technology including an online motor vehicle services system, which provides 21 applications and payment services to citizens.

Government-to-Citizen is the communication link between a government and private individuals or residents. Such G2C communication most often refers to that which takes place through Information and Communication Technologies (ICTs), but can also include direct mail and media campaigns. G2C can take place at the federal, state, and local levels. G2C stands in contrast to G2B, or Government-to-Business networks.

One such Federal G2C network is USA.gov, the United States' official web portal, though there are many other examples from governments around the world.

Concerns

A full switch to government-to-citizen e-governance will cost a large amount of money in development and implementation. In addition, government agencies do not always engage citizens in the development of their e-gov services or accept feedback. Customers identified the following barriers to government-to-customer e-governance: not everyone has Internet access, especially in rural or low-income areas, G2C technology can be problematic for citizens who lack computing skills. Some G2C sites have technology requirements (such as browser requirements and plug-ins) that won't allow access to certain services, language barriers, the necessity for an e-mail address to access certain services, and a lack of privacy.

Government to employees

"G2E" redirects here. For gaming trade show, see Global Gaming Expo.

E-governance to Employee partnership (G2E) Is one of four main primary interactions in the delivery model of E-governance. It is the relationship between online tools, sources, and articles that help employees to maintain the communication with the government and their own companies. E-governance relationship with Employees allows new learning technology in one simple place as the computer. Documents can now be stored and shared with other colleagues online. E-governance makes it possible for employees to become paperless and makes it easy for employees to send important documents back and forth to colleagues all over the world instead of having to print out these records or faxG2E services also include software for maintaining personal information and records of employees. Some of the benefits of G2E expansion include:

- E-payroll – maintaining the online sources to view paychecks, pay stubs, pay bills, and keep records for tax information.
- E-benefits – be able to look up what benefits an employee is receiving and what benefits they have a right to.
- E-training – allows for new and current employees to regularly maintain the training they have through the development of new technology and to allow new employees to train and learn over new materials in one convenient location. E-learning is another way to keep employees informed on the important materials they need to know through the use of visuals, animation, videos, etc. It is usually a computer-based learning tool, although not always. It is also a way for employees to learn at their own pace (distance learning), although it can be instructor-led.
- Maintaining records of personal information – Allows the system to keep all records in one easy location to update with every single bit of information that is relevant to a personal file. Examples being social security numbers, tax information, current address, and other information

Government-to-employees (abbreviated G2E) is the online interactions through instantaneous communication tools between government units and their employees. G2E is one out of the four primary delivery models of e-Government.

G2E is an effective way to provide e-learning to the employees, bring them together and to promote knowledge sharing among them. It also gives employees the possibility of accessing information in regard to compensation and benefits policies, training and learning opportunities and civil rights laws. G2E services also include software for maintaining personal information and records of employees.

G2E is adopted in many countries including the United States, Hong Kong, and New Zealand.

Government to government

E-government

From the start of 1990s e-commerce and e-product, there has rampant integration of e-forms of government process. Governments have now tried to use the efficiencies of their techniques to cut down on waste. E-government is a fairly broad subject matter, but all relate to how the services and representation are now delivered and how they are now being implemented.

Many governments around the world have gradually turned to Information technologies (IT) in an effort to keep up with today's demands. Historically, many governments in this sphere have only been reactive, but recently there has been a more proactive approach in developing comparable services such things as e-commerce and e-business.

Before, the structure emulated private-like business techniques. Recently that has all changed as e-government begins to make its own plan. Not only does e-government introduce a new form of record keeping, but it also continues to become more interactive to better the process of delivering services and promoting constituency participation.

The framework of such an organization is now expected to increase more than ever by becoming efficient and reducing the time it takes to complete an objective. Some examples include paying utilities, tickets, and applying for permits. So far, the biggest concern is accessibility to Internet technologies for the average citizen. In an effort to help, administrations are now trying to aid those who do not have the skills to fully participate in this new medium of governance, especially now as e-government progressing to more e-governance terms.

An overhaul of the structure is now required as every pre-existing sub-entity must now merge under one concept of e-government. As a result, Public Policy has also seen changes due to the emerging of constituent participation and the Internet. Many governments such as Canada's have begun to invest in developing new mediums of communication of issues and information through virtual communication and participation. In practice, this has led to several responses and adaptations by interest groups, activist, and lobbying groups. This new medium has changed the way the polis interacts with government.

Editorial

The purpose to include e-governance to government is to means more efficient in various aspects. Whether it means to reduce cost by reducing paper clutter, staffing cost, or communicating with private citizens or public government. E-government brings many advantages to play such as facilitating information delivery, application process/renewal between both business and private citizen, and participation with the constituency. There are both internal and external advantages to the emergence of IT in government, though not all municipalities are alike in size and participation.

In theory, there are currently 4 major levels of E-government in municipal governments:

- The establishment of a secure and cooperative interaction among governmental agencies
- Web-based service delivery
- The application of e-commerce for more efficient government transactions activities
- Digital democracy

These, along with 5 degrees of technical integration and interaction of users include:

- Simple information dissemination (one-way communication)
- Two-way communication (request and response)
- Service and financial transactions
- Integration (horizontal and vertical integration)
- Political participation

The adoption of e-government in municipalities evokes greater innovation in e-governance by being specialized and localized. The level success and feedback depends greatly on the city size and government type. A council-manager government municipality typically works the best with this method, as opposed to mayor-council government positions, which tend to be more political. Therefore, they have greater barriers towards its application. Council-Manager governments are also more inclined to be effective here by bringing innovation and reinvention of governance to e-governance.

The International City/County Management Association and Public Technology Inc. have done surveys over the effectiveness of this method. The results are indicating that most governments are still in either the primary stages (1 or stage 2), which revolves around public service requests. Though application of integration is now accelerating, there has been little to no instigating research to see its progression as e-governance to the government. We can only theorize it's still within the primitive stages of e-governance.

Overview

Government-to-Government (abbreviated G2G) is the online non-commercial interaction between Government organizations, departments, and authorities and other Government organizations, departments, and authorities.

Its use is common in the UK, along with G2C, the online non-commercial interaction of local and central Government and private individuals, and G2B the online non-commercial interaction of local and central Government and the commercial business sector.

G2G systems generally come in one of two types: Internal-facing - joining up a single Governments departments, agencies, organizations, and authorities - examples include the integration aspect of the Government Gateway, and the UK NHS Connecting for Health Data SPINE. External facing - joining up multiple Governments IS systems - an example would include the integration aspect of the Schengen Information System (SIS), developed to meet the requirements of the Schengen Agreement.

Objective

The strategic objective of e-governance, or in this case G2G is to support and simplify governance for government, citizens, and businesses. The use of ICT can connect all parties and support processes and activities. Other objectives are to make government administration more transparent, speedy and accountable while addressing the society's needs and expectations through efficient public services and effective interaction between the people, businesses, and government.

Government-to-government model

Delivery model

Within every of those interaction domains, four sorts of activities take place:

Pushing data over the internet, e.g.: regulative services, general holidays, public hearing schedules, issue briefs, notifications, etc. two-way communications between one governmental department and another, users will interact in dialogue with agencies and post issues, comments, or requests to the agency. Conducting transactions, e.g.: Lodging tax returns, applying for services and grants. Governance, e.g.: To alter the national transition from passive info access to individual participation by:

- Informing the individual
- Representing an individual
- Consulting an individual
- Involving the individual

Internal G2G (UK)

In the field of networking, the Government Secure Intranet (GSi) puts in place a secure link between central government departments. It is an IP-based virtual private network based on broadband technology introduced in April 1998 and further upgraded in February 2004. Among other things, it offers a variety of advanced services including file transfer and search facilities, directory services, email exchange facilities (both between network members and over the Internet) as well as voice and video services. An additional network is currently also under development: the Public Sector Network (PSN) will be the network to interconnect public authorities (including departments and agencies in England; devolved administrations and local governments) and facilitate in particular sharing of information and services among each other.

Government to business

"G2B" redirects here. For the scientific journal, see Genes, Brain and Behavior.

Government-to-Business (G2B) is the online non-commercial interaction between local and central government and the commercial business sector with the purpose of providing businesses information and advice on e-business best practices. G2B: Refers to the conduction through the Internet between government agencies and trading companies. B2G: Professional transactions between the company and the district, city, or federal regulatory agencies. B2G usually include recommendations to complete the measurement and evaluation of books and contracts.

Objective

The objective of G2B is to reduce difficulties for business, provide immediate information and enable digital communication by e-business (XML). In addition, the government should re-use the data in the report proper, and take advantage of commercial electronic transaction protocol. Government services are concentrated on the following groups: human services; community services; judicial services; transport services; land resources; business services; financial services and other. Each of the components listed above for each cluster of related services to the enterprise.

Benefits for business

E-government reduces costs and lowers the barrier of allowing companies to interact with the government. The interaction between the government and businesses reduces the time required for businesses to conduct a transaction. For instance, there is no need to commute to a government agency's office, and transactions may be conducted online instantly with the click of a mouse. This significantly reduces transaction time for the government and businesses alike.

E-Government provides a greater amount of information that the business needed, also it makes that information more clear. A key factor in business success is the ability to planand forecast through data-driven future. The government collected a lot of economic, demographic and other trends in the data. This makes the data more accessible to companies which may increase the chance of economic prosperity.

In addition, E-Government can help businesses navigate through government regulations by providing an intuitive site organization with a wealth of useful applications. The electronic filings of applications for environmental permits give an example of it. Companies often do not know how, when, and what they must apply. Therefore, failure to comply with environmental regulations up to 70%, a staggering figure most likely due to confusion about the requirements, rather than the product of willful disregard of the law.

Disadvantages

The government should concern that not all people are able to access the internet to gain online government services. The network reliability, as well as information on government bodies, can influence public opinion and prejudice hidden agenda. There are many considerations and implementation, designing e-government, including the potential impact of government and citizens of disintermediation, the impact on economic, social and political factors, vulnerable to cyber attacks, and disturbances to the status quo in these areas.

G2B rises the connection between government and businesses. Once the e-government began to develop, become more sophisticated, people will be forced to interact with e-government in the larger area. This may result in a lack of privacy for businesses as their government gets their more and more information. In the worst case, there is so much information in the electron transfer between the government and business, a system which is like totalitarian could be developed. As the government can access more information, the loss of privacy could be a cost.

The government site does not consider about "potential to reach many users including those who live in remote areas, are homebound, have low literacy levels, exist on poverty line incomes."

Examples

• e-Tender Box (ETB) system – ETB system was developed by Government Logistics Department (GLD) to replace Electronic Tendering System. Users can use ETB system to download the resources and gain the service from the GLD.

• e-Procurement Programme – e-Procurement Programme provides a simple, convenient online ways for suppliers of the participating bureaux/departments (B/Ds) and suppliers of Government Logistics Department and agree to provide the low-valued goods and service.

• Finance and support for your business – UK Government provide the online financial help for business, including grants, loans, business guide; what's more, it also offers the funding for the sunrise businesses (just start) or small-scale firms.

Overview

The main goal of government to business is to increase productivity by giving business more access to information in a more organize manner while lowering the cost of doing business as well as the ability to cut "red tape", save time, reduce operational cost and to create a more transparent business environment when dealing with government.

• Lowering cost of doing business – electronic transaction save time compared to conducting business in person.

• Cutting red tape – rules and regulation placed upon business normally take time and are most likely to cause a delay- in (G2B) will allow a much faster process with fewer delays and decreasing the number of rules and regulations

• Transparency – More information will be available, making G2B easier to communicate.

Government to business key points:

1. Reduce the burden on business by adopting a process that enables collecting data once for multiple uses and streamlining redundant data.

2. Key lines of business: regulations, economic development, trade, permits/licenses, grants/loans, and asset management.

Difference between G2B and B2G

• Government to business (G2B) – Refers to the conducting of transactions between government bodies and business via the internet.

• Business to the government (B2G) – Professional affairs conducted between companies and regional, municipal, or federal governing bodies. B2G typically encompasses the determination and evaluation of proposal and completion of the contract.

Conclusion:

The overall benefit of e-governance when dealing with business is that it enables the business to perform more efficiently.

Challenges – international position

E-governance is facing numerous challenges world over. These challenges are arising from administrative, legal, institutional and technological factors. The challenge includes security drawbacks such as spoofing, tampering, repudiation, disclosure, elevation of privilege, denial of service and other cyber crimes. Other sets of problems include implementation parts such as funding, management of change, privacy, authentication, delivery of services, standardization, technology issues and use of local languages.

9

The Cyberspace

Cyberspace is a domain characterized by the use of electronics and the electromagnetic spectrum to store, modify, and exchange data via networked systems and associated physical infrastructures. In effect, cyberspace can be thought of as the interconnection of human beings through computers and telecommunication, without regard to physical geography.

Cyberspace is widespread, interconnected digital technology. The term entered the popular culture from science fiction and the arts but is now used by technology strategists, security professionals, government, military and industry leaders and entrepreneurs to describe the domain of the global technology environment. Others consider cyberspace to be just a notional environment in which communication over computer networks occurs. The word became popular in the 1990s when the uses of the Internet, networking, and digital communication were all growing dramatically and the term "cyberspace" was able to represent the many new ideas and phenomena that were emerging. It has been called the largest unregulated and uncontrolled domain in the history of mankind, and is also unique because it is a domain created by people vice the traditional physical domains.

The parent term of cyberspace is "cybernetics", derived from the Ancient Greek (kybernētēs, steersman, governor, pilot, or rudder), a word introduced by Norbert Wiener for his pioneering work in electronic communication and control science. This word cyberspace first appeared in the art installation of the same name by danish artist Susanne Ussing, 1968).

As a social experience, individuals can interact, exchange ideas, share information, provide social support, conduct business, direct actions, create artistic media, play games, engage in political discussion, and so on, using this global network. They are sometimes referred to as cybernauts. The term cyberspace has become a conventional means to describe anything associated with the Internetand the diverse Internet culture. The United States government recognizes the interconnected information technology and the interdependent network of information technology infrastructures operating across this medium as part of the US national critical infrastructure. Amongst individuals on cyberspace, there is believed to be a code of shared rules and ethics mutually beneficial for all to follow, referred to as cyberethics. Many view the right to privacy as most important to a functional code of cyberethics. Such moral responsibilities go hand in hand when working online with global networks, specifically, when opinions are involved with online social experiences.

According to Chip Morningstar and F. Randall Farmer, cyberspace is defined more by the social interactions involved rather than its technical implementation. In their view, the computational medium in cyberspace is an augmentation of the communication channel between real people; the core characteristic of cyberspace is that it offers an environment that consists of many participants with the ability to affect and influence each other. They derive this concept from the observation that people seek richness, complexity, and depth within a virtual world.

The term "cyberspace" first appeared in the visual arts in the late 1960s, when Danish artist Susanne Ussing (1940-1998) and her partner architect Carsten Hoff (b. 1934) constituted themselves as Atelier Cyberspace. Under this name the two made a series of installations and images entitled "sensory spaces" that were based on the principle of open systems adaptable to various influences, such as human movement and the behaviour of new materials.

Atelier Cyberspace worked at a time when the Internet did not exist and computers were more or less off-limit to artists and creative engagement. In a 2015-interview with Scandinavian art magazine Kunstkritikk, Carsten Hoff recollects, that although Atelier Cyberspace did try to implement computers, they had no interest in the virtual space as such:

To us, "cyberspace" was simply about managing spaces. There was nothing esoteric about it. Nothing digital, either. It was just a tool. The space was concrete, physical.

And in the same interview Hoff continues:

Our shared point of departure was that we were working with physical settings, and we were both frustrated and displeased with the architecture from the period, particularly when it came to spaces for living. We felt that there was a need to loosen up the rigid confines of urban planning, giving back the gift of creativity to individual human beings and allowing them to shape and design their houses or dwellings themselves – instead of having some clever architect pop up, telling you how you should live. We were thinking in terms of open-ended systems where things could grow and evolve as required.

For instance, we imagined a kind of mobile production unit, but unfortunately the drawings have been lost. It was a kind of truck with a nozzle at the back. Like a bee building its hive. The nozzle would emit and apply material that grew to form amorphous mushrooms or whatever you might imagine. It was supposed to be computer-controlled, allowing you to create interesting shapes and sequences of spaces. It was a merging of organic and technological systems, a new way of structuring the world. And a response that counteracted industrial uniformity. We had this idea that sophisticated software might enable us to mimic the way in which nature creates products – where things that belong to the same family can take different forms. All oak trees are oak trees, but no two oak trees are exactly alike. And then a whole new material – polystyrene foam – arrived on the scene. It behaved like nature in the sense that it grew when its two component parts were mixed. Almost like a fungal growth. This made it an obvious choice for our work in Atelier Cyberspace.

The works of Atelier Cyberspace were originally shown at a number of Copenhagen venues and have later been exhibited at The National Gallery of Denmark in Copenhagen as part of the exhibition "What's Happening?"

The term "cyberspace" first appeared in fiction in the 1980s in the work of cyberpunk science fiction author William Gibson, first in his 1982 short story "Burning Chrome" and later in his 1984 novel Neuromancer. In the next few years, the word became prominently identified with online computer networks. The portion of Neuromancer cited in this respect is usually the following:

Cyberspace. A consensual hallucination experienced daily by billions of legitimate operators, in every nation, by children being taught mathematical concepts... A graphic representation of data abstracted from the banks of every computer in the human system. Unthinkable complexity. Lines of light ranged in the nonspace of the mind, clusters and constellations of data. Like city lights, receding.

Now widely used, the term has since been criticized by Gibson, who commented on the origin of the term in the 2000 documentary No Maps for These Territories:

All I knew about the word "cyberspace" when I coined it, was that it seemed like an effective buzzword. It seemed evocative and essentially meaningless. It was suggestive of something, but had no real semantic meaning, even for me, as I saw it emerge on the page.

Metaphorical

Don Slater uses a metaphor to define cyberspace, describing the "sense of a social setting that exists purely within a space of representation and communication ... it exists entirely within a computer space, distributed across increasingly complex and fluid networks." The term "Cyberspace" started to become a de facto synonym for the Internet, and later the World Wide Web, during the 1990s, especially in academic circles and activist communities. Author Bruce Sterling, who popularized this meaning, credits John Perry Barlow as the first to use it to refer to "the present-day nexus of computer and telecommunications networks". Barlow describes it thus in his essay to announce the formation of the Electronic Frontier Foundation (note the spatial metaphor) in June 1990:

In this silent world, all conversation is typed. To enter it, one forsakes both body and place and becomes a thing of words alone. You can see what your neighbors are saying (or recently said), but not what either they or their physical surroundings look like. Town meetings are continuous and discussions rage on everything from sexual kinks to depreciation schedules. Whether by one telephonic tendril or millions, they are all connected to one another. Collectively, they form what their inhabitants call the Net. It extends across that immense region of electron states, microwaves, magnetic fields, light pulses and thought which sci-fi writer William Gibson named Cyberspace.

—John Perry Barlow, "Crime and Puzzlement", 1990-06-08

As Barlow, and the EFF, continued public education efforts to promote the idea of "digital rights", the term was increasingly used during the Internet boom of the late 1990s.

Virtual environments

Although the present-day, loose use of the term "cyberspace" no longer implies or suggests immersion in a virtual reality, current technology allows the integration of a number of capabilities (sensors, signals, connections, transmissions, processors, and controllers) sufficient to generate a virtual interactive experience that is accessible regardless of a geographic location. It is for these reasons cyberspace has been described as the ultimate tax haven.

In 1989, Autodesk, an American multinational corporation that focuses on 2D and 3D design software, developed a virtual design system called Cyberspace.

Recent definitions of Cyberspace

Although several definitions of cyberspace can be found both in scientific literature and in official governmental sources, there is no fully agreed official definition yet. According to F. D. Kramer there are 28 different definitions of the term cyberspace. See in particular the following links: "Cyberpower and National Security: Policy Recommendations for a Strategic Framework," in Cyberpower and National Security, FD Kramer, S. Starr, L.K. Wentz (ed.), National Defense University Press, Washington (DC) 2009; see also Mayer, M., Chiarugi, I., De Scalzi, N., https://www.academia.edu/14336129/International_Politics_in_the_Digital_Age.

The most recent draft definition is the following:

Cyberspace is a global and dynamic domain (subject to constant change) characterized by the combined use of electrons and electromagnetic spectrum, whose purpose is to create, store, modify, exchange, share and extract, use, eliminate information and disrupt physical resources. Cyberspace includes: a) physical infrastructures and telecommunications devices that allow for the connection of technological and communication system networks, understood in the broadest sense (SCADA devices, smartphones/tablets, computers, servers, etc.); b) computer systems (see point a) and the related (sometimes embedded) software that guarantee the domain's basic operational functioning and connectivity; c) networks between computer systems; d) networks of networks that connect computer systems (the distinction between networks and networks of networks is mainly organizational); e) the access nodes of users and intermediaries routing nodes; f) constituent data (or resident data). Often, in common parlance (and sometimes in commercial language), networks of networks are called Internet (with a lowercase i), while networks between computers are called intranet. Internet (with a capital I, in journalistic language sometimes called the Net) can be considered a part of the system a). A distinctive and constitutive feature of cyberspace is that no central entity exercises control over all the networks that make up this new domain.

Just as in the real world there is no world government, cyberspace lacks an institutionally predefined hierarchical center. To cyberspace, a domain without a hierarchical ordering principle, we can therefore extend the definition of international politics coined by Kenneth Waltz: as being "with no system of law enforceable." This does not mean that the dimension of power in cyberspace is absent, nor that power is dispersed and scattered into a thousand invisible streams, nor that it is evenly spread across myriad people and organizations, as some scholars had predicted. On the contrary, cyberspace is characterized by a precise structuring of hierarchies of power.

The Joint Chiefs of Staff of the United States Department of Defense define cyberspace as one of five interdependent domains, the remaining four being land, air, maritime, and space. See United States Cyber Command

Cyberspace as an Internet metaphor

While cyberspace should not be confused with the Internet, the term is often used to refer to objects and identities that exist largely within the communication network itself, so that a website, for example, might be metaphorically said to "exist in cyberspace". According to this interpretation, events taking place on the Internet are not happening in the locations where participants or servers are physically located, but "in cyberspace". The philosopher Michel Foucault used the term heterotopias, to describe such spaces which are simultaneously physical and mental.

Firstly, cyberspace describes the flow of digital data through the network of interconnected computers: it is at once not "real", since one could not spatially locate it as a tangible object, and clearly "real" in its effects. There have been several attempts to create a concise model about how cyberspace works since it is not a physical thing that can be looked at. Secondly, cyberspace is the site of computer-mediated communication (CMC), in which online relationships and alternative forms of online identity were enacted, raising important questions about the social psychology of Internet use, the relationship between "online" and "offline" forms of life and interaction, and the relationship between the "real" and the virtual. Cyberspace draws attention to remediation of culture through new media technologies: it is not just a communication tool but a social destination, and is culturally significant in its own right. Finally, cyberspace can be seen as providing new opportunities to reshape society and culture through "hidden" identities, or it can be seen as borderless communication and culture.

Cyberspace is the "place" where a telephone conversation appears to occur. Not inside your actual phone, the plastic device on your desk. Not inside the other person's phone, in some other city. The place between the phones. [...] in the past twenty years, this electrical "space," which was once thin and dark and one-dimensional—little more than a narrow speaking-tube, stretching from phone to phone—has flung itself open like a gigantic jack-in-the-box. Light has flooded upon it, the eerie light of the glowing computer screen. This dark electric netherworld has become a vast flowering electronic landscape. Since the 1960s, the world of the telephone has cross-bred itself with computers and television, and though there is still no substance to cyberspace, nothing you can handle, it has a strange kind of physicality now. It makes good sense today to talk of cyberspace as a place all its own.

—Bruce Sterling, Introduction to The Hacker Crackdown

The "space" in cyberspace has more in common with the abstract, mathematical meanings of the term (see space) than physical space. It does not have the duality of positive and negative volume (while in physical space for example a room has the negative volume of usable space delineated by positive volume of walls, Internet users cannot enter the screen and explore the unknown part of the Internet as an extension of the space they are in), but spatial meaning can be attributed to the relationship between different pages (of books as well as web servers), considering the unturned pages to be somewhere "out there." The concept of cyberspace therefore refers not to the content being presented to the surfer, but rather to the possibility of surfing among different sites, with feedback loops between the user and the rest of the system creating the potential to always encounter something unknown or unexpected.

Video games differ from text-based communication in that on-screen images are meant to be figures that actually occupy a space and the animation shows the movement of those figures. Images are supposed to form the positive volume that delineates the empty space. A game adopts the cyberspace metaphor by engaging more players in the game, and then figuratively representing them on the screen as avatars. Games do not have to stop at the avatar-player level, but current implementations aiming for more immersive playing space (i.e. Laser tag) take the form of augmented reality rather than cyberspace, fully immersive virtual realities remaining impractical.

Although the more radical consequences of the global communication network predicted by some cyberspace proponents (i.e. the diminishing of state influence envisioned by John Perry Barlow) failed to materialize and the word lost some of its novelty appeal, it remains current as of 2006.

Some virtual communities explicitly refer to the concept of cyberspace, for example Linden Lab calling their customers "Residents" of Second Life, while all such communities can be positioned "in cyberspace" for explanatory and comparative purposes (as did Sterling in The Hacker Crackdown, followed by many journalists), integrating the metaphor into a wider cyber-culture.

The metaphor has been useful in helping a new generation of thought leaders to reason through new military strategies around the world, led largely by the US Department of Defense (DoD). The use of cyberspace as a metaphor has had its limits, however, especially in areas where the metaphor becomes confused with physical infrastructure. It has also been critiqued as being unhelpful for falsely employing a spatial metaphor to describe what is inherently a network.

Alternate realities in philosophy and art

Predating computers

A forerunner of the modern ideas of cyberspace is the Cartesian notion that people might be deceived by an evil demon that feeds them a false reality. This argument is the direct predecessor of modern ideas of a brain in a vat and many popular conceptions of cyberspace take Descartes's ideas as their starting point.

Visual arts have a tradition, stretching back to antiquity, of artifacts meant to fool the eye and be mistaken for reality. This questioning of reality occasionally led some philosophers and especially theologians to distrust art as deceiving people into entering a world which was not real (see Aniconism). The artistic challenge was resurrected with increasing ambition as art became more and more realistic with the invention of photography, film (see Arrival of a Train at La Ciotat), and immersive computer simulations.

Influenced by computers

Philosophy

American counterculture exponents like William S. Burroughs (whose literary influence on Gibson and cyberpunk in general is widely acknowledged) and Timothy Learywere among the first to extol the potential of computers and computer networks for individual empowerment.

Some contemporary philosophers and scientists (e.g. David Deutsch in The Fabric of Reality) employ virtual reality in various thought experiments. For example, Philip Zhai in Get Real: A Philosophical Adventure in Virtual Reality connects cyberspace to the platonic tradition:

Let us imagine a nation in which everyone is hooked up to a network of VR infrastructure. They have been so hooked up since they left their mother's wombs. Immersed in cyberspace and maintaining their life by teleoperation, they have never imagined that life could be any different from that. The first person that thinks of the possibility of an alternative world like ours would be ridiculed by the majority of these citizens, just like the few enlightened ones in Plato's allegory of the cave.

Note that this brain-in-a-vat argument conflates cyberspace with reality, while the more common descriptions of cyberspace contrast it with the "real world".

Cyber-Geography

The "Geography of Notopia" (Papadimitriou, 2006) theorizes about the complex interplay of cyber-cultures and the geographical space. This interplay has several philosophical and psychological facets (Papadimitriou, 2009).

A New Communication Model

The technological convergence of the mass media is the result of a long adaptation process of their communicative resources to the evolutionary changes of each historical moment. Thus, the new media became (plurally) an extension of the traditional media on the cyberspace, allowing to the public access information in a wide range of digital devices. In other words, it is a cultural virtualization of human reality as a result of the migration from physical to virtual space (mediated by the ICTs), ruled by codes, signs and particular social relationships. Forwards, arise instant ways of communication, interaction and possible quick access to information, in which we are no longer mere senders, but also producers, reproducers, co-workers and providers. New technologies also help to "connect" people from different cultures outside the virtual space, what was unthinkable fifty years ago. In this giant relationships web, we mutually absorb each other's beliefs, customs, values, laws and habits, cultural legacies perpetuated by a physical-virtual dynamics in constant metamorphosis (ibidem). In this sense, Professor Doctor Marcelo Mendonça Teixeira created, in 2013, a new model of communication to the virtual universe, based in Claude Elwood Shannon (1948) article "A Mathematical Theory of Communication".

Art

Having originated among writers, the concept of cyberspace remains most popular in literature and film. Although artists working with other media have expressed interest in the concept, such as Roy Ascott, "cyberspace" in digital art is mostly used as a synonym for immersive virtual reality and remains more discussed than enacted.

Computer crime

Cyberspace also brings together every service and facility imaginable to expedite money laundering. One can purchase anonymous credit cards, bank accounts, encrypted global mobile telephones, and false passports. From there one can pay professional advisors to set up IBCs (International Business Corporations, or corporations with anonymous ownership) or similar structures in OFCs (Offshore Financial Centers). Such advisors are loath to ask any penetrating questions about the wealth and activities of their clients, since the average fees criminals pay them to launder their money can be as much as 20 percent.

5-level model

In 2010, a five-level model was designed in France. According to this model, cyberspace is composed of five layers based on information discoveries: language, writing, printing, Internet, etc. This original model links the world of information to telecommunication technologies.

Popular culture examples

- The anime Digimon is set in a variant of the cyberspace concept called the "Digital World". The Digital World is a parallel universe made up of data from the Internet. Similar to cyberspace, except that people could physically enter this world instead of merely using a computer.

- The anime Ghost in the Shell is set in the future where cyberization of humanity is commonplace and the world is connected by a vast electronic network.

• The CGI series, ReBoot, takes place entirely inside cyberspace, which is composed of two worlds: the Net and the Web.

• In the film Tron, a programmer was physically transferred to the program world, where programs were personalities, resembling the forms of their creators.

• In the film Virtuosity a program encapsulating a super-criminal within a virtual world simulation escapes into the "real world".

• In the novel Simulacron-3 the author Daniel F. Galouye explores multiple levels of "reality" represented by the multiple levels of computer simulation involved.

• The idea of "the matrix" in the film The Matrix resembles a complex form of cyberspace where people are "jacked in" from birth and do not know that the reality they experience is virtual.

• In the televised remote controlled robot competition series Robot Wars, the Megahurtz and subsequently Terrorhurtz team and their robot were introduced as being "from Cyberspace", a nod to their online collaborative formation.

• In the 1984 novel Neuromancer the author William Gibson introduces the idea of a virtual reality data space called "the Matrix".

• The British 1960s spy/fantasy TV show The Avengers used antagonists called Cybernauts. Their nature, however, was merely that of murderous remote-controlled humanoid robots.

Domain name

Domain Names are the names for the information's address on the Internet and are used to locate information on the Internet. This has been possible due to Domain Name System (DNS), which translates these domain names to the IP addresses of the computers.

The Internet Corporation for Assigned Names and Numbers (ICANN) is responsible for the administration of Top Level Domain Names.

The domain names are allocated by the administrator of the Top Level Domain (TLD), if the requested domain name is not already assigned previoulsy.

The management and operations of .IN Registry are managed by the National Internet Exchange of India (NIXI). IN Registry is now the official registry for registration but this registry does not carry out the functions itself, but through accredits registrars.

Like a trademark, a domain name too is associated with a particular firm and creates a unique identity. In today's world when most of the work is done on the World Wide Web it can help preventing other people from misleading customers. Hence it is very important to get a domain name registered.

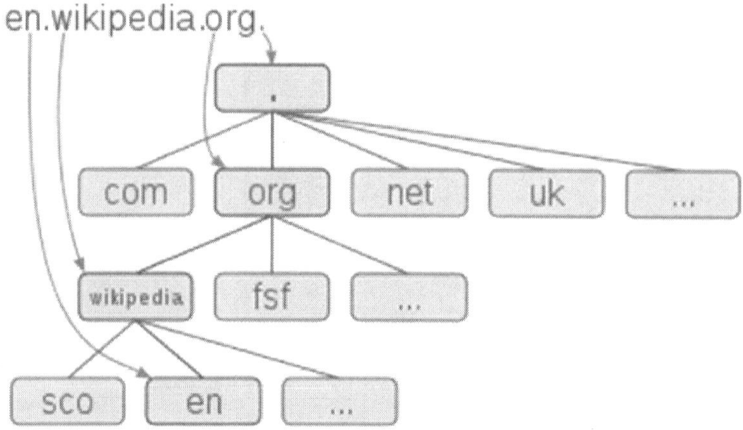

The hierarchy of labels in a fully qualified domain name.

A domain name is an identification string that defines a realm of administrative autonomy, authority or control within the Internet. Domain names are formed by the rules and procedures of the Domain Name System (DNS). Any name registered in the DNS is a domain name. Domain names are used in various networking contexts and for application-specific naming and addressing purposes. In general, a domain name represents an Internet Protocol (IP) resource, such as a personal computer used to access the Internet, a server computer hosting a web site, or the web site itself or any other service communicated via the Internet. In 2017, 330.6 million domain names had been registered.

Domain names are organized in subordinate levels (subdomains) of the DNS root domain, which is nameless. The first-level set of domain names are the top-level domains (TLDs), including the generic top-level domains (gTLDs), such as the prominent domains com, info, net, edu, and org, and the country code top-level domains (ccTLDs). Below these top-level domains in the DNS hierarchy are the second-level and third-level domain names that are typically open for reservation by end-users who wish to connect local area networks to the Internet, create other publicly accessible Internet resources or run web sites.

The registration of these domain names is usually administered by domain name registrars who sell their services to the public.

A fully qualified domain name (FQDN) is a domain name that is completely specified with all labels in the hierarchy of the DNS, having no parts omitted. Labels in the Domain Name System are case-insensitive, and may therefore be written in any desired capitalization method, but most commonly domain names are written in lowercase in technical contexts.

Purpose

Domain names serve to identify Internet resources, such as computers, networks, and services, with a text-based label that is easier to memorize than the numerical addresses used in the Internet protocols. A domain name may represent entire collections of such resources or individual instances. Individual Internet host computers use domain names as host identifiers, also called host names. The term host name is also used for the leaf labels in the domain name system, usually without further subordinate domain name space. Host names appear as a component in Uniform Resource Locators (URLs) for Internet resources such as web sites (e.g., en.wikipedia.org).

Domain names are also used as simple identification labels to indicate ownership or control of a resource. Such examples are the realm identifiers used in the Session Initiation Protocol (SIP), the Domain Keys used to verify DNS domains in e-mail systems, and in many other Uniform Resource Identifiers (URIs).

An important function of domain names is to provide easily recognizable and memorizable names to numerically addressed Internet resources. This abstraction allows any resource to be moved to a different physical location in the address topology of the network, globally or locally in an intranet. Such a move usually requires changing the IP address of a resource and the corresponding translation of this IP address to and from its domain name.

Domain names are used to establish a unique identity. Organizations can choose a domain name that corresponds to their name, helping Internet users to reach them easily.

A generic domain is a name that defines a general category, rather than a specific or personal instance, for example, the name of an industry, rather than a company name. Some examples of generic names are books.com, music.com, and travel.info. Companies have created brands based on generic names, and such generic domain names may be valuable

Domain names are often simply referred to as domains and domain name registrants are frequently referred to as domain owners, although domain name registration with a registrar does not confer any legal ownership of the domain name, only an exclusive right of use for a particular duration of time. The use of domain names in commerce may subject them to trademark law.

History

The practice of using a simple memorable abstraction of a host's numerical address on a computer network dates back to the ARPANET era, before the advent of today's commercial Internet. In the early network, each computer on the network retrieved the hosts file (host.txt) from a computer at SRI (now SRI International), which mapped computer host names to numerical addresses. The rapid growth of the network made it impossible to maintain a centrally organized hostname registry and in 1983 the Domain Name System was introduced on the ARPANET and published by the Internet Engineering Task Force as RFC 882 and RFC 883.

Domain name space

Today, the Internet Corporation for Assigned Names and Numbers (ICANN) manages the top-level development and architecture of the Internet domain name space. It authorizes domain name registrars, through which domain names may be registered and reassigned.

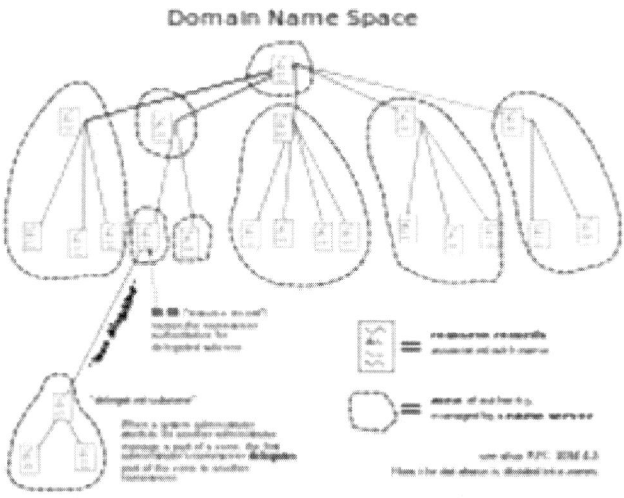

The hierarchical domain name system, organized into zones, each served by domain name servers.

The domain name space consists of a tree of domain names. Each node in the tree holds information associated with the domain name. The tree sub-divides into zones beginning at the DNS root zone.

Domain name syntax

A domain name consists of one or more parts, technically called labels, that are conventionally concatenated, and delimited by dots, such as example. com.

- The right-most label conveys the top-level domain; for example, the domain name www.example.com belongs to the top-level domain com.

• The hierarchy of domains descends from the right to the left label in the name; each label to the left specifies a subdivision, or subdomainof the domain to the right. For example: the label example specifies a node example. com as a subdomain of the com domain, and www is a label to create www. example.com, a subdomain of example.com. Each label may contain from 1 to 63 octets. The empty label is reserved for the root node and when fully qualified is expressed as the empty label terminated by a dot. The full domain name may not exceed a total length of 253 ASCII characters in its textual representation. Thus, when using a single character per label, the limit is 127 levels: 127 characters plus 126 dots have a total length of 253. In practice, some domain registries may have shorter limits.

• A hostname is a domain name that has at least one associated IP address. For example, the domain names www.example.com and example. com are also hostnames, whereas the com domain is not. However, other top-level domains, particularly country code top-level domains, may indeed have an IP address, and if so, they are also hostnames.

• Hostnames impose restrictions on the characters allowed in the corresponding domain name. A valid hostname is also a valid domain name, but a valid domain name may not necessarily be valid as a hostname.

Top-level domains

The top-level domains (TLDs) such as com, net and org are the highest level of domain names of the Internet. Top-level domains form the DNS root zone of the hierarchical Domain Name System. Every domain name ends with a top-level domain label.

When the Domain Name System was devised in the 1980s, the domain name space was divided into two main groups of domains. The country code top-level domains (ccTLD) were primarily based on the two-character territory codes of ISO-3166 country abbreviations. In addition, a group of seven generic top-level domains (gTLD) was implemented which represented a set of categories of names and multi-organizations. These were the domains gov, edu, com, mil, org, net, and int.

During the growth of the Internet, it became desirable to create additional generic top-level domains. As of October 2009, 21 generic top-level domains and 250 two-letter country-code top-level domains existed. In addition, the ARPA domain serves technical purposes in the infrastructure of the Domain Name System.

During the 32nd International Public ICANN Meeting in Paris in 2008, ICANN started a new process of TLD naming policy to take a "significant step forward on the introduction of new generic top-level domains." This program envisions the availability of many new or already proposed domains, as well as a new application and implementation process.Observers believed that the new rules could result in hundreds of new top-level domains to be registered. In 2012, the program commenced, and received 1930 applications.By 2016, the milestone of 1000 live gTLD was reached.

The Internet Assigned Numbers Authority (IANA) maintains an annotated list of top-level domains in the DNS root zone database.

For special purposes, such as network testing, documentation, and other applications, IANA also reserves a set of special-use domain names. This list contains domain names such as example, local, localhost, and test. Other top-level domain names containing trade marks are registered for corporate use. Cases include brands such as BMW, Google, and Canon.

Second-level and lower level domains

Below the top-level domains in the domain name hierarchy are the second-level domain (SLD) names. These are the names directly to the left of .com, .net, and the other top-level domains. As an example, in the domain example.co.uk, co is the second-level domain.

Next are third-level domains, which are written immediately to the left of a second-level domain. There can be fourth- and fifth-level domains, and so on, with virtually no limitation. An example of an operational domain name with four levels of domain labels is sos.state.oh.us. Each label is separated by a full stop (dot). 'sos' is said to be a sub-domain of 'state.oh.us', and 'state' a sub-domain of 'oh.us', etc. In general, subdomains are domains subordinate to their parent domain. An example of very deep levels of subdomain ordering are the IPv6 reverse resolution DNS zones, e.g., 1.0.0.0.0.0.0.0.0.0.0.0.0.0.0.0.0.0.0.0 .0.0.0.0.0.0.0.0.0.0.0.0.ip6.arpa, which is the reverse DNS resolution domain name for the IP address of a loopback interface, or the localhost name.

Second-level (or lower-level, depending on the established parent hierarchy) domain names are often created based on the name of a company (e.g., bbc.co.uk), product or service (e.g. hotmail.com). Below these levels, the next domain name component has been used to designate a particular host server. Therefore, ftp.example.com might be an FTP server, www.example.com would be a World Wide Web server, and mail.example.com could be an email server, each intended to perform only the implied function. Modern technology allows multiple physical servers with either different (cf. load balancing) or even identical addresses (cf. anycast) to serve a single hostname or domain name, or multiple domain names to be served by a single computer. The latter is very popular in Web hosting service centers, where service providers host the websites of many organizations on just a few servers.

The hierarchical DNS labels or components of domain names are separated in a fully qualified name by the full stop (dot, .).

Internationalized domain names

The character set allowed in the Domain Name System is based on ASCII and does not allow the representation of names and words of many languages in their native scripts or alphabets. ICANN approved the Internationalized domain name (IDNA) system, which maps Unicode strings used in application user interfaces into the valid DNS character set by an encoding called Punycode. For example, københavn.eu is mapped to xn--kbenhavn-54a.eu. Many registries have adopted IDNA.

Domain name registration

History

The first commercial Internet domain name, in the TLD com, was registered on 15 March 1985 in the name symbolics.com by Symbolics Inc., a computer systems firm in Cambridge, Massachusetts.

By 1992, fewer than 15,000 com domains had been registered.

In the first quarter of 2015, 294 million domain names had been registered. A large fraction of them are in the com TLD, which as of December 21, 2014, had 115.6 million domain names, including 11.9 million online business and e-commerce sites, 4.3 million entertainment sites, 3.1 million finance related sites, and 1.8 million sports sites. As of July 2012 the com TLD had more registrations than all of the ccTLDs combined.

Administration

The right to use a domain name is delegated by domain name registrars, which are accredited by the Internet Corporation for Assigned Names and Numbers (ICANN), the organization charged with overseeing the name and number systems of the Internet. In addition to ICANN, each top-level domain (TLD) is maintained and serviced technically by an administrative organization operating a registry. A registry is responsible for maintaining the database of names registered within the TLD it administers. The registry receives registration information from each domain name registrar authorized to assign names in the corresponding TLD and publishes the information using a special service, the WHOISprotocol.

Registries and registrars usually charge an annual fee for the service of delegating a domain name to a user and providing a default set of name servers. Often, this transaction is termed a sale or lease of the domain name, and the registrant may sometimes be called an "owner", but no such legal relationship is actually associated with the transaction, only the exclusive right to use the domain name. More correctly, authorized users are known as "registrants" or as "domain holders".

ICANN publishes the complete list of TLD registries and domain name registrars. Registrant information associated with domain names is maintained in an online database accessible with the WHOIS protocol. For most of the 250 country code top-level domains (ccTLDs), the domain registries maintain the WHOIS (Registrant, name servers, expiration dates, etc.) information.

Some domain name registries, often called network information centers (NIC), also function as registrars to end-users. The major generic top-level domain registries, such as for the com, net, org, info domains and others, use a registry-registrar model consisting of hundreds of domain name registrars (see lists at ICANN or VeriSign). In this method of management, the registry only manages the domain name database and the relationship with the registrars. The registrants (users of a domain name) are customers of the registrar, in some cases through additional layers of resellers.

Technical requirements and process

In the process of registering a domain name and maintaining authority over the new name space created, registrars use several key pieces of information connected with a domain:

- Administrative contact. A registrant usually designates an administrative contact to manage the domain name. The administrative contact usually has the highest level of control over a domain. Management functions delegated to the administrative contacts may include management of all business information, such as name of record, postal address, and contact information of the official registrant of the domain and the obligation to conform to the requirements of the domain registry in order to retain the right to use a domain name. Furthermore, the administrative contact installs additional contact information for technical and billing functions.

- Technical contact. The technical contact manages the name servers of a domain name. The functions of a technical contact include assuring conformance of the configurations of the domain name with the requirements of the domain registry, maintaining the domain zone records, and providing continuous functionality of the name servers (that leads to the accessibility of the domain name).

- Billing contact. The party responsible for receiving billing invoices from the domain name registrar and paying applicable fees.

- Name servers. Most registrars provide two or more name servers as part of the registration service. However, a registrant may specify its own authoritative name servers to host a domain's resource records. The registrar's policies govern the number of servers and the type of server information required. Some providers require a hostname and the corresponding IP address or just the hostname, which must be resolvable either in the new domain, or exist elsewhere. Based on traditional requirements (RFC 1034), typically a minimum of two servers is required.

A domain name consists of one or more labels, each of which is formed from the set of ASCII letters, digits, and hyphens (a-z, A-Z, 0-9, -), but not starting or ending with a hyphen. The labels are case-insensitive; for example, 'label' is equivalent to 'Label' or 'LABEL'. In the textual representation of a domain name, the labels are separated by a full stop (period).

Business models

Domain names are often seen in analogy to real estate in that domain names are foundations on which a website can be built, and the highest quality domain names, like sought-after real estate, tend to carry significant value, usually due to their online brand-building potential, use in advertising, search engine optimization, and many other criteria.

A few companies have offered low-cost, below-cost or even free domain registration with a variety of models adopted to recoup the costs to the provider. These usually require that domains be hosted on their website within a framework or portal that includes advertising wrapped around the domain holder's content, revenue from which allows the provider to recoup the costs. Domain registrations were free of charge when the DNS was new. A domain holder may provide infinite number of subdomains in their domain. For example, the owner of example.org could provide subdomains such as foo.example.org and foo.bar.example.org to interested parties.

Many desirable domain names are already assigned and users must search for other acceptable names, using Web-based search features, or WHOIS and dig operating system tools. Many registrars have implemented domain name suggestion tools which search domain name databases and suggest available alternative domain names related to keywords provided by the user.

Resale of domain names

The business of resale of registered domain names is known as the domain aftermarket. Various factors influence the perceived value or market value of a domain name. Most of the high-prize domain sales are carried out privately.

Domain name confusion

Intercapping is often used to emphasize the meaning of a domain name. However, DNS names are not case-sensitive, and some names may be misinterpreted in certain uses of capitalization. For example: Who Represents, a database of artists and agents, chose whorepresents.com, which can be misread as whore presents. Similarly, a therapists' network is named therapistfinder.com. In such situations, the proper meaning may be clarified by use of hyphens in the domain name. For instance, Experts Exchange, a programmers' discussion site, for a long time used expertsexchange.com, but ultimately changed the name to experts-exchange.com.

Use in web site hosting

The domain name is a component of a uniform resource locator (URL) used to access web sites, for example:

- URL: http://www.example.net/index.html
- Top-level domain: net
- Second-level domain: example
- Host name: www

A domain name may point to multiple IP addresses to provide server redundancy for the services offered, a feature that is used to manage the traffic of large, popular web sites.

Web hosting services, on the other hand, run servers that are typically assigned only one or a few addresses while serving websites for many domains, a technique referred to as virtual web hosting. Such IP address overloading requires that each request identifies the domain name being referenced, for instance by using the HTTP request header field Host:, or Server Name Indication.

Abuse and regulation

Critics often claim abuse of administrative power over domain names. Particularly noteworthy was the VeriSign Site Finder system which redirected all unregistered .com and .net domains to a VeriSign webpage. For example, at a public meeting with VeriSign to air technical concerns about SiteFinder, numerous people, active in the IETF and other technical bodies, explained how they were surprised by VeriSign's changing the fundamental behavior of a major component of Internet infrastructure, not having obtained the customary consensus. SiteFinder, at first, assumed every Internet query was for a website, and it monetized queries for incorrect domain names, taking the user to VeriSign's search site. Unfortunately, other applications, such as many implementations of email, treat a lack of response to a domain name query as an indication that the domain does not exist, and that the message can be treated as undeliverable. The original VeriSign implementation broke this assumption for mail, because it would always resolve an erroneous domain name to that of SiteFinder. While VeriSign later changed SiteFinder's behaviour with regard to email, there was still widespread protest about VeriSign's action being more in its financial interest than in the interest of the Internet infrastructure component for which VeriSign was the steward.

Despite widespread criticism, VeriSign only reluctantly removed it after the Internet Corporation for Assigned Names and Numbers (ICANN) threatened to revoke its contract to administer the root name servers. ICANN published the extensive set of letters exchanged, committee reports, and ICANN decisions.

There is also significant disquiet regarding the United States' political influence over ICANN. This was a significant issue in the attempt to create a .xxx top-level domain and sparked greater interest in alternative DNS roots that would be beyond the control of any single country.

Additionally, there are numerous accusations of domain name front running, whereby registrars, when given whois queries, automatically register the domain name for themselves. Network Solutions has been accused of this.

Truth in Domain Names Act

In the United States, the Truth in Domain Names Act of 2003, in combination with the PROTECT Act of 2003, forbids the use of a misleading domain name with the intention of attracting Internet users into visiting Internet pornography sites.

The Truth in Domain Names Act follows the more general Anticybersquatting Consumer Protection Act passed in 1999 aimed at preventing typosquatting and deceptive use of names and trademarks in domain names.

Seizures

In the early 21st century, the US Department of Justice (DOJ) pursued the seizure of domain names, based on the legal theory that domain names constitute property used to engage in criminal activity, and thus are subject to forfeiture. For example, in the seizure of the domain name of a gambling website, the DOJ referenced 18 U.S.C. § 981 and 18 U.S.C. § 1955(d).[1] In 2013 the US government seized Liberty Reserve, citing 18 U.S.C. § 982(a)(1).

The U.S. Congress passed the Combating Online Infringement and Counterfeits Act in 2010. Consumer Electronics Association vice president Michael Petricone was worried that seizure was a blunt instrument that could harm legitimate businesses. After a joint operation in February 15, 2011, the DOJ and the Department of Homeland Security claimed to have seized ten domains of websites involved in advertising and distributing child pornography, but also mistakenly seized the domain name of a large DNS provider, temporarily replacing 84,000 websites with seizure notices.

In the United Kingdom, the Police Intellectual Property Crime Unit has been attempting to seize domain names from registrars without court orders.

Suspensions

PIPCU and other UK law enforcement organisations make domain suspension requests to Nominet which they process on the basis of breach of terms and conditions. Around 16,000 domains are suspended annually, and about 80% of the requests originate from PIPCU.

Fictitious domain name

A fictitious domain name is a domain name used in a work of fiction or popular culture to refer to a domain that does not actually exist, often with invalid or unofficial top-level domains such as ".web", a usage exactly analogous to the dummy 555 telephone number prefix used in film and other media. The canonical fictitious domain name is "example.com", specifically set aside by IANA in RFC 2606 for such use, along with the .example TLD.

Domain names used in works of fiction have often been registered in the DNS, either by their creators or by cybersquatters attempting to profit from it. This phenomenon prompted NBC to purchase the domain name Hornymanatee.com after talk-show host Conan O'Brien spoke the name while ad-libbing on his show. O'Brien subsequently created a website based on the concept and used it as a running gag on the show.

10

Intellectual Property

Every new invention in the field of technology experiences a variety of threats. Internet is one such threat, which has captured the physical marketplace and have converted it into a virtual marketplace.

To safeguard the business interest, it is vital to create an effective property management and protection mechanism keeping in mind the considerable amount of business and commerce taking place in the Cyber Space.

Today it is critical for every business to develop an effective and collaborative IP management mechanism and protection strategy. The ever-looming threats in the cybernetic world can thus be monitored and confined.

Various approaches and legislations have been designed by the law-makers to up the ante in delivering a secure configuration against such cyber-threats. However it is the duty of the intellectual property right (IPR) owner to invalidate and reduce such mala fide acts of criminals by taking proactive measures.

Intellectual property (IP) is a category of property that includes intangible creations of the human intellect. Intellectual property encompasses two types of rights; industrial property rights (trademarks, patents, designations of origin, industrial designs and models) and copyright. It was not until the 19th century that the term "intellectual property" began to be used, and not until the late 20th century that it became commonplace in the majority of the world.

The main purpose of intellectual property law is to encourage the creation of a large variety of intellectual goods. To achieve this, the law gives people and businesses property rights to the information and intellectual goods they create – usually for a limited period of time. This gives economic incentive for their creation, because it allows people to profit from the information and intellectual goods they create. These economic incentives are expected to stimulate innovation and contribute to the technological progress of countries, which depends on the extent of protection granted to innovators.

The intangible nature of intellectual property presents difficulties when compared with traditional property like land or goods. Unlike traditional property, intellectual property is "indivisible" – an unlimited number of people can "consume" an intellectual good without it being depleted. Additionally, investments in intellectual goods suffer from problems of appropriation – a landowner can surround their land with a robust fence and hire armed guards to protect it, but a producer of information or an intellectual good can usually do very little to stop their first buyer from replicating it and selling it at a lower price. Balancing rights so that they are strong enough to encourage the creation of intellectual goods but not so strong that they prevent the goods' wide use is the primary focus of modern intellectual property law.

(261)

Anno Octavo

Annæ Reginæ.

An Act for the Encouragement of Learning, by Vesting the Copies of Printed Books in the Authors or Purchasers of such Copies, during the Times therein mentioned.

The Statute of Anne came into force in 1710

The Statute of Monopolies (1624) and the British Statute of Anne (1710) are seen as the origins of patent law and copyright respectively,firmly establishing the concept of intellectual property.

The first known use of the term intellectual property dates to 1769, when a piece published in the Monthly Review used the phrase. The first clear example of modern usage goes back as early as 1808, when it was used as a heading title in a collection of essays.

The German equivalent was used with the founding of the North German Confederation whose constitution granted legislative power over the protection of intellectual property (Schutz des geistigen Eigentums) to the confederation. When the administrative secretariats established by the Paris Convention (1883) and the Berne Convention (1886) merged in 1893, they located in Berne, and also adopted the term intellectual property in their new combined title, the United International Bureaux for the Protection of Intellectual Property.

The organization subsequently relocated to Geneva in 1960, and was succeeded in 1967 with the establishment of the World Intellectual Property Organization (WIPO) by treaty as an agency of the United Nations. According to legal scholar Mark Lemley, it was only at this point that the term really began to be used in the United States (which had not been a party to the Berne Convention), and it did not enter popular usage there until passage of the Bayh-Dole Act in 1980.

"The history of patents does not begin with inventions, but rather with royal grants by Queen Elizabeth I (1558–1603) for monopoly privileges... Approximately 200 years after the end of Elizabeth's reign, however, a patent represents a legal rightobtained by an inventor providing for exclusive control over the production and sale of his mechanical or scientific invention... [demonstrating] the evolution of patents from royal prerogative to common-law doctrine."

The term can be found used in an October 1845 Massachusetts Circuit Court ruling in the patent case Davoll et al. v. Brown., in which Justice Charles L. Woodbury wrote that "only in this way can we protect intellectual property, the labors of the mind, productions and interests are as much a man's own...as the wheat he cultivates, or the flocks he rears." The statement that "discoveries are..property" goes back earlier. Section 1 of the French law of 1791 stated, "All new discoveries are the property of the author; to assure the inventor the property and temporary enjoyment of his discovery, there shall be delivered to him a patent for five, ten or fifteen years." In Europe, French author A. Nion mentioned propriété intellectuelle in his Droits civils des auteurs, artistes et inventeurs, published in 1846.

Until recently, the purpose of intellectual property law was to give as little protection as possible in order to encourage innovation. Historically, therefore, they were granted only when they were necessary to encourage invention, limited in time and scope. This is mainly as a result of knowledge being traditionally viewed as a public good, in order to allow its extensive dissemination and improvement thereof.

The concept's origins can potentially be traced back further. Jewish law includes several considerations whose effects are similar to those of modern intellectual property laws, though the notion of intellectual creations as property does not seem to exist – notably the principle of Hasagat Ge'vul (unfair encroachment) was used to justify limited-term publisher (but not author) copyright in the 16th century. In 500 BCE, the government of the Greek state of Sybaris offered one year's patent "to all who should discover any new refinement in luxury".

According to Jean-Frédéric Morin, "the global intellectual property regime is currently in the midst of a paradigm shift". Indeed, up until the early 2000s the global IP regime used to be dominated by high standards of protection characteristic of IP laws from Europe or the United States, with a vision that uniform application of these standards over every country and to several fields with little consideration over social, cultural or environmental values or of the national level of economic development. Morin argues that "the emerging discourse of the global IP regime advocates for greater policy flexibility and greater access to knowledge, especially for developing countries." Indeed, with the Development Agenda adopted by WIPO in 2007, a set of 45 recommendations to adjust WIPO's activities to the specific needs of developing countries and aim to reduce distortions especially on issues such as patients' access to medicines, Internet users' access to information, farmers' access to seeds, programmers' access to source codes or students' access to scientific articles.However, this paradigm shift has not yet manifested itself in concrete legal reforms at the international level.

Similarly, it is based on these background that the Trade-Related Aspects of Intellectual Property Rights (TRIPS) agreement requires members of the WTO to set minimum standards of legal protection, but its objective to have a "one-fits-all" protection law on Intellectual Property has been viewed with controversies regarding differences in the development level of countries. Despite the controversy, the agreement has extensively incorporated intellectual property rights into the global trading system for the first time in 1995, and has prevailed as the most comprehensive agreement reached by the world.

Intellectual property rights

Intellectual property rights include patents, copyright, industrial design rights, trademarks, plant variety rights, trade dress, geographical indications, and in some jurisdictions trade secrets. There are also more specialized or derived varieties of sui generis exclusive rights, such as circuit design rights (called mask work rights in the US) and supplementary protection certificates for pharmaceutical products (after expiry of a patent protecting them) and database rights (in European law). The term "industrial property" is sometimes used to refer to a large subset of intellectual property rights including patents, trademarks, industrial designs, utility models, service marks, trade names, and geographical indications.

Patents

A patent is a form of right granted by the government to an inventor or their successor-in-title, giving the owner the right to exclude others from making, using, selling, offering to sell, and importing an invention for a limited period of time, in exchange for the public disclosure of the invention. An invention is a solution to a specific technological problem, which may be a product or a process and generally has to fulfill three main requirements: it has to be new, not obvious and there needs to be an industrial applicability. To enrich the body of knowledge and stimulate innovation, it is an obligation for patent owners to disclose valuable information about their inventions to the public.

Copyright

A copyright gives the creator of an original work exclusive rights to it, usually for a limited time. Copyright may apply to a wide range of creative, intellectual, or artistic forms, or "works". Copyright does not cover ideas and information themselves, only the form or manner in which they are expressed.

Industrial design rights

An industrial design right (sometimes called "design right" or design patent) protects the visual design of objects that are not purely utilitarian. An industrial design consists of the creation of a shape, configuration or composition of pattern or color, or combination of pattern and color in three-dimensional form containing aesthetic value. An industrial design can be a two- or three-dimensional pattern used to produce a product, industrial commodity or handicraft. Generally speaking, it is what makes a product look appealing, and as such, it increases the commercial value of goods.

Plant varieties

Plant breeders' rights or plant variety rights are the rights to commercially use a new variety of a plant. The variety must amongst others be novel and distinct and for registration the evaluation of propagating material of the variety is considered.

Trademarks

A trademark is a recognizable sign, design or expression which distinguishes products or services of a particular trader from the similar products or services of other traders.

Trade dress

Trade dress is a legal term of art that generally refers to characteristics of the visual and aesthetic appearance of a product or its packaging (or even the design of a building) that signify the source of the product to consumers.

Trade secrets

A trade secret is a formula, practice, process, design, instrument, pattern, or compilation of information which is not generally known or reasonably ascertainable, by which a business can obtain an economic advantage over competitors and customers. There is no formal government protection granted; each business must take measures to guard its own trade secrets (e.g., Formula of its soft drinks is a trade secret for Coca-Cola.)

Object of intellectual property law

The main purpose of intellectual property law is to encourage the creation of a wide variety of intellectual goods for consumers. To achieve this, the law gives people and businesses property rights to the information and intellectual goods they create, usually for a limited period of time. Because they can then profit from them, this gives economic incentive for their creation. The intangible nature of intellectual property presents difficulties when compared with traditional property like land or goods. Unlike traditional property, intellectual property is indivisible – an unlimited number of people can "consume" an intellectual good without it being depleted. Additionally, investments in intellectual goods suffer from problems of appropriation – while a landowner can surround their land with a robust fence and hire armed guards to protect it, a producer of information or an intellectual good can usually do very little to stop their first buyer from replicating it and selling it at a lower price. Balancing rights so that they are strong enough to encourage the creation of information and intellectual goods but not so strong that they prevent their wide use is the primary focus of modern intellectual property law.

By exchanging limited exclusive rights for disclosure of inventions and creative works, society and the patentee/copyright owner mutually benefit, and an incentive is created for inventors and authors to create and disclose their work. Some commentators have noted that the objective of intellectual property legislators and those who support its implementation appears to be "absolute protection". "If some intellectual property is desirable because it encourages innovation, they reason, more is better. The thinking is that creators will not have sufficient incentive to invent unless they are legally entitled to capture the full social value of their inventions". This absolute protection or full value view treats intellectual property as another type of "real" property, typically adopting its law and rhetoric. Other recent developments in intellectual property law, such as the America Invents Act, stress international harmonization. Recently there has also been much debate over the desirability of using intellectual property rights to protect cultural heritage, including intangible ones, as well as over risks of commodification derived from this possibility. The issue still remains open in legal scholarship.

Financial incentive

These exclusive rights allow owners of intellectual property to benefit from the property they have created, providing a financial incentive for the creation of an investment in intellectual property, and, in case of patents, pay associated research and development costs. In the United States Article I Section 8 Clause 8 of the Constitution, commonly called the Patent and Copyright Clause, reads; "[The Congress shall have power] 'To promote the progress of science and useful arts, by securing for limited times to authors and inventors the exclusive right to their respective writings and discoveries.'" "Some commentators, such as David Levine and Michele Boldrin, dispute this justification.

In 2013 the United States Patent & Trademark Office approximated that the worth of intellectual property to the U.S. economy is more than US $5 trillion and creates employment for an estimated 18 million American people. The value of intellectual property is considered similarly high in other developed nations, such as those in the European Union. In the UK, IP has become a recognised asset class for use in pension-led funding and other types of business finance. However, in 2013, the UK Intellectual Property Office stated: "There are millions of intangible business assets whose value is either not being leveraged at all, or only being leveraged inadvertently".

Economic growth

The WIPO treaty and several related international agreements underline that the protection of intellectual property rights is essential to maintaining economic growth. The WIPO Intellectual Property Handbook gives two reasons for intellectual property laws:

One is to give statutory expression to the moral and economic rights of creators in their creations and the rights of the public in access to those creations. The second is to promote, as a deliberate act of Government policy, creativity and the dissemination and application of its results and to encourage fair trading which would contribute to economic and social development.

The Anti-Counterfeiting Trade Agreement (ACTA) states that "effective enforcement of intellectual property rights is critical to sustaining economic growth across all industries and globally".

Economists estimate that two-thirds of the value of large businesses in the United States can be traced to intangible assets. "IP-intensive industries" are estimated to generate 72 percent more value added (price minus material cost) per employee than "non-IP-intensive industries".

A joint research project of the WIPO and the United Nations University measuring the impact of IP systems on six Asian countries found "a positive correlation between the strengthening of the IP system and subsequent economic growth."

Morality

According to Article 27 of the Universal Declaration of Human Rights, "everyone has the right to the protection of the moral and material interests resulting from any scientific, literary or artistic production of which he is the author". Although the relationship between intellectual property and human rights is a complex one, there are moral arguments for intellectual property.

The arguments that justify intellectual property fall into three major categories. Personality theorists believe intellectual property is an extension of an individual. Utilitarians believe that intellectual property stimulates social progress and pushes people to further innovation. Lockeans argue that intellectual property is justified based on deservedness and hard work.

Various moral justifications for private property can be used to argue in favor of the morality of intellectual property, such as:

1. Natural Rights/Justice Argument: this argument is based on Locke's idea that a person has a natural right over the labour and/or products which is produced by his/her body. Appropriating these products is viewed as unjust. Although Locke had never explicitly stated that natural right applied to products of the mind, it is possible to apply his argument to intellectual property rights, in which it would be unjust for people to misuse another's ideas. Locke's argument for intellectual property is based upon the idea that laborers have the right to control that which they create. They argue that we own our bodies which are the laborers, this right of ownership extends to what we create. Thus, intellectual property ensures this right when it comes to production.

2. Utilitarian-Pragmatic Argument: according to this rationale, a society that protects private property is more effective and prosperous than societies that do not. Innovation and invention in 19th century America has been attributed to the development of the patent system. By providing innovators with "durable and tangible return on their investment of time, labor, and other resources", intellectual property rights seek to maximize social utility. The presumption is that they promote public welfare by encouraging the "creation, production, and distribution of intellectual works". Utilitarians argue that without intellectual property there would be a lack of incentive to produce new ideas. Systems of protection such as Intellectual property optimize social utility.

3. "Personality" Argument: this argument is based on a quote from Hegel: "Every man has the right to turn his will upon a thing or make the thing an object of his will, that is to say, to set aside the mere thing and recreate it as his own". European intellectual property law is shaped by this notion that ideas are an "extension of oneself and of one's personality". Personality theorists argue that by being a creator of something one is inherently at risk and vulnerable for having their ideas and designs stolen and/or altered. Intellectual property protects these moral claims that have to do with personality.

Lysander Spooner (1855) argues "that a man has a natural and absolute right—and if a natural and absolute, then necessarily a perpetual, right—of property, in the ideas, of which he is the discoverer or creator; that his right of property, in ideas, is intrinsically the same as, and stands on identically the same grounds with, his right of property in material things; that no distinction, of principle, exists between the two cases".

Writer Ayn Rand argued in her book Capitalism: The Unknown Ideal that the protection of intellectual property is essentially a moral issue. The belief is that the human mind itself is the source of wealth and survival and that all property at its base is intellectual property. To violate intellectual property is therefore no different morally than violating other property rights which compromises the very processes of survival and therefore constitutes an immoral act.

Infringement, misappropriation, and enforcement

Violation of intellectual property rights, called "infringement" with respect to patents, copyright, and trademarks, and "misappropriation" with respect to trade secrets, may be a breach of civil law or criminal law, depending on the type of intellectual property involved, jurisdiction, and the nature of the action.

As of 2011 trade in counterfeit copyrighted and trademarked works was a $600 billion industry worldwide and accounted for 5–7% of global trade.

Patent infringement

Patent infringement typically is caused by using or selling a patented invention without permission from the patent holder. The scope of the patented invention or the extent of protection is defined in the claims of the granted patent. There is safe harbor in many jurisdictions to use a patented invention for research. This safe harbor does not exist in the US unless the research is done for purely philosophical purposes, or in order to gather data in order to prepare an application for regulatory approval of a drug. In general, patent infringement cases are handled under civil law (e.g., in the United States) but several jurisdictions incorporate infringement in criminal law also (for example, Argentina, China, France, Japan, Russia, South Korea).

Copyright infringement

Copyright infringement is reproducing, distributing, displaying or performing a work, or to make derivative works, without permission from the copyright holder, which is typically a publisher or other business representing or assigned by the work's creator. It is often called "piracy". While copyright is created the instant a work is fixed, generally the copyright holder can only get money damages if the owner registers the copyright. Enforcement of copyright is generally the responsibility of the copyright holder. The ACTA trade agreement, signed in May 2011 by the United States, Japan, Switzerland, and the EU, and which has not entered into force, requires that its parties add criminal penalties, including incarceration and fines, for copyright and trademark infringement, and obligated the parties to active police for infringement. There are limitations and exceptions to copyright, allowing limited use of copyrighted works, which does not constitute infringement. Examples of such doctrines are the fair use and fair dealing doctrine.

Trademark infringement

Trademark infringement occurs when one party uses a trademark that is identical or confusingly similar to a trademark owned by another party, in relation to products or services which are identical or similar to the products or services of the other party. In many countries, a trademark receives protection without registration, but registering a trademark provides legal advantages for enforcement. Infringement can be addressed by civil litigation and, in several jurisdictions, under criminal law.

Trade secret misappropriation

Trade secret misappropriation is different from violations of other intellectual property laws, since by definition trade secrets are secret, while patents and registered copyrights and trademarks are publicly available. In the United States, trade secrets are protected under state law, and states have nearly universally adopted the Uniform Trade Secrets Act. The United States also has federal law in the form of the Economic Espionage Act of 1996 (18 U.S.C. §§ 1831–1839), which makes the theft or misappropriation of a trade secret a federal crime. This law contains two provisions criminalizing two sorts of activity. The first, 18 U.S.C. § 1831(a), criminalizes the theft of trade secrets to benefit foreign powers. The second, 18 U.S.C. § 1832, criminalizes their theft for commercial or economic purposes. (The statutory penalties are different for the two offenses.) In Commonwealth common lawjurisdictions, confidentiality and trade secrets are regarded as an equitable right rather than a property right but penalties for theft are roughly the same as in the United States.

Criticisms

Demonstration in Sweden in support of file sharing, 2006.

"Copying is not theft!" badge with a character resembling Mickey Mouse in reference to the in popular culture rationale behind the Sonny Bono Copyright Term Extension Act of 1998

The term "intellectual property"

Criticism of the term intellectual property ranges from discussing its vagueness and abstract overreach to direct contention to the semantic validity of using words like property and rights in fashions that contradict practice and law. Many detractors think this term specially serves the doctrinal agenda of parties opposing reform in the public interest or otherwise abusing related legislations; and that it disallows intelligent discussion about specific and often unrelated aspects of copyright, patents, trademarks, etc.

Free Software Foundation founder Richard Stallman argues that, although the term intellectual property is in wide use, it should be rejected altogether, because it "systematically distorts and confuses these issues, and its use was and is promoted by those who gain from this confusion". He claims that the term "operates as a catch-all to lump together disparate laws [which] originated separately, evolved differently, cover different activities, have different rules, and raise different public policy issues" and that it creates a "bias" by confusing these monopolies with ownership of limited physical things, likening them to "property rights". Stallman advocates referring to copyrights, patents and trademarks in the singular and warns against abstracting disparate laws into a collective term. He argues that "to avoid spreading unnecessary bias and confusion, it is best to adopt a firm policy not to speak or even think in terms of 'intellectual property'."

Similarly, economists Boldrin and Levine prefer to use the term "intellectual monopoly" as a more appropriate and clear definition of the concept, which they argue, is very dissimilar from property rights. They further argued that "stronger patents do little or nothing to encourage innovation", mainly explained by its tendency to create market monopolies, thereby restricting further innovations and technology transfer.

On the assumption that intellectual property rights are actual rights, Stallman says that this claim does not live to the historical intentions behind these laws, which in the case of copyright served as a censorship system, and later on, a regulatory model for the printing press that may have benefited authors incidentally, but never interfered with the freedom of average readers. Still referring to copyright, he cites legal literature such as the United States Constitution and case law to demonstrate that the law is meant to be an optional and experimental bargain to temporarily trade property rights and free speech for public, not private, benefits in the form of increased artistic production and knowledge. He mentions that "if copyright were a natural right nothing could justify terminating this right after a certain period of time".

Law professor, writer and political activist Lawrence Lessig, along with many other copyleft and free software activists, has criticized the implied analogy with physical property (like land or an automobile). They argue such an analogy fails because physical property is generally rivalrous while intellectual works are non-rivalrous (that is, if one makes a copy of a work, the enjoyment of the copy does not prevent enjoyment of the original). Other arguments along these lines claim that unlike the situation with tangible property, there is no natural scarcity of a particular idea or information: once it exists at all, it can be re-used and duplicated indefinitely without such re-use diminishing the original. Stephan Kinsella has objected to intellectual property on the grounds that the word "property" implies scarcity, which may not be applicable to ideas.

Entrepreneur and politician Rickard Falkvinge and hacker Alexandre Oliva have independently compared George Orwell's fictional dialect Newspeak to the terminology used by intellectual property supporters as a linguistic weapon to shape public opinion regarding copyright debate and DRM.

Alternative terms

In civil law jurisdictions, intellectual property has often been referred to as intellectual rights, traditionally a somewhat broader concept that has included moral rights and other personal protections that cannot be bought or sold. Use of the term intellectual rights has declined since the early 1980s, as use of the term intellectual property has increased.

Alternative terms monopolies on information and intellectual monopoly have emerged among those who argue against the "property" or "intellect" or "rights" assumptions, notably Richard Stallman. The backronyms intellectual protectionism and intellectual poverty, whose initials are also IP, have found supporters as well, especially among those who have used the backronym digital restrictions management.

The argument that an intellectual property right should (in the interests of better balancing of relevant private and public interests) be termed an intellectual monopoly privilege (IMP) has been advanced by several academics including Birgitte Andersen and Thomas Alured Faunce.

Objections to overbroad intellectual property laws

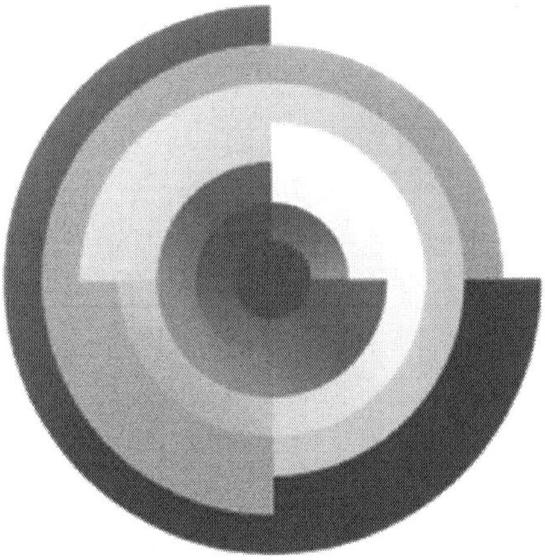

The free culture movementchampions the production of contentthat bears little or no restrictions.

Some critics of intellectual property, such as those in the free culture movement, point at intellectual monopolies as harming health (in the case of pharmaceutical patents), preventing progress, and benefiting concentrated interests to the detriment of the masses, and argue that the public interest is harmed by ever-expansive monopolies in the form of copyright extensions, software patents, and business method patents. More recently scientists and engineers are expressing concern that patent thickets are undermining technological development even in high-tech fields like nanotechnology.

Petra Moser has asserted that historical analysis suggests that intellectual property laws may harm innovation:

Overall, the weight of the existing historical evidence suggests that patent policies, which grant strong intellectual property rights to early generations of inventors, may discourage innovation. On the contrary, policies that encourage the diffusion of ideas and modify patent laws to facilitate entry and encourage competition may be an effective mechanism to encourage innovation.

In support of that argument, Jörg Baten, Nicola Bianchi and Petra Moser find historical evidence that especially compulsory licensing – which allows governments to license patents without the consent of patent-owners – encouraged invention in Germany in the early 20th century by increasing the threat of competition in fields with low pre-existing levels of competition.

Peter Drahos notes, "Property rights confer authority over resources. When authority is granted to the few over resources on which many depend, the few gain power over the goals of the many. This has consequences for both political and economic freedoms with in a society."

The World Intellectual Property Organization (WIPO) recognizes that conflicts may exist between the respect for and implementation of current intellectual property systems and other human rights. In 2001 the UN Committee on Economic, Social and Cultural Rights issued a document called "Human rights and intellectual property" that argued that intellectual property tends to be governed by economic goals when it should be viewed primarily as a social product; in order to serve human well-being, intellectual property systems must respect and conform to human rights laws. According to the Committee, when systems fail to do so they risk infringing upon the human right to food and health, and to cultural participation and scientific benefits. In 2004 the General Assembly of WIPO adopted The Geneva Declaration on the Future of the World Intellectual Property Organizationwhich argues that WIPO should "focus more on the needs of developing countries, and to view IP as one of many tools for development—not as an end in itself".

Further along these lines, The ethical problems brought up by IP rights are most pertinent when it is socially valuable goods like life-saving medicines are given IP protection. While the application of IP rights can allow companies to charge higher than the marginal cost of production in order to recoup the costs of research and development, the price may exclude from the market anyone who cannot afford the cost of the product, in this case a life-saving drug. "An IPR driven regime is therefore not a regime that is conductive to the investment of R&D of products that are socially valuable to predominately poor populations".

Libertarians have differing views on intellectual property. Stephan Kinsella, an anarcho-capitalist on the right-wing of libertarianism, argues against intellectual property because allowing property rights in ideas and information creates artificial scarcity and infringes on the right to own tangible property. Kinsella uses the following scenario to argue this point:

> [I]magine the time when men lived in caves. One bright guy—let's call him Galt-Magnon—decides to build a log cabin on an open field, near his crops. To be sure, this is a good idea, and others notice it. They naturally imitate Galt-Magnon, and they start building their own cabins. But the first man to invent a house, according to IP advocates, would have a right to prevent others from building houses on their own land, with their own logs, or to charge them a fee if they do build houses. It is plain that the innovator in these examples becomes a partial owner of the tangible property (e.g., land and logs) of others, due not to first occupation and use of that property (for it is already owned), but due to his coming up with an idea. Clearly, this rule flies in the face of the first-user homesteading rule, arbitrarily and groundlessly overriding the very homesteading rule that is at the foundation of all property rights.

Thomas Jefferson once said in a letter to Isaac McPherson on August 13, 1813:

> "If nature has made any one thing less susceptible than all others of exclusive property, it is the action of the thinking power called an idea, which an individual may exclusively possess as long as he keeps it to himself; but the moment it is divulged, it forces itself into the possession of every one, and the receiver cannot dispossess himself of it. Its peculiar character, too, is that no one possesses the less, because every other possesses the whole of it. He who receives an idea from me, receives instruction himself without lessening mine; as he who lights his taper at mine, receives light without darkening me."

In 2005 the RSA launched the Adelphi Charter, aimed at creating an international policy statement to frame how governments should make balanced intellectual property law.

Another aspect of current U.S. Intellectual Property legislation is its focus on individual and joint works; thus, copyright protection can only be obtained in 'original' works of authorship.

Expansion in nature and scope of intellectual property laws

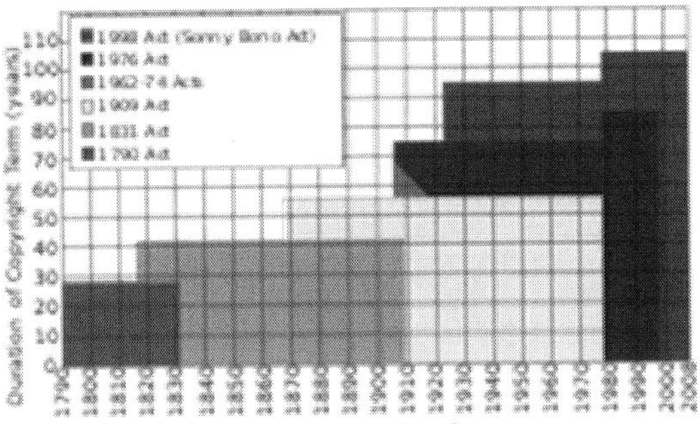

Expansion of U.S. copyright law (Assuming authors create their works by age 35 and live for seventy years)

Other criticism of intellectual property law concerns the expansion of intellectual property, both in duration and in scope.

In addition, as scientific knowledge has expanded and allowed new industries to arise in fields such as biotechnology and nanotechnology, originators of technology have sought IP protection for the new technologies. Patents have been granted for living organisms, (and in the United States, certain living organisms have been patentable for over a century).

The increase in terms of protection is particularly seen in relation to copyright, which has recently been the subject of serial extensions in the United States and in Europe. With no need for registration or copyright notices, this is thought to have led to an increase in orphan works (copyrighted works for which the copyright owner cannot be contacted), a problem that has been noticed and addressed by governmental bodies around the world.

Also with respect to copyright, the American film industry helped to change the social construct of intellectual property via its trade organization, the Motion Picture Association of America. In amicus briefs in important cases, in lobbying before Congress, and in its statements to the public, the MPAA has advocated strong protection of intellectual-property rights. In framing its presentations, the association has claimed that people are entitled to the property that is produced by their labor. Additionally Congress's awareness of the position of the United States as the world's largest producer of films has made it convenient to expand the conception of intellectual property. These doctrinal reforms have further strengthened the industry, lending the MPAA even more power and authority.

RIAA representative Hilary Rosentestifies before the Senate Judiciary Committee on the future of digital music (July 11, 2000)

The growth of the Internet, and particularly distributed search engines like Kazaa and Gnutella, have represented a challenge for copyright policy.

The Recording Industry Association of America, in particular, has been on the front lines of the fight against copyright infringement, which the industry calls "piracy". The industry has had victories against some services, including a highly publicized case against the file-sharing company Napster, and some people have been prosecuted for sharing files in violation of copyright. The electronic age has seen an increase in the attempt to use software-based digital rights management tools to restrict the copying and use of digitally based works. Laws such as the Digital Millennium Copyright Act have been enacted that use criminal law to prevent any circumvention of software used to enforce digital rights management systems. Equivalent provisions, to prevent circumvention of copyright protection have existed in EU for some time, and are being expanded in, for example, Article 6 and 7 the Copyright Directive. Other examples are Article 7 of the Software Directive of 1991 (91/250/EEC), and the Conditional Access Directive of 1998 (98/84/EEC). This can hinder legal uses, affecting public domain works, limitations and exceptions to copyright, or uses allowed by the copyright holder. Some copyleft licenses, like GNU GPL 3, are designed to counter that. Laws may permit circumvention under specific conditions like when it is necessary to achieve interoperability with the circumventor's program, or for accessibility reasons; however, distribution of circumvention tools or instructions may be illegal.

In the context of trademarks, this expansion has been driven by international efforts to harmonise the definition of "trademark", as exemplified by the Agreement on Trade-Related Aspects of Intellectual Property Rights ratified in 1994, which formalized regulations for IP rights that had been handled by common law, or not at all, in member states. Pursuant to TRIPs, any sign which is "capable of distinguishing" the products or services of one business from the products or services of another business is capable of constituting a trademark.

Use in corporate tax avoidance

Intellectual property has become a core tool in corporate tax planning and tax avoidance. IP is a key component of the leading multinational tax avoidance base erosion and profit shifting (BEPS) tools, which the OECD estimates costs $100–240 billion in lost annual tax revenues, and includes:

i. Using IP royalty payment schemes to profit shift income from higher-tax locations to lower-tax locations (such as the Facebook 2012 double Irish and the Microsoft 2015 single malt BEPS tax schemes);

ii. Using IP royalty payment schemes to overcome EU withholding tax protections (such as the circa 2007 Google dutch sandwichBEPS tax scheme);

iii.Using advanced IP GAAP accounting to create intangible assets which can be expensed against taxation in certain IP-beneficial regimes (such as the Apple 2015 Irish capital allowances for intangible assets BEPS tax scheme);

iv.Using advanced IP GAAP accounting to maximize the effect of corporate relocations to low-tax regimes (used by Accenture in their 2009 U.S. corporate tax inversion to Ireland).

In 2017-2018, both the U.S. and the EU Commission simultaneously decided to depart from the OECD BEPS Project timetable, which was set up in 2013 to combat IP BEPS tax tools like the above, and launch their own anti-IP BEPS tax regimes:

- U.S. Tax Cuts and Jobs Act of 2017, which has several anti-IP BEPS abuse tax regimes, including GILTI tax and the BEAT tax regimes.
- EU Commission 2018 Digital Services Tax, which is less advanced than the U.S. TCJA, but does seek to override IP BEPS tools via a quasi-VAT.

The departure of the U.S. and EU Commission from the OECD BEPS Project process, is attributed to frustrations with the rise in IP as a key BEPS tax tool, creating intangible assets, which are then turned into royalty payment BEPS schemes (double Irish), and/or capital allowanceBEPS schemes (capital allowances for intangibles). In contrast, the OECD has spent years developing and advocating intellectual property as a legal and a GAAP accounting concept.

The EU Commission's €13 billion fine of Apple's pre 2015 double Irish IP BEPS tax scheme, is the largest corporate tax fine in history.

Trade Marks

Trade Marks are registerable words and logos which distinguish the goods and services of one entity from those of another. Well known trade mark words include names such as COCA COLA, FORD and GUCCI while well known logo marks include the green LAND ROVER oval device, the large yellow MACDONALDS "M" device and the square ORANGE device. However, the registration and ownership of trade marks is not only for global giants such as Coca Cola and Macdonalds: small business proprietors (such as online traders, pub owners or beauty salons) may do well to register trade marks for their businesses, particularly with greater expansion as they may want to prevent competitor businesses from possibly using their marks and ideas without permission, and thereby riding on the good reputation of the original business' trade marks. A good and growing reputation in a trade mark is worth protecting by registering the mark.

In the United Kingdom, one can apply for registration of a UK trade mark (which affords protection of the mark in the UK) and/ or a Community Trade Mark ("CTM" – which affords protection in all countries of the European Union). UK trade marks are registered at the Intellectual Property Office and CTM's can be applied for at the Office for Harmonisation in the Internal Market.

Trade Marks that Can and Cannot be Registered

The Trade Marks Act 1994 stipulates which marks can and cannot be registered. In order for a trade mark to be registerable, it must be distinctive. In other words, it must be able to distinguish the goods or services of one entity from that of another so that there can be no confusion in the mind of the public as to the source of the goods or services. In other words, the mark, word or sign for which trade mark protection is being sought must be unique to a particular entity in relation to the nature of his business. Confusing similarities with the mark of another must be avoided. Trade marks that cannot be registered include:

- Trade marks that are already in existence
- Marks that are not distinctive or are deceptive (or confusingly similar to existing marks)
- Offensive marks
- Illegal marks
- Descriptive names or names which show the purpose of the goods or indicate where the goods or services originate
- Marks which have acquired a generic use within a particular trade or industry

Rights Afforded by Registration, Cost and Duration

There are various international, numbered classes of trade marks for the various possible goods and services. For example, vehicle parts and related services are registered under Class 12. The cost of registration of a trade mark in the UK is £200 (plus £50 per Class) – at the time of the drafting hereof. A trade mark owner has the exclusive right to use the registered mark in trade in the UK (and EU, depending on registration) and the law affords 10 years exclusivity and protection for the mark, and the registered mark is renewable after 10 years at the same cost as registration.

Means of Protection and Enforcement of Rights

A wide range of enforcement is afforded the trade mark owner, including delivery up and destruction of infringing goods or signage, search orders, disclosure orders, payment of damages and injunctions, to name a few.

Domain Name Infringement

A domain name is simply a website address. Some domain name traders (also known as "cyber squatters") often register numerous domain names containing well-known registered trade marks with the intention of selling these domain names to the rightful trade mark owners for inflated profit. Unauthorised and non-descriptive registration and use of a registered trade mark (belonging to another entity) in a domain name or email address amounts to trade mark infringement.

Copyright

Copyright is probably the most common IP right. We create and encounter copyright daily. The creation of copyright is governed by the Copyright, Designs and Patents Act 1998 and provides for rights in the creation of literary, dramatic, musical, artistic, visual, audiovisual, broadcasts and electronic works.

Copyright cannot be registered but subsists in the mere creation of the work by the author, artist, film maker, musician, programmer, publisher, broadcaster, or photographer, as the case may be. Therefore, even to the drafter of a personal letter is granted automatic copyright protection by law. For a work to enjoy copyright protection is must be an original work.

The Extent of Copyright Protection

Usually, the creator of the work is the automatic copyright owner and the copyright owner has the exclusive right to copy the work, to reproduce it, to adapt it, to issue it to the public; thus to publish it, show, display, broadcast, or play it in public.

There are exceptions to the rule that only the copyright owner may exercise the above rights. Mainstream exceptions to these include:

- Where a work is created by an employee, copyright belongs to the employer
- Where a work has been commissioned, copyright belongs to the commissioner
- Where permission or a licence has been granted to another party
- Making backup copies (e.g. of a computer programme) for private use
- Works copied for research or private study
- Copies made for educational purposes
- Quoting for media creations
- Parliamentary or judicial proceedings
- Fair dealing for criticism, review or news reporting

Patents

Patents are probably the most complex of the Intellectual Property Rights and the patent attorney often requires a strong technical and scientific background to deal with innovations in the broad fields of technology and medical science, amongst others. The patent attorney needs to fully understand the workings of complex inventions and must know how to apply the law to these to determine whether an idea qualifies as a patent and, if so, how to ensure complete protection for the invention.

The Purpose of Registering a Patent

A patent affords the owner the exclusive right to reproduce/ manufacture the patented item or concept, to grant licences to others to manufacture the patented concept, to import or export, to sell and profit by the patent.

Once a patent is registered, it must be renewed every year after five years for up to the maximum of 20 years. The reason for this maximum period of protection is to avoid an endless monopoly and to allow the broader economic community to benefit from the introduction of the patent.

Inventions that Can and Cannot be Patented

A patent must be novel, new; it must contain an inventive step; it must be an advancement on the state of the art (i.e. new and progressive in relation to those patents which already exist in the public domain) and it must be capable of being used within trade and industry. An inventor needs to keep the invention confidential and take care not to disclose the patent to the public before suitable rights are in place, as this may affect the essential requirement of novelty.

Legislation also provides that the following cannot be patented:

- a mathematical or scientific method or theory, literary
- a literary, dramatic or artistic work, a way of performing a mental act, playing a game, or doing business
- the presentation of information or a computer programme
- an immoral or offensive item

Application

In deciding whether or not your idea is patentable, it is advisable that to discuss your invention with a qualified and reputable patent attorney. This will add to the £200 it will cost to submit an application with the Intellectual Property Office (IPO) in the UK, but one would not want to risk compromising or jeopardising a potentially valuable and hard-earned invention.

In short, a patent application will comprise completion and submission of a number of documents, which include (but are not limited to):

- A Statement of Application declaring who the inventor of the patent is
- The Claims, a document which lists the innovative and distinguishing technical features of the invention

- The Description, which sets out in detail exactly how the invention functions, how it can be reproduced, and points to its nature and use
- Along with the Description, Drawings must be supplied to illustrate the parts and working of the invention
- An Abstract, a short summary of what the invention is – a title of the invention

It may happen that disputes arise where there is conflict between a patent application and an earlier application or existing patent. If the inventor has not made use of a patent attorney in the application phase, it is advisable to seek the expertise of a patent attorney should any dispute arise.

Design Rights

To qualify for protection as a design right, the design must be new and unique (not common to the public), different from all other known designs in its character and impression. The design can, for example, be the unique shape of a cool drink bottle or the ornamentation on a business logo. But the scope is vast. A creation that does not meet the legal requirement for a design cannot be registered. Nor can functional items where the design is central to the function. Offensive designs and national insignia cannot be registered, and obviously not designs already registered. It is possible to search for and compare designs to avoid conflict by referring to the IPO website.

As with copyright, the actual owner of an unregistered design right is the person who commissioned a design, as is the employer where an employee has created a design in the course of employment.

Registration of a Design Right

Registration of a design right can afford the owner the right to later sell the registered IP right, or to license others to use the design. An unregistered design may have protection under another type of IP right, possibly copyright or unregistered design right, but such cover will not be as firm or comprehensive.

The length and scope of design right protection differs from unregistered UK design right to registered UK design right to unregistered Community design right.

11

Copyrights

Registrar of Copyrights in India

The Registrar of Copyrights is the head of the Copyright Office under the Department of Industrial Policy and Promotion of the Ministry of Commerce and Industry and in-charge of implementation of Copyright Act. The appointment of the Registrar is done by the central government. The registrar of copyrights is also the secretary of the copyright board.

Copyright symbol

Section 9 of the Copyright Act requires for establishment of an office to be called the Copyright Office for the purpose of the Act. The Copyright Office is to be under the immediate control of a Registrar of Copyrights to be appointed by the Central Government, who would act under the superintendence and directions of the Central Government. The Copyright Office has been set up to provide registration facilities to all types of works and is headed by a

Registrar of Copyrights and is located at G-30, August Kranti Bhawan Bhikaji Cama Place, New Delhi, 110066. The applications for registration of works can be filled at the counter provided at the Copyright Office from 2.30 P.M. to 4.30. P.M. from Monday to Friday. The applications are also accepted by post. On-line registration through "E-filing facility " has been provided from 8 September 2009, which facilitates the applicants to file applications at the time and place chosen by them.

Types of Works

The types of work Copyright office is involved with includes:

1. Artistic Work
2. Literary Work
3. Software
4. Music
5. Sound Recording
6. Cinematograph films
7. Lyric
8. Lyric Book
9. Story Book
10. Story Themes

Copyright law of India

The Copyright Act 1957 (as amended by the Copyright Amendment Act 2012) governs the subject of copyright law in India. The Act is applicable from 21 January 1958. The history of copyright law in India can be traced back to its colonial era under the British Empire. The Copyright Act 1957 was the first post-independence copyright legislation in India and the law has been amended six times since 1957. The most recent amendment was in the year 2012, through the Copyright (Amendment) Act 2012. India is a member of most of the important international conventions governing the area of copyright law, including the Berne Convention of 1886 (as modified at Paris in 1971), the Universal Copyright Convention of 1951, the Rome Convention of 1961 and the Agreement on Trade Related Aspects of Intellectual Property Rights (TRIPS). But India is not a member of the WIPO Copyright Treaty (WCT) and the WIPO Performances and Phonograms Treaty (WPPT).

Applicable Copyright Act before 1958

Prior to 21 January 1958, The Indian Copyright Act, 1914, was applicable in India and still applicable for works created prior to 21 January 1958, when the new Act came into force(the Copyright Act of 1911 passed by the

Parliament of the United Kingdom as modified in its application to India by the Indian Copyright Act, 1914). According to this Act, the period of copyright for photographs was 50 years from the time it was first published. (Act language is:"the term for which copyright shall subsist in photographs shall be fifty years from the making of the original negative from which the photograph was directly or indirectly derived, and the person who was owner of such negative at the time when such negative was made shall be deemed to be the author of the work, and, where such owner is a body corporate, the body corporate shall be deemed for the purposes of this Act to reside within the parts of His Majesty's dominions to which this Act extends if it has established a place of business within such parts.") For photographs published, before 21 January 1958 in India, the period of copyright is thus 50 years, as for them the old Act is applicable.

Definition of copyright

Copyright is a bundle of rights given by the law to the creators of literary, dramatic, musical and artistic works and the producers of cinematograph films and sound recordings. The rights provided under Copyright law include the rights of reproduction of the work, communication of the work to the public, adaptation of the work and translation of the work. The scope and duration of protection provided under copyright law varies with the nature of the protected work.

In a 2016 copyright lawsuit, the Delhi High Court states that copyright is "not an inevitable, divine, or natural right that confers on authors the absolute ownership of their creations. It is designed rather to stimulate activity and progress in the arts for the intellectual enrichment of the public. Copyright is intended to increase and not to impede the harvest of knowledge. It is intended to motivate the creative activity of authors and inventors in order to benefit the public."

Types of works protected

The Indian copyright law protects literary works, dramatic works, musical works, artistic works, cinematograph films and sound recordings.

Foreign works

Copyrights of works of the countries mentioned in the International Copyright Order are protected in India, as if such works are Indian works. The term of copyright in a work shall not exceed that which is enjoyed by it in its country of origin.

Ownership of copyright under the Copyright Act 1957

The author of a work is generally considered as the first owner of the copyright under the Copyright Act 1957. However, for works made in the course of an author's employment under a "contract of service" or apprenticeship, the employer is considered as the first owner of copyright, in the absence of any agreement to the contrary.

The concept of joint authorship is recognised in Section. 2(z) of the Act which provides that "a work produced by the collaboration of two or more authors in which the contribution of one author is not distinct from the contribution of the other author or authors" is a work of joint authorship. This concept has been elucidated in cases like Najma Heptulla v. Orient Longman Ltd. and Ors.

Section 19 of the Copyright Act 1957 lays down the modes of assignment of copyright in India. Assignment can only be in writing and must specify the work, the period of assignment and the territory for which assignment is made. If the period of assignment is not specified in the agreement, it shall be deemed to be 5 years and if the territorial extent of assignment is not specified, it shall be presumed to be limited to the territories of India. In a recent judgement (Pine Labs Private Limited vs Gemalto Terminals India Limited), a division bench of the Delhi High Court confirmed this position and held that in cases wherein the duration of assignment is not specified, the duration shall be deemed to be five years and the copyright shall revert to the author after five years.

Exceptions to copyright infringement in India

The Copyright Act 1957 exempts certain acts from the ambit of copyright infringement. While many people tend to use the term fair use to denote copyright exceptions in India, it is a factually wrong usage. While the US and certain other countries follow the broad fair use exception, India follows a different approach towards copyright exceptions. India follows a hybrid approach that allows-

- fair dealing with any copyrighted work for certain specifically mentioned purposes and
- certain specific activities enumerated in the statute.

While the fair use approach followed in the US can be applied for any kind of uses, the fair dealing approach followed in India is clearly limited towards the purposes of

1. private or personal use, including research, and education,
2. criticism or review,
3. reporting of current events and current affairs, including the reporting of a lecture delivered in public.

While the term fair dealing has not been defined anywhere in the Copyright Act 1957, the concept of 'fair dealing' has been discussed in different judgments, including the decision of the Supreme Court of India in Academy of General Education v. B. Malini Mallya (2009) and the decision of the High Court of Kerala in Civic Chandran v. Ammini Amma.

In September 2016, the Delhi High Court ruled in Delhi University's Rameshwari Photocopy Service shop case, which sold photocopies of chapters from academic textbooks was not infringing on their publisher's copyright, arguing that the use of copyright to "stimulate activity and progress in the arts for the intellectual enrichment of the public" outweighed its use by the publishers to maintain commercial control of their property. However, in December 2016, the ruling was reversed and taken back to court, citing that there were "triable issues" in the case.

Remedies available against copyright infringement in India

The Copyright Act 1957 provides three kinds of remedies - administrative remedies, civil remedies and criminal remedies. The administrative remedies provided under the statute include detention of the infringing goods by the customs authorities. The civil remedies are provided under Chapter XII of the Copyright Act 1957 and the remedies provided include injunctions, damages and account of profits. The criminal remedies are provided under Chapter XIII of the statute and the remedies provided against copyright infringement include imprisonment (up to 3 years) along with a fine (up to 200,000 Rupees).

Jurisdiction [Place of Suing] Under Copyright Act, 1957 - Recently in 2015 the Jurisdiction law regarding Copyright Violation has gone a drastic change by the following judgement of the Hon'ble Supreme Court - Jagdish Singh Khehar and Arun Mishra, JJ. – Civil Appeal Nos. 10643 – 10644 of 2010 with 4912 of 2015 [arising out of SLP [c] No. 8253 of 2013], Dated 01/07/2015 – Indian Performing Rights Society Ltd. Vs. Sanjay Dalia and another - - Copyright Act [14 of 1957], Section 62 – Trade Marks Act [47 of 1999], Section 134 – Civil Procedure Code Section 20 – Suit for infringement of Copyright of Trade Mark – Place of suing – Place where plaintiff resides or carries on business or works for gain – Is an additional forum made available to plaintiff by Section 62 of 1957 Act and Section 134 of 1999 Act – Applicability of Section 20 of Civil Procedure Code is not completely ousted thereby – If cause of action has arisen wholly or in part in place where plaintiff resides or is doing business suit has to be filed at such place – Plaintiff cannot drag defendant to far off place under guise that he carries business there also. --- Interpretation of statutes – Mischief Rule – Construction that suppresses even counter mischief has to be adopted. – Interpretation of statutes – words notwithstanding anything contained in any other law – do not always completely exclude applicability of other law. ---- Words and phrases – "Notwithstanding anything contained --- being in force" – Do not necessarily exclude applicability of other law.

Copyright infringement

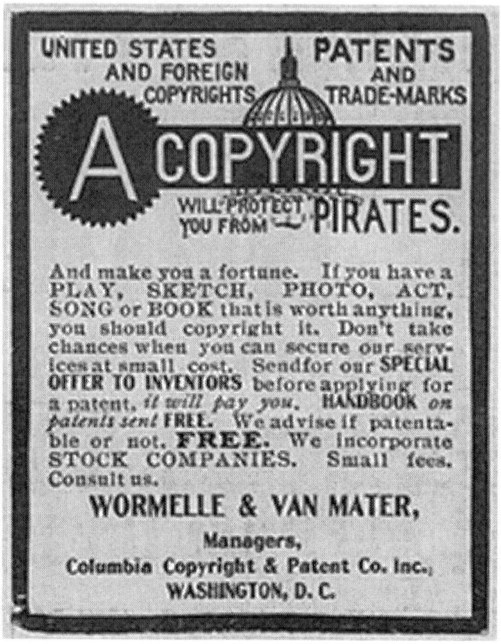

An advertisement for copyright and patent preparation services from 1906, when copyright registration formalitieswere still required in the US

Copyright infringement (colloquially referred to as piracy) is the use of works protected by copyright law without permission, infringing certain exclusive rights granted to the copyright holder, such as the right to reproduce, distribute, display or perform the protected work, or to make derivative works. The copyright holder is typically the work's creator, or a publisher or other business to whom copyright has been assigned. Copyright holders routinely invoke legal and technological measures to prevent and penalize copyright infringement.

Copyright infringement disputes are usually resolved through direct negotiation, a notice and take down process, or litigation in civil court. Egregious or large-scale commercial infringement, especially when it involves counterfeiting, is sometimes prosecuted via the criminal justicesystem. Shifting public expectations, advances in digital technology, and the increasing reach of the Internet have led to such widespread, anonymous infringement that copyright-dependent industries now focus less on pursuing individuals who seek and share copyright-protected content online, and more on expanding copyright law to recognize and penalize, as indirect infringers, the service providers and software distributors who are said to facilitate and encourage individual acts of infringement by others.

Estimates of the actual economic impact of copyright infringement vary widely and depend on many factors. Nevertheless, copyright holders, industry representatives, and legislators have long characterized copyright infringement as piracy or theft – language which some U.S. courts now regard as pejorative or otherwise contentious.

The terms piracy and theft are often associated with copyright infringement. The original meaning of piracy is "robbery or illegal violence at sea", but the term has been in use for centuries as a synonym for acts of copyright infringement. Theft, meanwhile, emphasizes the potential commercial harm of infringement to copyright holders. However, copyright is a type of intellectual property, an area of law distinct from that which covers robbery or theft, offenses related only to tangible property. Not all copyright infringement results in commercial loss, and the U.S. Supreme Court ruled in 1985 that infringement does not easily equate with theft.

This was taken further in the case MPAA v. Hotfile, where Judge Kathleen M. Williams granted a motion to deny the MPAA the usage of words whose appearance was primarily "pejorative". This list included the word "piracy", the use of which, the motion by the defense stated, serves no court purpose but to misguide and inflame the jury.

"Piracy"

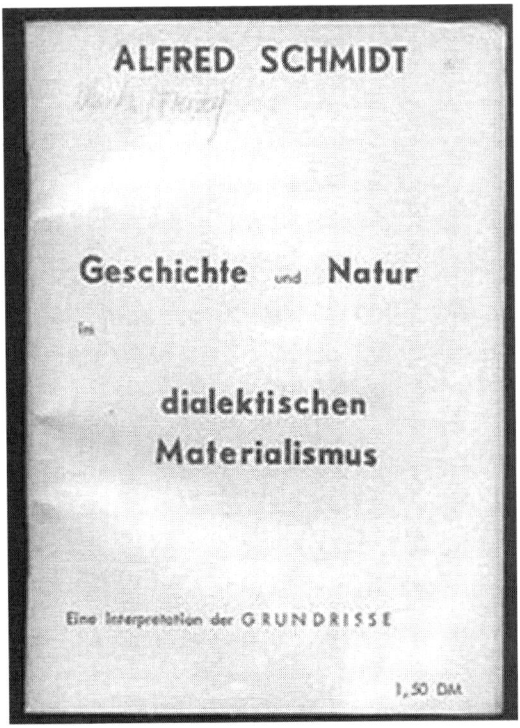

Pirated edition of German philosopher Alfred Schmidt(Amsterdam, ca. 1970)

The term "piracy" has been used to refer to the unauthorized copying, distribution and selling of works in copyright. The practice of labelling the infringement of exclusive rights in creative works as "piracy" predates statutory copyright law. Prior to the Statute of Anne in 1710, the Stationers' Company of London in 1557, received a Royal Charter giving the company a monopoly on publication and tasking it with enforcing the charter. Those who violated the charter were labelled pirates as early as 1603. Article 12 of the 1886 Berne Convention for the Protection of Literary and Artistic Works uses the term "piracy" in relation to copyright infringement, stating "Pirated works may be seized on importation into those countries of the Union where the original work enjoys legal protection." Article 61 of the 1994 Agreement on Trade-Related Aspects of Intellectual Property Rights (TRIPs) requires criminal procedures and penalties in cases of "willful trademark counterfeiting or copyright piracy on a commercial scale." Piracy traditionally refers to acts of copyright infringement intentionally committed for financial gain, though more recently, copyright holders have described online copyright infringement, particularly in relation to peer-to-peer file sharing networks, as "piracy".

Richard Stallman and the GNU Project have criticized the use of the word "piracy" in these situations, saying that publishers use the word to refer to "copying they don't approve of" and that "they [publishers] imply that it is ethically equivalent to attacking ships on the high seas, kidnapping and murdering the people on them."

"Theft"

Copyright holders frequently refer to copyright infringement as theft. In copyright law, infringement does not refer to theft of physical objects that take away the owner's possession, but an instance where a person exercises one of the exclusive rights of the copyright holder without authorization. Courts have distinguished between copyright infringement and theft. For instance, the United States Supreme Court held in Dowling v. United States (1985) that bootleg phonorecords did not constitute stolen property. Instead,

"interference with copyright does not easily equate with theft, conversion, or fraud. The Copyright Act even employs a separate term of art to define one who misappropriates a copyright: '[...] an infringer of the copyright.'"

The court said that in the case of copyright infringement, the province guaranteed to the copyright holder by copyright law – certain exclusive rights – is invaded, but no control, physical or otherwise, is taken over the copyright, nor is the copyright holder wholly deprived of using the copyrighted work or exercising the exclusive rights held.

A 1979 East German court ruling found that software was "neither a scientific work nor a creative achievement" and ineligible for copyright protection, legalizing software copying in the country.

"Freebooting"

The term "freebooting" has been used to describe the unauthorized copying of online media, particularly videos, onto websites such as Facebook, YouTube or Twitter. The word itself had already been in use since the 16th century, referring to pirates, and meant "looting" or "plundering". This form of the word – a portmanteau of "freeloading" and "bootlegging" – was suggested by YouTuber and podcaster Brady Haran in the podcast Hello Internet. Haran advocated the term in an attempt to find a phrase more emotive than "copyright infringement", yet more appropriate than "theft". The phrase was also the title of the episode the phrase was coined on. An alternative proposed by co-host CGP Grey is viewjacking.

Motivation

Some of the motives for engaging in copyright infringement are the following:

- Pricing – unwillingness or inability to pay the price requested by the legitimate sellers
- Testing and evaluation – try before paying for what may be bad value
- Unavailability – no legitimate sellers providing the product in the language or country of the end-user: not yet launched there, already withdrawn from sales, never to be sold there, geographical restrictions on online distribution and international shipping
- Usefulness – the legitimate product comes with various means (DRM, region lock, DVD region code, Blu-ray region code) of restricting legitimate use (backups, usage on devices of different vendors, offline usage) or comes with non-skippable advertisements and anti-piracy disclaimers, which are removed in the unauthorized product making it more desirable for the end-user
- Shopping experience – no legitimate sellers providing the product with the required quality through online distribution and through a shopping system with the required level of user-friendliness
- Anonymity – downloading works does not require identification whereas downloads directly from the website of the copyright owner often require a valid email address and/ or other credentials
- Freedom of Information – Not believing that the idea of copyright law can or should exist

Sometimes only partial compliance with license agreements is the cause. For example, in 2013, the US Army settled a lawsuit with Texas-based company Apptricity, which makes software that allows the army to track their soldiers in real time. In 2004, the US Army paid US$4.5 million for a license of 500 users, while allegedly installing the software for more than 9000 users; the case was settled for US$50 million. Major anti-piracy organizations, like the BSA, conduct software licensing audits regularly to ensure full compliance.

Cara Cusumano, director of the Tribeca Film Festival, stated in April 2014: "Piracy is less about people not wanting to pay and more about just wanting the immediacy – people saying, 'I want to watch Spiderman right now' and downloading it". The statement occurred during the third year that the festival used the Internet to present its content, while it was the first year that it featured a showcase of content producers who work exclusively online. Cusumano further explained that downloading behavior is not merely conducted by people who merely want to obtain content for free:

I think that if companies were willing to put that material out there, moving forward, consumers will follow. It's just that they [consumers] want to consume films online and they're ready to consume films that way and we're not necessarily offering them in that way. So it's the distribution models that need to catch up. People will pay for the content.

In response to Cusumano's perspective, Screen Producers Australia executive director Matt Deaner clarified the motivation of the film industry: "Distributors are usually wanting to encourage cinema-going as part of this process [monetizing through returns] and restrict the immediate access to online so as to encourage the maximum number of people to go to the cinema." Deaner further explained the matter in terms of the Australian film industry, stating: "there are currently restrictions on quantities of tax support that a film can receive unless the film has a traditional cinema release."

In a study published in the Journal of Behavioural and Experimental Economics, and reported on in early May 2014, researchers from the University of Portsmouth in the UK discussed findings from examining the illegal downloading behavior of 6,000 Finnish people, aged seven to 84. The list of reasons for downloading given by the study respondents included money saving; the ability to access material not on general release, or before it was released; and assisting artists to avoid involvement with record companies and movie studios.

In a public talk between Bill Gates, Warren Buffett, and Brent Schlender at the University of Washington in 1998, Bill Gates commented on piracy as a means to an end, whereby people who use Microsoft software illegally will eventually pay for it, out of familiarity, as a country's economy develops and legitimate products become more affordable to businesses and consumers:

Although about three million computers get sold every year in China, people don't pay for the software. Someday they will, though. And as long as they're going to steal it, we want them to steal ours. They'll get sort of addicted, and then we'll somehow figure out how to collect sometime in the next decade.

Developing world

In Media Piracy in Emerging Economies, the first independent international comparative study of media piracy with center on Brazil, India, Russia, South Africa, Mexico, Turkey and Bolivia, "high prices for media goods, low incomes, and cheap digital technologies" are the chief factors that lead to the global spread of media piracy, especially in emerging markets.

According to the same study, even though digital piracy inflicts additional costs on the production side of media, it also offers the main access to media goods in developing countries. The strong tradeoffs that favor using digital piracy in developing economies dictate the current neglected law enforcements toward digital piracy. In China, the issue of digital infringement is not merely legal, but social – originating from the high demand for cheap and affordable goods as well as the governmental connections of the businesses which produce such goods.

Motivations due to censorship

There have been instances where a country's government bans a movie, resulting in the spread of copied videos and DVDs. Romanian-born documentary maker Ilinca Calugareanu wrote a New York Times article telling the story of Irina Margareta Nistor, a narrator for state TV under Nicolae Ceauşescu's regime. A visitor from the west gave her bootlegged copies of American movies, which she dubbed for secret viewings through Romania. According to the article, she dubbed more than 3,000 movies and became the country's second-most famous voice after Ceauşescu, even though no one knew her name until many years later.

Existing and proposed laws

Demonstration in Sweden in support of file sharing, 2006

The Pirate Bay logo, a retaliation to the stereotypical image of piracy

Most countries extend copyright protections to authors of works. In countries with copyright legislation, enforcement of copyright is generally the responsibility of the copyright holder. However, in several jurisdictions there are also criminal penalties for copyright infringement.

Civil law

Copyright infringement in civil law is any violation of the exclusive rights of the owner. In U.S. law, those rights include reproduction, the preparation of derivative works, distributing copies by sale or rental, and public performance or display.

In the U.S., copyright infringement is sometimes confronted via lawsuits in civil court, against alleged infringers directly, or against providers of services and software that support unauthorized copying. For example, major motion-picture corporation MGM Studios filed suit against P2P file-sharing services Grokster and Streamcast for their contributory role in copyright infringement. In 2005, the Supreme Court ruled in favor of MGM, holding that such services could be held liable for copyright infringement since they functioned and, indeed, willfully marketed themselves as venues for acquiring copyrighted movies. The MGM v. Grokster case did not overturn the earlier Sony v. Universal City Studios decision, but rather clouded the legal waters; future designers of software capable of being used for copyright infringement were warned.

In the United States, copyright term has been extended many times over from the original term of 14 years with a single renewal allowance of 14 years, to the current term of the life of the author plus 70 years. If the work was produced under corporate authorship it may last 120 years after creation or 95 years after publication, whichever is sooner.

Article 50 of the Agreement on Trade-Related Aspects of Intellectual Property Rights (TRIPs) requires that signatory countries enable courtsto remedy copyright infringement with injunctions and the destruction of infringing products, and award damages. Some jurisdictions only allow actual, provable damages, and some, like the U.S., allow for large statutory damage awards intended to deter would-be infringers and allow for compensation in situations where actual damages are difficult to prove.

In some jurisdictions, copyright or the right to enforce it can be contractually assigned to a third party which did not have a role in producing the work. When this outsourced litigator appears to have no intention of taking any copyright infringement cases to trial, but rather only takes them just far enough through the legal system to identify and exact settlements from suspected infringers, critics commonly refer to the party as a "copyright troll". Such practices have had mixed results in the U.S.

Criminal law

Punishment of copyright infringement varies case-by-case across countries. Convictions may include jail time and/or severe fines for each instance of copyright infringement. In the United States, willful copyright infringement carries a maximum penalty of $150,000 per instance.

Article 61 of the Agreement on Trade-Related Aspects of Intellectual Property Rights (TRIPs) requires that signatory countries establish criminal procedures and penalties in cases of "willful trademark counterfeiting or copyright piracy on a commercial scale". Copyright holders have demanded that states provide criminal sanctions for all types of copyright infringement.

The first criminal provision in U.S. copyright law was added in 1897, which established a misdemeanor penalty for "unlawful performances and representations of copyrighted dramatic and musical compositions" if the violation had been "willful and for profit." Criminal copyright infringement requires that the infringer acted "for the purpose of commercial advantage or private financial gain." 17 U.S.C. § 506. To establish criminal liability, the prosecutor must first show the basic elements of copyright infringement: ownership of a valid copyright, and the violation of one or more of the copyright holder's exclusive rights. The government must then establish that defendant willfully infringed or, in other words, possessed the necessary mens rea. Misdemeanor infringement has a very low threshold in terms of number of copies and the value of the infringed works.

The ACTA trade agreement, signed in May 2011 by the United States, Japan, and the EU, requires that its parties add criminal penalties, including incarceration and fines, for copyright and trademark infringement, and obligated the parties to actively police for infringement.

United States v. LaMacchia 871 F.Supp. 535 (1994) was a case decided by the United States District Court for the District of Massachusetts which ruled that, under the copyright and cybercrime laws effective at the time, committing copyright infringement for non-commercial motives could not be prosecuted under criminal copyright law. The ruling gave rise to what became known as the "LaMacchia Loophole", wherein criminal charges of fraud or copyright infringement would be dismissed under current legal standards, so long as there was no profit motive involved.

The United States No Electronic Theft Act (NET Act), a federal law passed in 1997, in response to LaMacchia, provides for criminal prosecution of individuals who engage in copyright infringement under certain circumstances, even when there is no monetary profit or commercial benefit from the infringement. Maximum penalties can be five years in prison and up to $250,000 in fines. The NET Act also raised statutory damages by 50%. The court's ruling explicitly drew attention to the shortcomings of current law that allowed people to facilitate mass copyright infringement while being immune to prosecution under the Copyright Act.

Proposed laws such as the Stop Online Piracy Act broaden the definition of "willful infringement", and introduce felony charges for unauthorized media streaming. These bills are aimed towards defeating websites that carry or contain links to infringing content, but have raised concerns about domestic abuse and internet censorship.

Noncommercial file sharing

Legality of downloading

To an extent, copyright law in some countries permits downloading copyright-protected content for personal, noncommercial use. Examples include Canada and European Union(EU) member states like Poland, and The Netherlands.

The personal copying exemption in the copyright law of EU member states stems from the EU Copyright Directive of 2001, which is generally devised to allow EU members to enact laws sanctioning making copies without authorization, as long as they are for personal, noncommercial use. The Copyright Directive was not intended to legitimize file-sharing, but rather the common practice of space shifting copyright-protected content from a legally purchased CD (for example) to certain kinds of devices and media, provided rights holders are compensated and no copy protection measures are circumvented. Rights-holder compensation takes various forms, depending on the country, but is generally either a levy on "recording" devices and media, or a tax on the content itself. In some countries, such as Canada, the applicability of such laws to copying onto general-purpose storage devices like computer hard drives, portable media players, and phones, for which no levies are collected, has been the subject of debate and further efforts to reform copyright law.

In some countries, the personal copying exemption explicitly requires that the content being copied was obtained legitimately – i.e., from authorized sources, not file-sharing networks. Other countries, such as the Netherlands, make no such distinction; the exemption there had been assumed, even by the government, to apply to any such copying, even from file-sharing networks. However, in April 2014, the Court of Justice of the European Union ruled that "national legislation which makes no distinction between private copies made from lawful sources and those made from counterfeited or pirated sources cannot be tolerated."

Legality of uploading

Although downloading or other private copying is sometimes permitted, public distribution – by uploading or otherwise offering to share copyright-protected content – remains illegal in most, if not all countries. For example, in Canada, even though it was once legal to download any copyrighted file as long as it was for noncommercial use, it was still illegal to distribute the copyrighted files (e.g. by uploading them to a P2P network).

Relaxed penalties

Some countries, like Canada and Germany, have limited the penalties for non-commercial copyright infringement. For example, Germany has passed a bill to limit the fine for individuals accused of sharing movies and series to €800-900. Canada's Copyright Modernization Act claims that statutory damages for non-commercial copyright infringement are capped at C$5,000 but this only applies to copies that have been made without the breaking of any "digital lock". However, this only applies to "bootleg distribution" and not non-commercial use.

DMCA and anti-circumvention laws

Title I of the U.S. DMCA, the WIPO Copyright and Performances and Phonograms Treaties Implementation Act has provisions that prevent persons from "circumvent[ing] a technological measure that effectively controls access to a work". Thus if a distributor of copyrighted works has some kind of software, dongle or password access device installed in instances of the work, any attempt to bypass such a copy protection scheme may be actionable – though the US Copyright Office is currently reviewing anticircumvention rulemaking under DMCA – anti-circumvention exemptions that have been in place under the DMCA include those in software designed to filter websites that are generally seen to be inefficient (child safety and public library website filtering software) and the circumvention of copy protection mechanisms that have malfunctioned, have caused the instance of the work to become inoperable or which are no longer supported by their manufacturers. According to Abby House Media Inc v. Apple Inc., it is legal to point users to DRM-stripping software and inform them how to use it because of lack of evidence that DRM stripping leads to copyright infringement.

Online intermediary liability

Whether Internet intermediaries are liable for copyright infringement by their users is a subject of debate and court cases in a number of countries.

Definition of intermediary

Internet intermediaries were formerly understood to be internet service providers (ISPs). However, questions of liability have also emerged in relation to other Internet infrastructure intermediaries, including Internet backbone providers, cable companies and mobile communications providers.

In addition, intermediaries are now also generally understood to include Internet portals, software and games providers, those providing virtual information such as interactive forums and comment facilities with or without a moderation system, aggregators of various kinds, such as news aggregators, universities, libraries and archives, web search engines, chat rooms, web blogs, mailing lists, and any website which provides access to third party content through, for example, hyperlinks, a crucial element of the World Wide Web.

Litigation and legislation concerning intermediaries

Early court cases focused on the liability of Internet service providers (ISPs) for hosting, transmitting or publishing user-supplied content that could be actioned under civil or criminal law, such as libel, defamation, or pornography. As different content was considered in different legal systems, and in the absence of common definitions for "ISPs", "bulletin boards" or "online publishers", early law on online intermediaries' liability varied widely from country to country. The first laws on online intermediaries' liability were passed from the mid-1990s onwards.

The debate has shifted away from questions about liability for specific content, including that which may infringe copyright, towards whether online intermediaries should be generallyresponsible for content accessible through their services or infrastructure.

The U.S. Digital Millennium Copyright Act (1998) and the European E-Commerce Directive (2000) provide online intermediaries with limited statutory immunity from liability for copyright infringement. Online intermediaries hosting content that infringes copyright are not liable, so long as they do not know about it and take actions once the infringing content is brought to their attention. In U.S. law this is characterized as "safe harbor" provisions. Under European law, the governing principles for Internet Service Providers are "mere conduit", meaning that they are neutral 'pipes' with no knowledge of what they are carrying; and 'no obligation to monitor' meaning that they cannot be given a general mandate by governments to monitor content. These two principles are a barrier for certain forms of online copyright enforcement and they were the reason behind an attempt to amend the European Telecoms Package in 2009 to support new measures against copyright infringement.

Peer-to-peer issues

Peer-to-peer file sharing intermediaries have been denied access to safe harbor provisions in relation to copyright infringement. Legal action against such intermediaries, such as Napster, are generally brought in relation to principles of secondary liability for copyright infringement, such as contributory liability and vicarious liability.

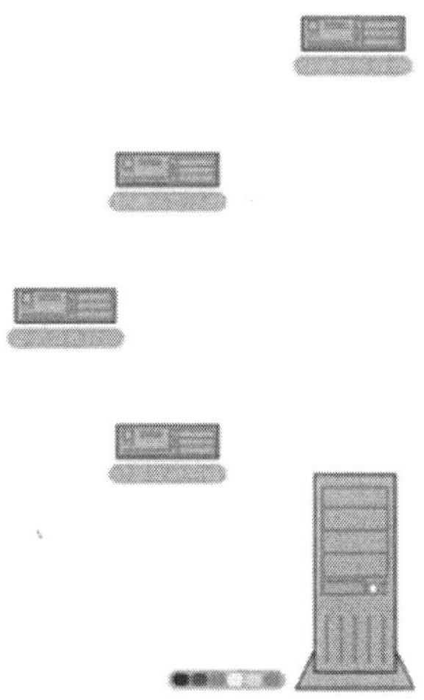

The BitTorrent protocol: In this animation, the colored bars beneath all of the seven clients in the upper region above represent the file, with each color representing an individual piece of the file. After the initial pieces transfer from the seed (large system at the bottom), the pieces are individually transferred from client to client. The original seeder only needs to send out one copy of the file for all the clients to receive a copy.

These types of intermediaries do not host or transmit infringing content, themselves, but may be regarded in some courts as encouraging, enabling or facilitating infringement by users. These intermediaries may include the author, publishers and marketers of peer-to-peer networking software, and the websites that allow users to download such software. In the case of the BitTorrent protocol, intermediaries may include the torrent tracker and any websites or search engines which facilitate access to torrent files. Torrent files don't contain copyrighted content, but they may make reference to files that do, and they may point to trackers which coordinate the sharing of those files. Some torrent indexing and search sites, such as The Pirate Bay, now encourage the use of magnet links, instead of direct links to torrent files, creating another layer of indirection; using such links, torrent files are obtained from other peers, rather than from a particular website.

Since the late 1990s, copyright holders have taken legal actions against a number of peer-to-peer intermediaries, such as pir, Grokster, eMule, SoulSeek, BitTorrent and Limewire, and case law on the liability of Internet service providers (ISPs) in relation to copyright infringement has emerged primarily in relation to these cases.

Nevertheless, whether and to what degree any of these types of intermediaries have secondary liability is the subject of ongoing litigation. The decentralised structure of peer-to-peer networks, in particular, does not sit easily with existing laws on online intermediaries' liability. The BitTorrent protocol established an entirely decentralised network architecture in order to distribute large files effectively. Recent developments in peer-to-peer technology towards more complex network configurations are said to have been driven by a desire to avoid liability as intermediaries under existing laws.

Limitations

Copyright law does not grant authors and publishers absolute control over the use of their work. Only certain types of works and kinds of uses are protected; only unauthorized uses of protected works can be said to be infringing.

Non-infringing uses

Article 10 of the Berne Convention mandates that national laws provide for limitations to copyright, so that copyright protection does not extend to certain kinds of uses that fall under what the treaty calls "fair practice", including but not limited to minimal quotations used in journalism and education. The laws implementing these limitations and exceptions for uses that would otherwise be infringing broadly fall into the categories of either fair use or fair dealing. In common law systems, these fair practice statutes typically enshrine principles underlying many earlier judicial precedents, and are considered essential to freedom of speech.

Another example is the practice of compulsory licensing, which is where the law forbids copyright owners from denying a license for certain uses of certain kinds of works, such as compilations and live performances of music.

Compulsory licensing laws generally say that for certain uses of certain works, no infringement occurs as long as a royalty, at a rate determined by law rather than private negotiation, is paid to the copyright owner or representative copyright collective. Some fair dealing laws, such as Canada's, include similar royalty requirements.

In Europe, the copyright infringement case Public Relations Consultants Association Ltd v Newspaper Licensing Agency Ltd had two prongs; one concerned whether a news aggregator service infringed the copyright of the news generators; the other concerned whether the temporary web cache created by the web browser of a consumer of the aggregator's service, also infringed the copyright of the news generators. The first prong was decided in favor of the news generators; in June 2014 the second prong was decided by the Court of Justice of the European Union (CJEU), which ruled that the temporary web cache of consumers of the aggregator did not infringe the copyright of the news generators.

Non-infringing types of works

In order to qualify for protection, a work must be an expression with a degree of originality, and it must be in a fixed medium, such as written down on paper or recorded digitally. The idea itself is not protected. That is, a copy of someone else's original idea is not infringing unless it copies that person's unique, tangible expression of the idea. Some of these limitations, especially regarding what qualifies as original, are embodied only in case law (judicial precedent), rather than in statutes.

In the U.S., for example, copyright case law contains a substantial similarity requirement to determine whether the work was copied. Likewise, courts may require computer software to pass an Abstraction-Filtration-Comparison test (AFC Test) to determine if it is too abstract to qualify for protection, or too dissimilar to an original work to be considered infringing. Software-related case law has also clarified that the amount of R&D, effort and expense put into a work's creation doesn't affect copyright protection.

Evaluation of alleged copyright infringement in a court of law may be substantial; the time and costs required to apply these tests vary based on the size and complexity of the copyrighted material. Furthermore, there is no standard or universally accepted test; some courts have rejected the AFC Test, for example, in favor of narrower criteria.

The POSAR test, a recently devised forensic procedure for establishing software copyright infringement cases, is an extension or an enhancement of the AFC test. POSAR, with its added features and additional facilities, offers something more to the legal and the judicial domain than what the AFC test offers. These additional features and facilities make the test more sensitive to the technical and legal requirements of software copyright infringement.

Preventative measures

The BSA outlined four strategies that governments can adopt to reduce software piracy rates in its 2011 piracy study results:

- "Increase public education and raise awareness about software piracy and IP rights in cooperation with industry and law enforcement."
- "Modernize protections for software and other copyrighted materials to keep pace with new innovations such as cloud computing and the proliferation of networked mobile devices."
- "Strengthen enforcement of IP laws with dedicated resources, including specialized enforcement units, training for law enforcement and judiciary officials, improved cross-border cooperation among law enforcement agencies, and fulfillment of obligations under the World Trade Organization's Agreement on Trade-Related Aspects of Intellectual Property Rights (TRIPS)."
- "Lead by example by using only fully licensed software, implementing software asset management (SAM) programs, and promoting the use of legal software in state-owned enterprises, and among all contractors and suppliers."

Legal

Corporations and legislatures take different types of preventative measures to deter copyright infringement, with much of the focus since the early 1990s being on preventing or reducing digital methods of infringement. Strategies include education, civil & criminal legislation, and international agreements, as well as publicizing anti-piracy litigation successes and imposing forms of digital media copy protection, such as controversial DRM technology and anti-circumvention laws, which limit the amount of control consumers have over the use of products and content they have purchased.

Legislatures have reduced infringement by narrowing the scope of what is considered infringing. Aside from upholding international copyright treaty obligations to provide general limitations and exceptions, nations have enacted compulsory licensing laws applying specifically to digital works and uses. For example, in the U.S., the DMCA, an implementation of the 1996 WIPO Copyright Treaty, considers digital transmissions of audio recordings to be licensed as long as a designated copyright collective's royalty and reporting requirements are met. The DMCA also provides safe harbor for digital service providers whose users are suspected of copyright infringement, thus reducing the likelihood that the providers themselves will be considered directly infringing.

Some copyright owners voluntarily reduce the scope of what is considered infringement by employing relatively permissive, "open" licensing strategies: rather than privately negotiating license terms with individual users who must first seek out the copyright owner and ask for permission, the copyright owner publishes and distributes the work with a prepared license that anyone can use, as long as they adhere to certain conditions. This has the effect of reducing infringement – and the burden on courts – by simply permitting certain types of uses under terms that the copyright owner considers reasonable. Examples include free software licenses, like the GNU General Public License (GPL), and the Creative Commons licenses, which are predominantly applied to visual and literary works.

Protected distribution

To prevent piracy of films, the standard drill of film distribution is to have a movie first released through movie theaters (theatrical window), on average approximately 16 and a half weeks, before having it released to Blu-Ray and DVD (entering its video window). During the theatrical window, digital versions of films are often transported in data storage devices by couriers rather than by data transmission. The data can be encrypted, with the key being made to work only at specific times in order to prevent leakage between screens. Coded Anti-Piracy marks can be added to films to identify the source of illegal copies and shut them down.

Economic impact of copyright infringement

Organizations disagree on the scope and magnitude of copyright infringement's free rider economic effects and public support for the copyright regime.

The European Commission funded a study to analyze "the extent to which unauthorised online consumption of copyrighted materials (music, audiovisual, books and video games) displaces sales of online and offline legal content", across Germany, the United Kingdom, Spain, France, Poland and Sweden; the public funding behind the study provided a necessary basis for its neutrality. 30,000 users, including minors between 14 and 17 years, were surveyed among September and October 2014. While a negative impact was found for the film industry, videogame sales were positively affected by illegal consumption, possibly due to "the industry being successful in converting illegal users to paying users" and employing player-oriented strategies (for example, by providing additional bonus levels or items in the gameplay for a fee); finally, no evidence was found for any claims of sales displacement in the other market sectors. According to the European Digital Rights association, the study may have been censored: specifically, as of 2018, the European Commission has not published the results, except in the part where the film industry was found to be adversely affected by illegal content consumption. Access to the study was requested and obtained by Member of the European Parliament Julia Reda.

In relation to computer software, the Business Software Alliance (BSA) claimed in its 2011 piracy study: "Public opinion continues to support intellectual property (IP) rights: Seven PC users in 10 support paying innovators to promote more technological advances."

Following consultation with experts on copyright infringement, the United States Government Accountability Office (GAO) clarified in 2010 that "estimating the economic impact of IP [intellectual property] infringements is extremely difficult, and assumptions must be used due to the absence of data," while "it is difficult, if not impossible, to quantify the net effect of counterfeiting and piracy on the economy as a whole."

The U.S. GAO's 2010 findings regarding the great difficulty of accurately gauging the economic impact of copyright infringement was reinforced within the same report by the body's research into three commonly cited estimates that had previously been provided to U.S. agencies. The GAO report explained that the sources – a Federal Bureau of Investigation(FBI) estimate, a Customs and Border Protection (CBP) press release and a Motor and Equipment Manufacturers Association estimate – "cannot be substantiated or traced back to an underlying data source or methodology."

Deaner explained the importance of rewarding the "investment risk" taken by motion picture studios in 2014:

Usually movies are hot because a distributor has spent hundreds of thousands of dollars promoting the product in print and TV and other forms of advertising. The major Hollywood studios spend millions on this process with marketing costs rivalling the costs of production. They are attempting then to monetise through returns that can justify the investment in both the costs of promotion and production.

Motion picture industry estimates

In 2008, the Motion Picture Association of America (MPAA) reported that its six major member companies lost US$6.1 billion to piracy. A 2009 Los Angeles Daily News article then cited a loss figure of "roughly $20 billion a year" for Hollywood studios. According to a 2013 Wall Street Journal article, industry estimates in the United States range between $6.1B to $18.5B per year.

In an early May 2014 Guardian article, an annual loss figure of US$20.5 billion was cited for the movie industry. The article's basis is the results of a University of Portsmouth study that only involved Finnish participants, aged between seven and 84. The researchers, who worked with 6,000 participants, stated: "Movie pirates are also more likely to cut down their piracy if they feel they are harming the industry compared with people who illegally download music".

However, a study conducted on data from sixteen countries between 2005 and 2013, many of which had enacted anti-piracy measures to increase box office revenues of movies, found no significant increases in any markets attributable to policy interventions, which calls into doubt the claimed negative economic effects of digital piracy on the film industry.

Software industry estimates

Psion Software claimed in 1983 that software piracy cost it £2.9 million a year, 30% of its revenue. According to a 2007 BSA and International Data Corporation (IDC) study, the five countries with the highest rates of software piracy were: 1. Armenia (93%); 2. Bangladesh (92%); 3. Azerbaijan (92%); 4. Moldova (92%); and 5. Zimbabwe (91%). According to the study's results, the five countries with the lowest piracy rates were: 1. U.S. (20%); 2. Luxembourg (21%); 3. New Zealand (22%); 4. Japan (23%); and 5. Austria (25%). The 2007 report showed that the Asia-Pacific region was associated with the highest amount of loss, in terms of U.S. dollars, with $14,090,000, followed by the European Union, with a loss of $12,383,000; the lowest amount of U.S. dollars was lost in the Middle East/Africa region, where $2,446,000 was documented.

In its 2011 report, conducted in partnership with IDC and Ipsos Public Affairs, the BSA stated: "Over half of the world's personal computer users – 57 percent – admit to pirating software." The ninth annual "BSA Global Software Piracy Study" claims that the "commercial value of this shadow market of pirated software" was worth US$63.4 billion in 2011, with the highest commercial value of pirated PC software existent in the U.S. during that time period (US$9,773,000). According to the 2011 study, Zimbabwe was the nation with the highest piracy rate, at 92%, while the lowest piracy rate was present in the U.S., at 19%.

The GAO noted in 2010 that the BSA's research up until that year defined "piracy as the difference between total installed software and legitimate software sold, and its scope involved only packaged physical software."

Music industry estimates

In 2007, the Institute for Policy Innovation (IPI) reported that music piracy took $12.5 billion from the U.S. economy. According to the study, musicians and those involved in the recording industry are not the only ones who experience losses attributed to music piracy. Retailers have lost over a billion dollars, while piracy has resulted in 46,000 fewer production-level jobs and almost 25,000 retail jobs. The U.S. government was also reported to suffer from music piracy, losing $422 million in tax revenue.

A report from 2013, released by the European Commission Joint Research Centre suggests that illegal music downloads have almost no effect on the number of legal music downloads. The study analyzed the behavior of 16,000 European music consumers and found that although music piracy negatively affects offline music sales, illegal music downloads had a positive effect on legal music purchases. Without illegal downloading, legal purchases were about two percent lower.

The study has received criticism, particularly from The International Federation of the Phonographic Industry, which believes the study is flawed and misleading. One argument against the research is that many music consumers only download music illegally. The IFPI also points out that music piracy affects not only online music sales but also multiple facets of the music industry, which is not addressed in the study.

Criticism of industry estimates

The methodology of studies utilized by industry spokespeople has been heavily criticized. Inflated claims for damages and allegations of economic harm are common in copyright disputes. Some studies and figures, including those cited by the MPAA and RIAA with regards to the economic effects of film and music downloads, have been widely disputed as based on questionable assumptions which resulted in statistically unsound numbers.

In one extreme example, the RIAA claimed damages against LimeWire totaling $75 trillion – more than the global GDP – and "respectfully" disagreed with the judge's ruling that such claims were "absurd".

However, this $75 trillion figure is obtained through one specific interpretation of copyright law that would count each song downloaded as an infringement of copyright. After the conclusion of the case, LimeWire agreed to pay $105 million to RIAA.

The judicial system has also found flaws in industry estimates and calculations. In one decision, US District Court Judge James P. Jones found that the "RIAA's request problematically assumes that every illegal download resulted in a lost sale," indicating profit-loss estimates were likely extremely off.

Other critics of industry estimates argue that those who use peer-to-peer sharing services, or practice "piracy" are actually more likely to pay for music. A Jupiter Research study in 2000 found that "Napster users were 45 percent more likely to have increased their music purchasing habits than online music fans who don't use the software were." This indicated that users of peer-to-peer sharing didn't hurt the profits of the music industry, but in fact may have increased it.

Professor Aram Sinnreich, in his book The Piracy Crusade, states that the connection between declining music sales and the creation of peer to peer file sharing sites such as Napster is tenuous, based on correlation rather than causation. He argues that the industry at the time was undergoing artificial expansion, what he describes as a "'perfect bubble'—a confluence of economic, political, and technological forces that drove the aggregate value of music sales to unprecedented heights at the end of the twentieth century".

Sinnreich cites multiple causes for the economic bubble, including the CD format replacement cycle; the shift from music specialty stores to wholesale suppliers of music and 'minimum advertised pricing'; and the economic expansion of 1991–2001. He believes that with the introduction of new digital technologies, the bubble burst, and the industry suffered as a result.

Economic impact of infringement in emerging markets

The 2011 Business Software Alliance Piracy Study Standard, estimates the total commercial value of illegally copied software to be at $59 billion in 2010, with emerging markets accounting for $31.9 billion, over half of the total. Furthermore, mature markets for the first time received less PC shipments than emerging economies in 2010. In addition with software infringement rates of 68 percent comparing to 24 percent of mature markets, emerging markets thus possess the majority of the global increase in the commercial value of counterfeit software. China continues to have the highest commercial value of such software at $8.9 billion among developing countries and second in the world behind the US at $9.7 billion in 2011. In 2011, the Business Software Alliance announced that 83 percent of software deployed on PCs in Africa has been pirated (excluding South Africa).

Some countries distinguish corporate piracy from private use, which is tolerated as a welfare service. This is the leading reason developing countries refuse to accept or respect copyright laws. Traian Băsescu, the president of Romania, stated that "piracy helped the young generation discover computers. It set off the development of the IT industry in Romania."

Pro-open culture organizations

Main articles: Anti-copyright and Free culture movement

- Free Software Foundation (FSF)
- Electronic Frontier Foundation (EFF)
- Creative Commons (CC)
- Demand Progress
- Fight for the Future
- Pirate Party
- Plan S, by major funders of scientific research

Anti-copyright infringement organizations

- Business Software Alliance (BSA)
- Canadian Alliance Against Software Theft (CAAST)
- Entertainment Software Association (ESA)
- Federation Against Software Theft (FAST)
- International Intellectual Property Alliance (IIPA)

12

Obscenity and Pornography

An obscenity is any utterance or act that strongly offends the prevalent morality of the time. It is derived from the Latin obscaena (offstage) a cognate of the Ancient Greek root skene, because some potentially offensive content, such as murder or sex, was depicted offstage in classical drama. The word can be used to indicate a strong moral repugnance, in expressions such as "obscene profits" or "the obscenity of war". As a legal term, it usually refers to graphic depictions of people engaged in sexual and excretory activity.

United States obscenity law

Cover of an undated American edition of Fanny Hill, ca. 1910

In the United States of America, issues of obscenity raise issues of limitations on the freedom of speech and of the press, which are otherwise protected by the First Amendment to the Constitution of the United States.

Federal obscenity law in the U.S. is unusual in that there is no uniform national standard. Former Justice Potter Stewart of the Supreme Court of the United States, in attempting to classify what material constituted exactly "what is obscene," famously wrote, "I shall not today attempt further to define the kinds of material I understand to be embraced ... [b]ut I know it when I see it...." In the United States, the 1973 ruling of the Supreme Court of the United States in Miller v. California established a three-tiered test to determine what was obscene—and thus not protected, versus what was merely erotic and thus protected by the First Amendment.

Delivering the opinion of the court, Chief Justice Warren Burger wrote:

The basic guidelines for the trier of fact must be: (a) whether the average person, applying contemporary community standards would find that the work, taken as a whole, appeals to the prurient interest, (b) whether the work depicts or describes, in a patently offensive way, sexual conduct specifically defined by the applicable state law; and (c) whether the work, taken as a whole, lacks serious literary, artistic, political, or scientific value.

Non image-based obscenity cases in the U.S.

While most recent (2016) obscenity cases in the United States have revolved around images and films, the first obscenity cases dealt with textual works.

The classification of "obscene" and thus illegal for production and distribution has been judged on printed text-only stories starting with "Dunlop v. U.S., 165 U.S. 486 (1897)", which upheld a conviction for mailing and delivery of a newspaper called the 'Chicago Dispatch,' containing "obscene, lewd, lascivious, and indecent materials", which was later upheld in several cases. One of these was "A Book Named John Cleland's Memoirs of a Woman of Pleasure" v. Attorney General of Com. of Massachusetts, "383 U.S. 413 (1966)" wherein the book "Fanny Hill", written by John Cleland c. 1760, was judged to be obscene in a proceeding that put the book itself on trial rather than its publisher. Another was "Kaplan v. California, 413 U.S. 115 (1973)" whereby the court most famously determined that "Obscene material in book form is not entitled to any First Amendment protection merely because it has no pictorial content."

In 2005, the U.S. Department of Justice formed the Obscenity Prosecution Task Force in a push to prosecute obscenity cases. Red Rose Stories, a site dedicated to text-only fantasy stories, became one of many sites targeted by the FBI for shutdown. The government alleged that Red Rose Stories contained depictions of child rape. The publisher pleaded guilty. Extreme pornographer Max Hardcore served 30 months of a 46-month prison sentence for obscenity.

Many U.S. states have had bans on the sale of sex toys, regulating them as obscene devices. Some states have seen their sex toy bans ruled unconstitutional in the courts. That ruling leaves only Mississippi, Alabama, and Virginia with current bans on the sale of obscene devices.

Literature (non-fiction) communicating contraceptive information was prohibited by several states. The last such prohibition, in Connecticut, was overturned judicially in 1965.

Key U.S. court cases on obscenity

• In 1957, two associates of acclaimed poet Allen Ginsberg were arrested and jailed for selling his book "Howl and Other Poems" to undercover police officers at a beatnik bookstore in San Francisco. Eventually the California Supreme Court declared the literature to be of "redeeming social value" and therefore not classifiable as "obscene". Because the poem "Howl" contains pornographic slang and overt references to drugs and homosexuality, the poem was (and is) frequently censored and confiscated; however, it remains a landmark case.

• FCC v. Pacifica (1978) (external link) better known as the landmark "seven dirty words" case. In that ruling, the Court found that only "repetitive and frequent" use of the words in a time or place when a minor could hear can be punished.

• In State v. Henry (1987), the Oregon Supreme Court ruled that the Oregon state law that criminalized obscenity was an unconstitutional restriction of free speech under the free speech provision of the Oregon Constitution, with the ruling making Oregon the "first state in the nation to abolish the offense of obscenity."

• In Reno v. ACLU (1997), the Supreme Court struck down indecency laws applying to the Internet.

• In Miller v. California (1973) - the currently-binding Supreme Court precedent on the issue - the Court ruled materials were obscene if they appealed, "to a prurient interest", showed "patently offensive sexual conduct" that was specifically defined by a state obscenity law, and "lacked serious artistic, literary, political, or scientific value." Decisions regarding whether material was obscene should be based on local, not national, standards.

Standards superseded by the Miller Test include:

• Wepplo (1947): If material has a substantial tendency to deprave or corrupt its readers by inciting lascivious thoughts or arousing lustful desires.

(People v. Wepplo, 78 Cal. App.2d Supp. 959, 178 P.2d 853).

- Hicklin test (1868): the effect of isolated passages upon the most susceptible persons. (British common law, cited in Regina v. Hicklin, 1868. LR 3 QB 360 - overturned when Michigan tried to outlaw all printed matter that would 'corrupt the morals of youth' in Butler v. State of Michigan 352 U.S. 380 (1957))

- Roth Standard (1957): "Whether to the average person applying contemporary community standards, the dominant theme of the material, taken as a whole, appeals to the prurient interest". Roth v. United States 354 U.S. 476 (1957) - overturned by Miller

- Roth-Jacobellis (1964): "community standards" applicable to an obscenity are national, not local standards. Material is "utterly without redeeming social importance". Jacobellis v. Ohio 378 US 184 (1964) - famous quote: "I shall not today attempt further to define [hardcore pornography] ...But I know it when I see it."

- Roth-Jacobellis-Memoirs Test (1966): Adds that the material possesses "not a modicum of social value". (A Book Named John Cleland's Memoirs of a Woman of Pleasure v. Attorney General of Massachusetts, 383 U.S. 413 (1966))

FCC rules and federal law govern obscenity in broadcast media. Many historically important works have been described as obscene or prosecuted under obscenity laws, including the works of Charles Baudelaire, Lenny Bruce, William S. Burroughs, Allen Ginsberg, James Joyce, D. H. Lawrence, Henry Miller, Samuel Beckett, and the Marquis de Sade.

Criticism

Obscenity law has been criticized in the following areas:

- Federal law forbids obscenity in certain contexts (such as broadcast); however, the law does not define the term.

- The U.S. Supreme Court similarly has had difficulty defining the term. In Miller v. California, the court defers definition to two hypothetical entities, "contemporary community standards" and "hypothetical reasonable persons".

- The courts and the legislature have had similar problems defining this term because it is paradoxical, and thus impossible to define.

- Because the term "obscenity" is not defined by either the statutes or the case law, this law does not satisfy the Vagueness doctrine, which states that people must clearly be informed as to the prohibited behavior.

- Because the determination of what is obscene (offensive) is ultimately a personal preference, alleged violations of obscenity law are not actionable (actions require a right).

• Because no actual injury occurs when a mere preference is violated, alleged violations of obscenity law are not actionable (actions require an injury).

Obscenity laws remain enforceable under Miller despite these criticisms. Some states have passed laws mandating censorship in schools, universities, and libraries even if they are not receiving government aid that would require censorship in these institutions. These include Arizona, Kentucky, Michigan, Minnesota, South Carolina, and Tennessee. Twenty more states were considering such legislation in 2001–2002.

Child pornography

Child pornography refers to images or films (also known as child abuse images); as such, visual child pornography is a record of child sexual abuse. Abuse of the child occurs during the sexual acts that are recorded in the production of child pornography, and several professors of psychology state that memories of the abuse are maintained as long as visual records exist, are accessed, and are "exploited perversely." Some countries also bans writings— that depict sexually explicit activities involving a child.

In New York v. Ferber, 458 U.S. 747 (1982), the U.S. Supreme Court ruled that child pornography need not be legally obscene in order to be outlawed. The Court ruled that in contrast to the types of images considered in Miller, images that depicted underlying harm to children need not appeal to "the prurient interest of the average person," portray sexual conduct in "a patently offensive manner," nor be considered holistically, in order to be proscribed. Another difference between U.S. constitutional law concerning obscenity and that governing child pornography is that the Supreme Court ruled in Stanley v. Georgia, 394 U.S. 557 (1969), that possession of obscene material could not be criminalized, while in Osborne v. Ohio, 495 U.S. 103 (1990), the high court ruled that possession of child pornography could be criminalized. The reason was that the motive for criminalizing child pornography possession was "to destroy a market for the exploitative use of children" rather than to prevent the material from poisoning the minds of its viewers. The three dissenting justices in that case argued, "While the sexual exploitation of children is undoubtedly a serious problem, Ohio may employ other weapons to combat it."

Censorship in film

This is most notably shown with the "X" rating under which some films are categorized. The most notable films given an "X" rating were Deep Throat (1972) and The Devil in Miss Jones (1973). These films show explicit, non-simulated, penetrative sex that was presented as part of a reasonable plot with respectable production values. Some state authorities issued injunctions against such films to protect "local community standards"; in New York, the print of

Deep Throat was seized mid-run, and the film's exhibitors were found guilty of promoting obscenity. According to the documentary This Film Is Not Yet Rated, films that include gay sex (even if implied) or female pleasure have been more harshly censored than their heterosexual, male counterparts. The Motion Picture Association of America (MPAA) issues ratings for motion pictures exhibited and distributed commercially to the public in the United States; the ratings are issued through the Classification and Rating Administration (CARA). The intent of the rating system is to provide information about the content of motion pictures so parents can determine whether an individual motion picture is suitable for viewing by their children.

United Kingdom

In the United Kingdom, the Obscene Publications Acts sets the criteria for what material is allowed to be publicly accessed and distributed.

Stanley Kauffmann's novel The Philanderer was published by Penguin Books in 1957 and was unsuccessfully prosecuted for obscenity.

Sex crime has generated particular concern. In 1976 the BBFC claimed that, in that year, it had viewed 58 films depicting "explicit rape", declaring scenes that glorified it as "obscene". As opposed to questions of "indecency", which have been applied to sexual explicitness, films charged with being obscene have been viewed as having "a tendency to deprave and corrupt" and been liable to prosecution.

In 2008, the UK prosecuted a man for writing a fictional sex story (R v Walker). In 2009, the crown prosecution service (CPS) dropped the case.

Obscenity law in England and Wales is currently governed by the Obscene Publications Act, but obscenity law goes back much further into the English common law. The conviction in 1727 of Edmund Curll for the publication of Venus in the Cloister or the Nun in her Smock under the common law offence of disturbing the peace appears to be the first conviction for obscenity in the United Kingdom, and set a legal precedent for other convictions. These common law ideas of obscenity formed the original basis of obscenity law in other common law countries, such as the United States.

For visual works of art the main obscenity law in England and Wales was, until the 1960s, the Vagrancy Act 1838 which was successfully used in prosecutions against D.H. Lawrence for an exhibition of his paintings at the Warren Gallery, London, in 1929, and in 1966 against the British artist Stass Paraskos for an exhibition of his paintings held that year in the northern English city of Leeds. Parts of the Act were repealed shortly after the Paraskos trial and it has rarely been used since in relation to visual art.

The Obscene Publications act is notoriously vague, defining obscenity as material likely to "deprave and corrupt". The 1959 act was passed just as most

Western countries were about to enter a new phase of sexual freedom. The trial of Penguin Books over Lady Chatterley's Lover in 1960 failed to secure a conviction and the conviction in the 1971 trial of Oz magazine was overturned on appeal. An attempt to prosecute the University of Central England in 1997 over a copy of a library book by Robert Mapplethorpe was abandoned amidst derision from academics and the media.

During the 1960s and 1970s most Western countries legalised hardcore pornography. By the 1980s the UK was almost the only liberal democracy where the sale of hardcore pornography was still completely illegal, although ownership was not a criminal offence (except child pornography). Home videotape was a booming market and it was relatively simple for individuals to smuggle hardcore material in from Europe or the United States, where it had been purchased legally, either for personal use or to copy it for distribution. This resulted in a considerable black market of poor quality videotapes. Meanwhile, people attempting to buy pornography legally would often be stuck with heavily censored R18 certificate material.

While the authorities did their best to stay on top of illegal pornography they found that juries, while not particularly liking the material, were reluctant to convict defendants where the material was intended for private use among consenting adults. During the 1990s the advent of the internet made it easier than ever before for British citizens to access hardcore material. Finally, in 2000, following the dismissal of a test case brought by the BBFC, hardcore pornography was effectively legalised, subject to certain conditions and licensing restrictions. It is still an offence to sell obscene material by mail order.

After 1984 videotape sellers were more likely to be prosecuted under the Video Recordings Act rather than the OPA. The VRA requires that all videos must have a certificate from the BBFC. If the BBFC refuses a certificate a video is effectively banned for home viewing, but not necessarily in the cinema. Four films that were originally refused a certificate, The Exorcist, Straw Dogs, The Evil Dead and The Texas Chainsaw Massacre were granted a certificate in the late 1990s and have subsequently been screened on mainstream television.

New Zealand

In New Zealand, screening of Deep Throat (1972) was only cleared in 1986. However, the film has not been screened because the only cinema that has tried to organize a screening was thwarted by the city council that owned the building's lease.

Canada

Section 163 of the Canadian Criminal Code provides the country's legal definition of "obscenity". Officially termed as "Offences Tending to Corrupt Morals", the Canadian prohibited class of articles that are to be legally included as "obscene things" is very broad, including text-only written material, pictures, models (including statues), records or "any other thing whatsoever"—that according to Section 163(8)—has "a dominant characteristic of the publication is the undue exploitation of sex, or the combination of sex and at least one of crime, horror, cruelty or violence" is deemed to be "obscene" under the current law.

The current law states

163. (1) Every one commits an offense who

(a) makes, prints, publishes, distributes, circulates, or has in his possession for the purpose of publication, distribution or circulation any obscene written matter, picture, model, phonograph record or other thing whatever; or

(b) makes, prints, publishes, distributes, sells or has in his possession for the purposes of publication, distribution or circulation a crime comic.

"Crime comics" are stated to be books that glorify criminal activities and have at least one depiction of such criminal actions of the book's text.

The Canada Border Services Agency seizes items it labels obscene.

In 1993, Canadian police arrested the 19-year-old writer of a fictional sex story "The Forestwood Kids" however the case was dismissed in 1995.

In February 2009, citing its Policy On The Classification Of Obscene Material, the CBSA banned two Lucas Entertainment films because they show the "ingestion of someone else's urine... with a sexual purpose".

Brazil

Ever since 1940, in the Title VI of the Penal Code, naming crimes against sexual dignity (until 2009 crimes against social conventions), the fourth chapter is dedicated to a crime named "public outrage related to modesty" (Portuguese: ultraje público ao pudor, pronounced [uw□t□a□i □publikw aw pu□do□]).

It is composed of two articles, Art. 233 "Obscene Act", "to practice an obscene act in a public place, or open or exposed to the public", punished with arrest of 3 months to 1 year or a fine; and Art. 234 "Obscene Written Piece or Object", to do, import, export, purchase or have in one's property, to ends of trade, distribution or public display, any written, drew, painted, stamped or object piece of obscenity, punished with arrest of 6 months to 1 years or a fine.

Criticism to the legislation have included:

- They do not attack anyone's sexual dignity, instead causing outrage at best, but generally just slight discomfort or embarrassment, that can be easily avoided through not looking to such a scene.

• The Art. 234 is aside obsolete, unconstitutional, for the 1988 post-military dictatorship Constitution having in its Fifth Chapter: "[the people] are free to the expression of intellectual, artistic, scientific and communicative activity, independently of censorship and license", reason to which, instead of making it suffer penal restriction, gives any distribution of media the right to be fully exerted.

• The flourishing internet culture of Brazil, where such media is freely shared, as well as its pornographic industry and shops catered to the interests of enhancing apparatus to masturbatory and sexual activity.

It is often used against people who expose their nude bodies in public environments that were not warranted a license to cater to the demographic interested in such practice (the first such place was the Praia do Abricó in Rio de Janeiro, in 1994), even if no sexual action took place, and it may include for example a double standard for the chest area of women and men in which only women are penalized. Such a thing took place in FEMEN protests in São Paulo, in 2012.

South Korea

In 2017 the Supreme Court in South Korea ruled that an image of unclothed male genitalia is obscene if not contextualized in a cultural, artistic, medical or educational setting.

Other countries

Various countries have different standings on the types of materials that they as legal bodies permit their citizens to have access to and disseminate among their local populations. The set of these countries' permissible content vary widely accordingly with some having extreme punishment up to and including execution for members who violate their restrictions, as in the case of Iran where the current laws against pornography now include death sentences for those convicted of producing pornography.

In India the Obscenity law is the same as had been framed by the British Government. Charges of obscenity have been levelled against various writers and poets till date; the law has not yet been revised. The famous trials relate to the Hungryalists who were arrested and prosecuted in the 1960s.

Obscenity is a confounding area of First Amendment law

Obscenity remains one of the most controversial and confounding areas of First Amendment law, and Supreme Court justices have struggled mightily through the years to define it. Justice Potter Stewart could provide no definition for obscenity in Jacobellis v. Ohio (1964), but he did exclaim: "I know it when I see it." Stewart found that the Court was "faced with the task of trying to define what may be indefinable." In a later case, Interstate Circuit, Inc. v. Dallas (1968), Justice John Marshall Harlan II referred to this area as the "intractable obscenity problem."

controversial and confounding areas of First Amendment law, and Supreme Court justices have struggled mightily through the years to define it. Harry Reems co-star of the film "Deep Throat" is shown in this 1976 booking photo. The movie was a forerunner of today's hardcore adult-entertainment industry and a touchstone for obscenity laws. Reems was convicted of obscenity charges in 1976 for his role in the movie and faced a potential five-year prison term. Celebrities such as Jack Nicholson and Warren Beatty came to Reems' defense, and the conviction was later overturned. (AP Photo/ho, used with permission from the Associated Press)

The Hicklin rule was a broad and suppressive test

Several early U.S. courts adopted a standard for obscenity from the British case Regina v. Hicklin (1868). The Hicklin rule provided the following test for obscenity: "whether the tendency of the matter . . . is to deprave and corrupt those whose minds are open to such immoral influences, and into whose hands a publication of this sort may fall."

This test allowed material to be declared obscene based on isolated passages of a work and its effect on particularly susceptible persons. Using this broad test, the British court ruled obscene books deemed to be anti-religious. The two major problems with the Hicklin test were that it allowed works to be judged obscene based on isolated passages, and it focused on particularly susceptible persons instead of reasonable persons. This focus led to suppression of much free expression.

The Roth test focused on the theme of the material and the average, reasonable person

The Supreme Court squarely confronted the obscenity question in Roth v. United States (1957), a case contesting the constitutionality of a federal law prohibiting the mailing of any material that is "obscene, lewd, lascivious, or filthy . . . or other publication of an indecent character." The Court, in an opinion drafted by Justice William J. Brennan Jr., determined that "obscenity is not within the area of constitutionally protected speech or press." He articulated a new test for obscenity: "whether to the average person, applying contemporary community standards, the dominant theme of the material taken as a whole appeals to the prurient interest." The Roth test differed from the Hicklin test in that it focused on "the dominant theme" of the material as opposed to isolated passages and on the average person rather than the most susceptible person.

In Miller, the Court reasoned that individuals could not be convicted of obscenity charges unless the materials depict "patently offensive hard core sexual conduct." Under that reasoning, many sexually explicit materials — pornographic magazines, books, and movies — are not legally obscene. In this photo, Luther Campbell, leader of hip hop group of 2 Live Crew and president of its record label, points to the warning sticker on his shirt, identical to the one on the group's controversial album "Nasty As They Wanna Be" outside federal court Florida in 1990. The group filed a suit trying to stop obscenity arrests for the sales of their album. (AP Photo/Beth Keiser, used with permission from the Associated Press)

Brennan articulated a new test

The Court struggled with obscenity cases through the 1960s and 1970s. In Memoirs v. Massachusetts (1966), a plurality of the Court, in an opinion by Justice Brennan, articulated a new three-part test:

• "(a) the dominant theme of the material taken as a whole appeals to a prurient interest in sex;

• (b) the material is patently offensive because it affronts contemporary community standards relating to the description or representation of sexual matters;

• and (c) the material is utterly without redeeming social value."

The Miller test is now the leading test for obscenity cases

In the 1970s, the Burger Court determined that the obscenity standard was too rigid for prosecutors. Therefore, in Miller v. California (1973) the Court adopted a new three-part test — what Chief Justice Warren E. Burger called "guidelines" for jurors — that was more favorable to the prosecution:

• (1) whether the average person, applying contemporary community standards, would find that the work, taken as a whole, appeals to the prurient interest;

• (2) whether the work depicts or describes, in a patently offensive way, sexual conduct specifically defined by the applicable state law;

• and (3) whether the work, taken as a whole, lacks serious literary, artistic, political, or scientific value.

In Miller, the Court reasoned that individuals could not be convicted of obscenity charges unless the materials depict "patently offensive hard core sexual conduct." Under that reasoning, many sexually explicit materials — pornographic magazines, books, and movies — are not legally obscene. Ironically, Justice Brennan dissented in Miller and Paris Adult Theatre I v. Slaton (1973), changing his position on obscenity. He determined that obscenity laws were too vague and could not be applied without "jeopardizing fundamental First Amendment values."

The contemporary community standards prong of the Miller test is confusing in the Internet Age

The Miller test remains the leading test for obscenity cases, but it continues to stir debate. In its 1987 decision in Pope v. Illinois (1987), the Court clarified that the "serious value" prong of the Miller test was not to be judged by contemporary community standards. Obscenity prosecutions do, however, impose contemporary community standards, even though a distributor may transport materials to various communities. Thus interesting issues emerge when a defendant in California is prosecuted in a locale with more restrictive community standards.

This phenomenon has caused some legal experts and interested observers to call for the creation of a national standard, particularly in the age of the Internet. In Ashcroft v. American Civil Liberties Union (2002), several justices expressed concern about applying local community standards to the Internet as required by the Child Online Protection Act of 1998. For example, Justice Stephen G. Breyer wrote in his concurring opinion that "to read the statute as adopting the community standards of every locality in the United States would provide the most puritan of communities with a heckler's veto affecting the rest of the Nation." Similarly, Justice Sandra Day O'Connor, in her concurrence, wrote that "adoption of a national standard is necessary in my view for any reasonable regulation of Internet obscenity."

The Miller test remains the leading test for obscenity cases, but it continues to stir debate. In this photo, activists demonstrate in the streets of downtown Cincinnati, Ohio, on September 24, 1990, as jury selection began in the obscenity charges against the Contemporary Arts Center for exhibiting photographs by late artist Robert Mapplethorpe. (AP Photo, used with permission from the Associated Press)

The Court has resisted categorizing violence as obscenity

The Supreme Court has resisted efforts to extend the rationale of obscenity from hard-core sexual materials to hard-core violence. The state of California sought to advance the concept of violence as obscenity in defending its state law regulating the sale or rental of violent video games to minors. The Court invalidated the law in Brown v. Entertainment Merchants Association (2011), writing that "violence is not part of the obscenity that the Constitution permits to be regulated."

Federal and state obscenity prosecutions have continued

Federal obscenity prosecutions increased during the George W. Bush administration. States continued to pursue obscenity prosecutions against hard-core pornography, but also occasionally against other materials. For example, in 1994 a comic book artist was convicted of obscenity in Florida, and in 1999 the owner of gay bar in Nebraska was successfully prosecuted for displaying a gay art in a basement. Although obscenity laws have their critics, they likely will remain part of the legal system and First Amendment jurisprudence.

While federal obscenity prosecutions waned during the Barack Obama administration, state obscenity prosecutions continue in the 21 century. In this light, Professor Jennifer Kinsley refers to the argument that obscenity law is a thing of the past as "the myth of obsolete obscenity."

Pornography refers to material dealing with sex designed to arouse its readers or viewers. Webster's Dictionary defines "pornography" as "writings, pictures, etc. intended primarily to arouse sexual desire."

There are two types of pornography that receive no First Amendment protection — obscenity and child pornography. The First Amendment generally protects pornography that does not fall into one of these two categories — at least for adult viewers. Sometimes, material is classified as "harmful to minors" even though adults can have access to the same material.

Even a 1986 Attorney General Commission Report on Pornography said that "not all pornography is legally obscene." The question becomes what types of pornography cross the line into the unprotected categories of obscenity and child pornography. Or to put it another way, courts often struggle with whether pornography is too "hard core."

Obscenity

Obscenity remains one of the most controversial and confounding areas of First Amendment law. U.S. Supreme Court justices have struggled mightily through the years to define it. Justice Potter Stewart could provide no definition in Jacobellis v. Ohio other than exclaiming: "I know it when I see it." In that 1964 decision, Stewart also said that the Court was "faced with the task of trying to define what may be indefinable."

Justice Hugo Black expressed his frustration with determining whether certain pornography could be prohibited under the First Amendment when he wrote in Mishkin v. State of N.Y.: "I wish once more to express my objections to saddling this Court with the irksome and inevitably unpopular and unwholesome task of finally deciding by a case-by-case, sight-by-sight personal judgment of the members of this Court what pornography (whatever that means) is too hard core for people to see or read."

After grappling with the obscenity problem in many cases during the late 1950s and early 1960s, the Supreme Court laid out "basic guidelines" for jurors in obscenity cases in its 1973 decision Miller v. California. These include:

• Whether the average person, applying contemporary community standards, would find that the work, taken as a whole, appeals to the prurient interest.

• Whether the work depicts or describes, in a patently offensive way, sexual conduct specifically defined by the applicable state law.

• Whether the work, taken as a whole, lacks serious literary, artistic, political or scientific value.

The Court reasoned that individuals could not be convicted of obscenity charges unless the materials depict "patently offensive hard core sexual conduct." This means that many materials dealing with sex, including pornographic magazines, books, and movies, simply do not qualify as legally obscene.

Even more fundamentally, nudity does not equal obscenity. The Supreme Court recognized this in Jenkins v. Georgia, when it ruled that the film "Carnal Knowledge" was not obscene. Justice William Rehnquist wrote in that 1974 case that "nudity alone is not enough to make material legally obscene under the Miller standards."

A most troubling aspect of obscenity law concerns the application of community standards for defendants who ship materials of a sexual nature to different parts of the country. Should a defendant in California be subject to the mores of a more conservative locale?

The Court in Miller said that it was constitutional for different communities to articulate different community standards in obscenity cases. "To require a State to structure obscenity proceedings around evidence of a national community standard would be an exercise in futility," Chief Justice Warren Burger wrote.

"Nothing in the First Amendment requires that a jury must consider hypothetical and unascertainable 'national standards' when attempting to determine whether certain materials are obscene as a matter of fact," Burger continued. "It is neither realistic nor constitutionally sound to read the First Amendment as requiring that the people of Maine or Mississippi accept public depiction of conduct found tolerable in Las Vegas or New York City."

A pressing legal issue still to be resolved is whether federal law can apply local community standards to the global medium of the Internet. The Child Online Protection Act applies local community standards in determining whether material is harmful to minors. The 3rd U.S. Circuit Court of Appeals struck down the law in June 2000, writing that "Web publishers cannot restrict access to their site based on the geographic locale of the Internet user visiting their site."

In May 2002, the Supreme Court vacated the 3rd Circuit's ruling in Ashcroft v. ACLU, saying that the federal appeals court jumped the gun by invalidating the law based on the community-standards criterion at the early stages of litigation. However, several justices expressed uneasiness with applying local community standards to the Internet. For example, Justice Stephen Breyer wrote in his concurring opinion that "to read the statute as adopting the community standards of every locality in the United States would provide the most puritan of communities with a heckler's veto affecting the rest of the Nation."

After the Supreme Court's initial ruling, a federal district court granted a preliminary injunction preventing enforcement of the law pending a full trial. The 3rd Circuit affirmed, as did the Supreme Court in Ashcroft v. ACLU II,(2004).

"The Government has failed, at this point, to rebut the plaintiffs' contention that there are plausible less restrictive alternatives to the statute," Justice Anthony Kennedy wrote for the Court. "Substantial practical considerations, furthermore, argue in favor of upholding the injunction and allowing the case to proceed to trial."

The case returned to district court for a full trial in fall 2006. In March 2007, the district judge released his opinion striking down COPA. "Perhaps we do the minors of this country harm if First Amendment protections, which they will with age inherit fully, are chipped away in the name of their protection," wrote Senior U.S. District Judge Lowell Reed Jr. in ACLU v. Gonzalez.

In July 2008, a three-judge panel of the 3rd Circuit invalidated COPA in ACLU v. Mukasey, finding that it did not pass strict scrutiny because filtering presented a less speech-restrictive alternative. The Supreme Court refused to review this decision in January 2009.

Child pornography

Another type of pornography that receives no First Amendment protection is child pornography. In 1982, the Supreme Court ruled in New York v. Ferber that states could prohibit child pornography even if somehow the material in question did not meet the Miller obscenity standard. The high court noted that a work taken as a whole could have serious artistic value but also "embody the hardest core of child pornography."

The high court determined that the state had a compelling interest to prevent the sexual exploitation of minors in the making of child pornography. The Court called such an interest one of "surpassing importance." The Court did recognize that child-pornography laws could be applied in a heavy-handed way: "Like obscenity statutes, laws directed at the dissemination of child pornography run the risk of suppressing protected expression by allowing the hand of the censor to become unduly heavy."

In the 1990 case Osborne v. Ohio, the high court ruled that a state could punish even the private possession and viewing of child pornography. The defendant argued that the state was punishing a thought crime, but the majority of the Court disagreed. "Rather, Ohio has enacted ... [the law] ... in order to protect the victims of child pornography; it hopes to destroy a market for the exploitative use of children."

Not all child pornography statutes are immune from First Amendment challenge. In April 2002, the Court struck down two provisions of the 1996 Child Pornography Prevention Act in Ashcroft v. Free Speech Coalition.

CPPA expanded the definition of child pornography to include "any visual depiction" that "is, or appears to be, of a minor engaging in sexually explicit conduct." The other challenged provision banned any sexually explicit material that is advertised or promoted in a way that "conveys the impression" that a minor is engaging in sexually explicit conduct.

In other words, the "appears to be a minor" and "conveys the impression" clauses of the CPPA classified certain material as child pornography even though no actual minors were involved. The government asserted that it needed these provisions to target so-called "virtual child pornography." The government argued the law was needed to keep pace with technology — that it was becoming harder to determine if certain images contained pictures of actual children.

However, the majority of the Court was bothered by the breadth of the language in CPPA. The justices noted that the law could theoretically be applied to certain Hollywood movies that use youthful adult actors in sexual scenes or even to Renaissance paintings. The Court noted that CPPA "proscribes a significant universe of speech that is neither obscene under Miller nor child pornography under Ferber."

Congress responded to the Court's decision in Free Speech Coalition by passing the Prosecutorial Remedies and Other Tools to end the Exploitation of Children Today Act of 2003, better known as the PROTECT Act. The purpose of the law was to "restore the government's ability to prosecute child pornography offenses successfully." Prosecutors and legislators warned about the ability of defendants in child-porn cases to raise the "virtual child porn defense," arguing that the images in question did not contain pictures of actual minors.

A February 2003 Senate report on the PROTECT Act said prosecution of child pornography became more difficult for prosecutors because of the Free Speech Coalition ruling. "Many prosecutions, in fact, were dismissed," the report stated. "And even the prosecutions that remain have been significantly and adversely affected by the decision because prosecutors need to devote significantly more resources to each child pornography case than ever before."

The PROTECT Act, which was signed into law in April 2003, amended child- pornography laws in several ways. First, it created a new definition of child pornography to include pornographic pictures of children that are "virtually indistinguishable" from actual children. It also requires defendants to prove that the images they possess or distribute were not made with and do not depict actual children.

The PROTECT Act also created a new pandering offense by prohibiting offers to sell, trade or buy material purported to depict actual or obscene child pornography. The Supreme Court rejected a First Amendment challenge to this pandering provision from constitutional challenge in U.S. v. Williams (2008).

"Offers to engage in illegal transactions are categorically excluded from First Amendment protection," the Court wrote. "Offers to deal in illegal products or otherwise engage in illegal activity do not acquire First Amendment protection when the offeror is mistaken about the factual predicate of his offer." (See also"Virtual child pornography.")

Indecent speech

Much sexual expression does not meet the legal definition of obscenity or child pornography. But society simply doesn't want this material to fall into the hands of minors. Thus many states have regulated other forms of sexual speech that are "indecent" but not obscene.

The Supreme Court, for instance, ruled in 1978 that the Federal Communications Commission could limit the transmission of indecent speech on the radio during hours when children are likely to be listening. That case dealt with a fine imposed on a radio station that played George Carlin's "Filthy Words" monologue during daytime hours. The Court's ruling in FCC v. Pacificahas been largely confined to the broadcast medium.

The Supreme Court's ruling in Pacifica has been criticized. Recent broadcast indecency cases involving the brief display of Janet Jackson's breast at the Super Bowl and the use of the F-word by Sonny Bono and Nicole Richie at the Billboard Music awards have led to constitutional challenges, including arguments that FCC v. Pacifica should be overturned. However, in Fox Television v. FCC (2009), the Supreme Court declined to address the underlying First Amendment arguments and instead decided that the FCC did not act arbitrarily under the Administrative Procedure Act when it tightened its policy on indecency enforcement for the use of fleeting expletives.

Justice Clarence Thomas in a concurring opinion in the Fox case criticized the Court's differential treatment of different media in First Amendment cases. He concluded that he was "open to reconsideration" of Pacifica.

As for other media, the Court has ruled that the government cannot use the protection-of-minors rationale to shield adults from viewing indecent material. In the 1989 dial-a-porn case, Sable Communications of California, Inc. v. FCC,the Supreme Court bluntly stated that "sexual expression which is indecent but not obscene is protected by the First Amendment." The Court also has struck down prohibitions on indecent speech on the Internet and cable television.

Pornography in India

In India, watching or possessing pornographic material is legal. However, the production, publication, or distribution of such materials is illegal. Pornography is available in print magazines, but is mainly consumed using the internet. This consumption is increasing with the increased prevalence of smartphones and the internet. Despite the increased access, public discourse and attitudes on pornography remain muted and a taboo in many parts of India.

Types of publication

Print

Studies have found that print media is less widely accessible than internet media in India. A randomized survey of 96 random vendors, such as video stores, mobile downloads/recharge stores and cybercafés, in Haryana, India found that 17% displayed pornography openly, 34% displayed it semi-openly, and 49% kept it hidden. It is possible that cultural taboos and legal issues (such as those described below) make it more desirable to view pornography in India through internet mediums, such as computers or smartphones, for more privacy.

Internet

Internet pornography has become very popular in India with from 30% up to 70% of total traffic from porn websites. It has become a major portion of traffic and source of data revenue for telecom companies. A popular porn site released viewership data and national capital Delhi recorded up to 40% of all traffic.

One self reporting survey found that 63% of youths in urban areas such as Haryana reported watching pornography, with 74% accessing it through their mobile phones. As smartphone and internet access in India continues to increase, more people will be able to privately view pornography. Quartz has have found that 50% of Indian IP addresses accessed popular pornography websites on mobile phones. Online erotic comics have also become popular in India as the internet becomes more readily available to the common citizen.

Softcore pornography

Prior to the explosion of the internet, soft-core pornographic movies were popularly consumed in India.

Legality

The law as it pertains to pornography or "obscenity" is laid down in Section 292 of the Indian Penal Code, which was amended by the IT Act to include electronic data.

The Indian Penal Code, 1860 section 293 also makes the sale of obscene objects to minors illegal.

The Information Technology Act, 2000 (IT Act) section 67 Government of India specifies that, the transmission of online pornography through any electronic medium is a punishable offence.

Section 67A of IT Act details punishment for publishing or transmitting of material containing sexually explicit acts. This section also includes "causes to be published" and prohibits Internet Service Providers from transmitting adult content. But no ISP blocks adult content on their own. They prefer to invoke Section 79 3(B), to block only on the direction of the government. ISPs insist on a list of websites common for all ISPs.

Govt provided such a list of 857 websites and ISPs blocked them for 5-days in 2015, from 1-August till 5-August. Due to huge loss of revenue to ISPs, govt softened its stance and instructed to block only child pornography.

Section 67B of IT Act criminalises child pornography including browsing, downloading, creation, and publishing child pornography. The bill enables India's law enforcement agencies to take strict action against those seeking child pornography. For example, browsing for child pornography on the Internet can lead to a 5-year term of imprisonment and a ▯ 10 lakh fine.

In India, distributing pornography is illegal. However, enforcement is not severe and pornographic materials are easily available in public places. Softcore and hardcore pornography movies/photos are easily accessible through magazines, films, or the Internet.

Pornographic films in India are referred to as Blue Films and are available virtually anywhere; especially in areas where illegal material is already being sold. Despite the illegality, stores selling "X-rated" material are abundant in major cities and advertise openly; laws are rarely enforced in this case.

Ban

In Oct 2018, Internet Service Providers of India banned popular porn websites as per the directions of Uttarakhand High Court which imposed a strict ban on pornographic websites.

Judicial opinion

The Supreme Court of India, in Khoday Distilleries Ltd. and Ors. v. State of Karnataka and Ors. - (1995) 1 SCC 574, held that there is no fundamental right to carry on business of exhibiting and publishing pornographic or obscene films and literature.

Kamlesh Vaswani vs. Union of India and ors in 2013 (diary 5917, 2013), a PIL petition was filed in the Supreme Court of India seeking a ban on pornography in India. The Court issued a notice to the central government of India and sought its response. The government informed the Court that the Cyber Regulation Advisory Committee constituted under Section 88 of the IT Act, 2000 was assigned with a brief with regard to availability of pornography on the Internet and it was looking into the matter.

On 26 January 2016, the Supreme Court has asked the government to block websites having child pornography and rape videos.

Prajwala Letter dated 18.2.2015 VIDEOS OF SEXUAL VIOLENCE AND RECOMMENDATIONS, a suo moto PIL was admitted in Supreme Court (Diary No.- 6818 - 2015). Prajwala NGO pleaded to court to stop rampant circulation of rape videos through mobile application WhatsApp. Supreme court has ordered CBI probe to find and arrest the culprits clearly visible in the rape videos.

Socio-cultural attitudes

Many sex related topics, such as pornography, are considered taboo in traditional Indian households. This trend seems to be rapidly changing, especially in urbanized cities. Researchers have found that the primary sex education of youth born in the 1990s onwards in India comes from pornography and conversations amongst their peers, which has been known to cause long term sexual anxiety and frustration in other cultures where youth learn sexual attitudes from pornography. However, due to the internet and increased access for the common citizen, pornography has slowly entered the public discourse, most notably with the outrage towards a 2015 government order to censor 857 websites that contained explicit materials.

Homosexual pornography

Homosexual pornography is not widely available in print, due to the socio-culture taboo surrounding both pornography and homosexuality (see LGBT culture in India). However, Indian IP Addresses watch both lesbian and gay porn using the internet, with a 213% increase in searches for gay porn. Additionally, the most popular search for pornography amongst females in India, centers on lesbian and gay pornography.

Violence

Important people in media have argued that censoring pornography would decrease the rape culture in India. There has not been a link between pornography being a significant factor in the rate of crime and violence in India. Indian ministers quit after caught watching porn in parliament. Many Indian politicians, including a women's affairs minister, resigned after being caught watching pornography on a mobile phone during a session of state parliament.The link between pornography and sexual violence has not been observed in other countries.

Sex work

Some studies have speculated that pornography influences sex work in India. For instance, one study of 555 female sex workers found that 45% self-reported pornographic influence driving clientele desire for anal sex. In another study, female sex workers reported being asked to perform new sexual acts such as anal sex, masturbation and different sex positions, requests that they believed were due to an increased exposure to pornography. The implications of such work is currently unclear for public health policy in India.

Legal actions in Internet pornography

Due to the international nature of the Internet, Internet pornography carries with it special issues with regard to the law. There is no one set of laws that apply to the distribution, purchase, or possession of Internet pornography. This means that, for example, even if a pornographer is legally distributing pornography, the person receiving it may not be legally doing so due to local laws.

Child pornography and the Internet

Child pornography is illegal in most countries with coordinated enforcement by Interpol and policing institutions of various governments, including among others the United States Department of Justice. Even so, the UK based NSPCC said that worldwide an estimated 2% of websites still had not been removed a year after being identified. Recent investigations include Operation Cathedral that resulted in multi-national arrests and 7 convictions as well as uncovering 750,000 images with 1,200 unique identifiable faces being distributed over the web; Operation Amethyst which occurred in the Republic of Ireland; Operation Auxin; Operation Avalanche; Operation Ore based in the United Kingdom; Operation Pin; Operation Predator; the 2004 Ukrainian child pornography raids and the 2008 US child pornography raid. New technology that aids those who produce this material include inexpensive digital cameras and Internet distribution has made it easier than ever before to produce and distribute child pornography. The producers of child pornography try to avoid prosecution by distributing their material across national borders, though this issue is increasingly being addressed with regular arrests of suspects from a number of countries occurring over the last few years.

The legal status of simulated or "virtual" child pornography varies around the world. Simulated child pornography that do not pass the Miller test was banned in the United States in 2003 when the PROTECT Act was signed, it is illegal in the European Union, and in Australia its legal status is unclear and, as of 2007, untested in the courts. Child pornography may be simulated by the use of computers or adults made to look like children.

In 2008, it was discovered that the United States authorities will post fake hyperlinks claiming to be child pornography and then raiding, arresting, and prosecuting anyone who was found using the IP address that visited them, even someone whose computer was an open wifi. In 2008, a man in Middlesbrough, UK, was found guilty of downloading "child pornography" when he downloaded computer generated cartoons.

Internet pornography laws in various countries

United States

With the exception of child pornography, the legal status of accessing Internet pornography is still somewhat unsettled, though many individual states have indicated that the creation and distribution of adult films and photography are legally listed as prostitution within them.

The legality of pornography at the federal level has been traditionally determined by implementing the Miller test. This test dictates that the opinion of the local community on a specific pornographic piece is most important in determining its legality. Thus, if a local community determines a pornographic work to meet its standard for obscenity then it is more likely to be banned. This means that a pornographic magazine that might be legal in California could be illegal in Alabama. This standard on pornographic legality is extremely difficult to uphold for the internet given that the internet contains ubiquitous amounts of pornography. It has been argued that if the Miller test were applied to the Internet then, in effect, the community standards for the most conservative community would become the standard for all U.S.-based Web sites. The courts are currently examining this issue.

The first attempt to regulate pornography on the Internet was the federal Communications Decency Act of 1996, which prohibited the "knowing" transmission of "indecent" messages to minors and the publication of materials which depict, in a manner "patently offensive as measured by contemporary community standards, sexual or excretory activities or organs", unless those materials were protected from access by minors, for example by the use of credit card systems. Immediately challenged by a group of organizations spearheaded by the ACLU, both of these provisions were struck down by the U.S. Supreme Court in Reno v. American Civil Liberties Union (1997). The "indecent transmission" and "patently offensive display" provisions were ruled to limit the freedom of speech guarantee of the First Amendment.

A second attempt was made with the narrower Child Online Protection Act (COPA) of 1998, which forced all commercial distributors of "material harmful to minors" to protect their sites from access by minors. "Material harmful to minors" was defined as materials that by "contemporary community standards" are judged to appeal to the "prurient interest" and that show sexual acts or nudity (including female breasts). Several states have since passed similar laws. An injunction blocking the federal government from enforcing COPA was obtained in 1998. In 1999, the 3rd Circuit Court of Appeals upheld the injunction and struck down the law, ruling that it was too broad in using "community standards" as part of the definition of harmful materials. In May 2002, the Supreme Court reviewed this ruling, found the lower court's given reason insufficient and returned the case to the circuit court. In March 2003, the 3rd Circuit Court again struck down the law as unconstitutional, this time arguing that it would hinder protected speech among adults. The administration appealed; in June 2004 the Supreme Court upheld the injunction against the law, ruling that it was most likely unconstitutional but that a lower court should determine whether newer technical developments could affect this question. On March 22, 2007, COPA was found to violate the First and Fifth Amendments of the United States Constitution and was struck down.

Another act intended to protect children from access to Internet pornography is the Children's Internet Protection Act (CIPA) of 2000. It requires that public libraries, as a condition of receiving federal subsidies for Internet connectivity, employ filtering software to prevent patrons from using Internet terminals to view images of obscenity and child pornography, and to prevent children from viewing images "harmful to minors", a phrase encompassing pornography that has been held by the Supreme Court to be protected by the First Amendment for adults. The act allows librarians to disable the filtering software for adult patrons with "bona-fide research or other lawful purposes". The act was challenged by the American Library Association on First Amendment grounds, and enforcement of the act was blocked by a lower court. In June 2003, the Supreme Court reversed and ruled that the act was constitutional and could go into effect.

The production of sexually explicit materials is regulated under 18 U.S.C. 2257, requiring "original" producers to retain records showing that all performers were over the age of 18 at the time of the production for inspection by the Attorney General. The 18 U.S.C. 2257 disclaimer is common on Internet sites distributing pornography, but the Department of Justicehas rarely if ever enforced the provision. Although the law had been on the books for over 10 years, the Justice Department never actually inspected anyone. It was not until pressure from Congress, and conservative religious groups spurred the administration of George W. Bush and Attorney General Gonzales to begin inspections of larger commercial pornography companies primarily in the Los Angeles area. Despite fearing mass inspections, harassment, and prosecution, the Justice Department inspected less than two dozen companies (out of several thousand operating), and no prosecutions resulted from any of the inspections. Retired FBI agents conducted the inspections, and generally arrived with a list of videos whose records they wanted to examine (most likely, to avoid potential Fourth Amendment conflicts on issues of probable cause). According to pornography executives, the agents were always courteous and professional, suggesting changes or modifications to the companies' record-keeping processes. Once Attorney General Alberto Gonzales left the Justice Department, the inspections ended.

In 2005, the Department of Justice issued regulations that expand the definition of a "secondary producer" of sexually explicit material. As of June 23, 2005, federal regulations apply the 2257 record-keeping requirement to secondary producers, and defines them as including anyone who "inserts on a computer site or service a digital image of, or otherwise manages the sexually explicit content of a computer site or service that contains a visual depiction of, an actual human being engaged in actual or simulated sexually explicit conduct." 73 Fed. Reg. at 77,468.

On October 24, 2007, the Sixth Circuit Court of Appeals in Ohio issued a judgment against the 2257 law, ruling it as unconstitutional according to the First Amendment. However, the Sixth Circuit subsequently reheard the case en banc and issued an opinion on February 20, 2009, upholding the constitutionality of the record-keeping requirements, albeit with some dissents. The Sixth Circuit en banc decision was appealed to the US Supreme Court where on Monday October 5, 2009, the US Supreme Court denied certiorari without comment not addressing the Sixth Circuit decision that 18 USC 2257 is not constitutionally "vague and overbroad" and able to be enforced. See the one line denial on page nine of the Supreme Court order list for October 5, 2009.

In February 2001, Buffnet, a New York Internet Service Provider, pleaded guilty in state court to a misdemeanor count of knowingly providing access to child pornography, after being notified by police of the content and not taking action. The ISP faced a $5000 fine.

United Kingdom

The sale or distribution of hardcore pornography through any channel was prohibited until the rules were relaxed in 2002. However, pornographic videos sold or distributed legally within the UK must receive a certificate from the British Board of Film Classification (BBFC) and the rules are still quite strict.

In 1996, internet service providers started the Internet Watch Foundation to watch for pornographic content that is in violation of British law and report it to the police. The web filter Cleanfeed is used by the largest ISP, BT Group, to block sites on the Internet Watch Foundation's list, which include sites that are "criminally obscene" as well as child pornography. The government ordered all ISPs to have a Cleanfeed-like system by the end of 2007.

The possession of pornographic images for private use has traditionally not been an offence in the UK. This means that UK citizens have been able to access content on sites overseas without breaking any laws, except for child pornography. However, adult pornography that falls under the Government's classification of "extreme pornography" became illegal to possess as of January 26, 2009, carrying a three-year prison sentence. This was proposed by the Government after the murder of Jane Longhurst, claiming that such material was viewed by murderer Graham Coutts. Critics of the law have pointed out that it criminalises images of legal acts between consenting adults and have criticised the lack of evidence of a link between viewing such material, and violent crime.

In 2013, Prime Minister David Cameron introduced plans to filter internet pornography by default in the UK. By the end of 2014, access to internet pornography was blocked unless subscribers specifically chose to 'opt out' by contacting their ISP. This was done in an effort to reduce the number of children having access to pornography on the Internet. The plans were criticised as likely to sweep up non-pornographic content, disclose intimate information to the government, and as unwarranted censorship. In December 2014, the jurisdiction of the BBFC was extended with the Audiovisual Media Services Regulations 2014 to include pornography available over video on demand and streaming platforms, effectively aligning internet pornography laws with the Video Recordings Act 1984. This brought a renewed controversy over the banning of depiction of certain sex acts including depictions "physical or verbal abuse", "roleplay as non-adults", urolagnia, and female ejaculation, among others.

The Digital Economy Act 2017 includes powers to require age-verification for pornographic Internet sites and the government accepted an amendment to allow the regulator to require ISPs to block access to non-compliant sites. As the BBFC have been appointed as the regulator, this has caused discussion about ISPs being required to block content that is prohibited even under an R18 certificate, the prohibition of some of which is itself controversial.

Australia

Internet pornography in Australia is subject to a multifaceted regulatory framework. Criminal legislation is in force at the Commonwealth, state and territory levels targeting those involved in the production, dissemination and consumption of illegal internet pornography (including online child abuse pornography and online pornography featuring adults portrayed as children).

It is illegal for internet content providers within Australia to 'broadcast' internet pornography classified as MA15+ to R18+ unless such internet pornography is subject to an age verification system or internet pornography which may be classified as X18+ to RC content that is not subject to an Australian Communications and Media Authority (ACMA) infringement notice through exceptions.

Under an internet filter, proposed by Senator Stephen Conroy, internet pornography hosted outside Australia classified by the ACMA under the Classification Board legislation will be blocked if such internet pornography is deemed by the AMCA to be refused classification (RC), or 'potentially' refused classification. Refused classification (RC) does include real child abuse internet pornography and bestiality internet pornography, however it may also include content discussing or illustrating examples of internet pornography (including both, illegal internet pornography and internet pornography featuring adults portrayed as children) which may limit discussion and debate to authorised statutory persons only, rather than open and free public debate.

Criminal legislation is complemented by a further tier of regulation which provides a range of administrative remedies designed to deal with the availability of inappropriate content by removing it from the internet or by blocking access to it.

Online content scheme

Since January 1999, internet pornography considered offensive or illegal has been subject to a statutory scheme administered by ACMA as Australia's media regulator.

Established under Schedule 5 to the Broadcasting Services Act 1992, the online content scheme evolved from a tradition of Australian content regulation in broadcasting and other entertainment media. This tradition embodies the principle that – while adults should be free to see, hear and read what they want – children should be protected from material that may be unsuitable for (or harmful to) them, and everyone should be protected from material that is highly offensive.

The online content scheme seeks to achieve these objectives by a number of means such as complaint investigation processes, government and industry collaboration, and community awareness and empowerment. While administration of the scheme is the responsibility of ACMA, the principle of 'co-regulation' underpinning the scheme reflects parliament's intention that government, industry and the community each plays a role in managing internet safety issues in Australia.

Investigations into internet pornography

A central feature of the online content scheme is the complaints mechanism that allows members of the Australian public to submit complaints to ACMA about offensive and illegal internet content.

Offensive and illegal internet content will be 'prohibited' under the scheme if it meets certain classification thresholds, irrespective of where the content is hosted. If prohibited content is hosted in Australia, ACMA will direct the internet content host to remove the content from its service. If prohibited content is not hosted in Australia, ACMA will notify the content to the suppliers of accredited filters in accordance with the Internet Industry Association's internet content code of practice so that access to that content is blocked for users of those filters.

In addition, sufficiently serious internet content (for example, illegal material such as child pornography) will be referred by ACMA under specialized agreements to the appropriate law enforcement agency, or, where appropriate, to a fellow member of the Internet Hotline Providers' Association (INHOPE).

Between January 2000 and June 2006, ACMA received over 5,000 complaints from the public about offensive and illegal internet content hosted in Australia and overseas, resulting in the removal or blocking of almost 4,000 individual items of online content. Approximately 60% of such content was also referred to law enforcement agencies on the basis that it related to material classifiable as 'RC' (see below).

Classification of internet pornography

Internet pornography will be 'prohibited' by ACMA if certain classification thresholds are met. These thresholds form part of the National Classification Scheme (which also applies to other forms of media such as publications, films and video games) and are agreed by the Attorneys-General of the Commonwealth, States and Territories.

The thresholds are articulated in a National Classification Code and in Guidelines. The Classification Board (part of the Attorney-General's Department) is Australia's official classification body. In the course of investigating potentially prohibited internet content, ACMA may seek a formal classification decision from the Classification Board, or it may make its own assessment of the content against the National Classification Code and in Guidelines.

In summary, the following categories of internet content are prohibited: • Content classifiable as 'RC' ('refused classification'). Such content includes, for example, illegal material (such as child sexual abuse material) and other highly offensive material (such as bestiality). • Content classifiable as 'X18+'. Such content includes material containing real depictions of actual sexual activity. • Content hosted in Australia which is classified 'R18+' and not subject to a restricted access system which complies with criteria determined by ACMA. Content classified R18+ is not considered suitable for minors. Such content includes, for example, material containing implied (or simulated) sexual activity.

Internet pornography will be prohibited if it falls within the 'RC' or 'X18+' classifications or, for content hosted in Australia that is not restricted by an adult verification procedure, if it falls within the 'R18+' classification.

Victorian legislation

In Victoria, the law states that child pornography 'means a film, photograph, publication or computer game that describes or depicts a person who is, or who looks like, a minor under 18 engaging in sexual activity or depicted in an indecent manner or context. Under this law, 'publications' also include stories, poems, essays, drawings and cartoons.

Finland

Finnish law specifically prohibits either real or realistic imagery which sexually depicts children. The illegality thus excludes non-realistic imagery.

Indonesia

The legal situation in Indonesia tightened sharply in 2008 with the passing of the Bill against Pornography and Pornoaction. Law books of Indonesia KUHP (Kitab Undang-Undang Hukum Pidana) article number 282 says that "it is forbidden to spread pornographic content". But there have been Indonesian pornographic pay sites with Indonesian nude models that exploit legal loopholes.

Hong Kong

Pursuant to the Control of Obscene and Indecent Articles Ordinance (Cap 390), it is an offence to publish an obscene article. Publication covers distribution, circulation, selling, hiring, giving, or lending the obscene article. Distribution by email would fall within the definition of distribution, as would the placing of an obscene article on a web site. It should also be noted that distribution does not require any element of financial gain to be present. The definition of article includes "anything consisting of or containing material to be read or looked at or both read and looked at, any sound recording, and any film, video-tape, disc or other record of a picture or pictures." The article will be considered obscene if, by reason by its obscenity, "it is not suitable to be published by any person." Obscenity includes "violence, depravity and repulsiveness". The penalty for this offence is up to three years imprisonment and a fine of up to HK$1,000,000.

Related cases (see Edison Chen photo scandal):

- On January 27, 2008, The Hong Kong Police Force arrested suspects who were accused of uploading pornographic images after a multi-billion entertainment company filed a complaint about these photos available on the internet having been fabricated and might charge the offender for defamation.

Moreover, the Prevention of Child Pornography Ordinance, Cap.579, was enacted to deal with the problems associated with child pornography in Hong Kong. Under Section 3, dealing in any of the following manners with child pornography, such as "prints, makes, produces, reproduces, copies, imports or exports"; "publishes" or " has in his possession" is an offence. A child is a person under the age of 16. "Child pornography" means a photograph, film, computer-generated image or other visual depiction that is a pornographic depiction of a child. "Pornographic depiction" means a visual depiction that depicts a person as being engaged in explicit sexual conduct, whether or not the person is in fact engaged in such conduct; or a visual depiction that depicts, in a sexual manner or context, the genitals or anal region of a person or the breast of a female person. In Hong Kong, recent data shows that $14k is funded towards hentai/pornography companies. Producers are beginning to believe this is "A special skill and talent" or in other words, a paying job.

Gaza Strip

Hamas authorities of the Gaza Strip began blocking Internet pornography sites in late May 2008.

Malaysia

A limited number of pornographic websites are accessible in Malaysia, with blocks and government monitoring. The national government continues to block many porn websites, it has blocked over 3,000 sites as of 2018.

In July 2018, the Malaysian police announced the creation of the Malaysian Internet Crime Against Children Investigation Unit (MICAC) that is equipped with real-time mass internet surveillance software developed in the United States and is tasked with the monitoring of all Malaysian Internet users even on mobile phones, with a focus on pornography and child pornography. The system creates a "data library" of users which includes details such as IP addresses, websites, locations, duration and frequency of use and files uploaded and downloaded. Visiting these websites are subject to either questioning by police or imprisonment.

Philippines

Since January 14, 2017, several pornography sites including Pornhub and XVideos has been blocked in the Philippines by President Rodrigo Duterte as part of the Republic Act 9775 or the Anti-Child Pornography Law, but still can be accessed depending on the ISP.

Russia

Roskomnadzor, the Russian government's media overseer, has the power to order the blocking of pornographic websites. In 2015, the agency ordered the blocking of the Russian-language version of Pornhub and 10 other pornographic sites on the basis of a court ruling. In early 2015, the Roskomnadzor has blocked over 100 pornography sites, making it difficult to view in Russia. Two more websites PornHub and YouPorn were blocked in Russia in September 2016. PornHub was unblocked in 2017.

Singapore

The Media Development Authority, a government-run agency in Singapore, blocks a "symbolic" number of websites containing "mass impact objectionable" material, including Playboy, and Sex.com. In addition, the Ministry of Education, Singapore blocks access to pornographic websites.

South Africa

Since 2007, it is illegal to host a pornographic website in South Africa. However, accessing international porn websites is not an offence.

Thailand

A few pornographic websites are accessible in Thailand, mostly foreign, as long it's for personal use.

Ukraine

Pornography has become illegal in Ukraine since 2009, however the Internet porn websites are still accessible. No laws has been enforced yet.

13

Hacking on the Cyberspace and Internet

Computers have become mandatory to run a successful businesses. It is not enough to have isolated computers systems; they need to be networked to facilitate communication with external businesses. This exposes them to the outside world and hacking. Hacking means using computers to commit fraudulent acts such as fraud, privacy invasion, stealing corporate/personal data, etc. Cyber crimes cost many organizations millions of dollars every year. Businesses need to protect themselves against such attacks.

Cybercrime, or computer-oriented crime, is the crime that involves a computer and a network.The computer may have been used in the commission of a crime, or it may be the target.Cybercrimes can be defined as: "Offences that are committed against individuals or groups of individuals with a criminal motive to intentionally harm the reputation of the victim or cause physical or mental harm, or loss, to the victim directly or indirectly, using modern telecommunication networks such as Internet (networks including chat rooms, emails, notice boards and groups) and mobile phones (Bluetooth/SMS/MMS)". Cybercrime may threaten a person or a nation's security and financial health. Issues surrounding these types of crimes have become high-profile, particularly those surrounding hacking, copyright infringement, unwarranted mass-surveillance, sextortion, child pornography, and child grooming. There are also problems of privacy when confidential information is intercepted or disclosed, lawfully or otherwise. Debarati Halder and K. Jaishankar further define cybercrime from the perspective of gender and defined 'cybercrime against women' as "Crimes targeted against women with a motive to intentionally harm the victim psychologically and physically, using modern telecommunication networks such as internet and mobile phones". Internationally, both governmental and non-state actors engage in cybercrimes, including espionage, financial theft, and other cross-border crimes. Cybercrimes crossing international borders and involving the actions of at least one nation state is sometimes referred to as cyberwarfare.

A report (sponsored by McAfee), published in 2014, estimated that the annual damage to the global economy was $445 billion. Approximately $1.5 billion was lost in 2012 to online credit and debit card fraud in the US. In 2018, a study by Center for Strategic and International Studies (CSIS), in partnership with McAfee, concludes that close to $600 billion, nearly one percent of global GDP, is lost to cybercrime each year.

Classifications

Computer crime encompasses a broad range of activities.

Computer fraud is any dishonest misrepresentation of fact intended to let another to do or refrain from doing something which causes loss. In this context, the fraud will result in obtaining a benefit by:

- Altering in an unauthorized way. This requires little technical expertise and is common form of theft by employees altering the data before entry or entering false data, or by entering unauthorized instructions or using unauthorized processes;
- Altering, destroying, suppressing, or stealing output, usually to conceal unauthorized transactions. This is difficult to detect;
- Altering or deleting stored data;

Other forms of fraud may be facilitated using computer systems, including bank fraud, carding, identity theft, extortion, and theft of classified information.

Cyberterrorism

Government officials and information technology security specialists have documented a significant increase in Internet problems and server scans since early 2001. But there is a growing concern among government agencies such as the Federal Bureau of Investigations (FBI) and the Central Intelligence Agency (CIA) that such intrusions are part of an organized effort by cyberterrorists, foreign intelligence services, or other groups to map potential security holes in critical systems. A cyberterrorist is someone who intimidates or coerces a government or an organization to advance his or her political or social objectives by launching a computer-based attack against computers, networks, or the information stored on them.

Cyberterrorism in general can be defined as an act of terrorism committed through the use of cyberspace or computer resources (Parker 1983). As such, a simple propaganda piece in the Internet that there will be bomb attacks during the holidays can be considered cyberterrorism. There are also hacking activities directed towards individuals, families, organized by groups within networks, tending to cause fear among people, demonstrate power, collecting information relevant for ruining peoples' lives, robberies, blackmailing etc.

Cyberextortion

Cyberextortion occurs when a website, e-mail server, or computer system is subjected to or threatened with repeated denial of service or other attacks by malicious hackers. These hackers demand money in return for promising to stop the attacks and to offer "protection". According to the Federal Bureau of Investigation, cybercrime extortionists are increasingly attacking corporate websites and networks, crippling their ability to operate and demanding payments to restore their service. More than 20 cases are reported each month to the FBI and many go unreported in order to keep the victim's name out of the public domain. Perpetrators typically use a distributed denial-of-service attack. However, other cyberextortion techniques exist such as doxing extortion and bug poaching.

An example of cyberextortion was the attack on Sony Pictures of 2014.

Cyberwarfare

The U.S. Department of Defense (DoD) notes that the cyberspace has emerged as a national-level concern through several recent events of geostrategic significance. Among those are included, the attack on Estonia's infrastructure in 2007, allegedly by Russian hackers. "In August 2008, Russia again allegedly conducted cyberattacks, this time in a coordinated and synchronized kinetic and non-kinetic campaign against the country of Georgia. The December 2015 Ukraine power grid cyberattack has also been attributed to Russia and is considered the first successful cyberattack on a power grid. Fearing that such attacks may become the norm in future warfare among nation-states, the concept of cyberspace operations impacts and will be adapted by warfighting military commanders in the future.

Computer as a target

These crimes are committed by a selected group of criminals. Unlike crimes using the computer as a tool, these crimes require the technical knowledge of the perpetrators. As such, as technology evolves, so too does the nature of the crime. These crimes are relatively new, having been in existence for only as long as computers have—which explains how unprepared society and the world in general is towards combating these crimes. There are numerous crimes of this nature committed daily on the internet.

Crimes that primarily target computer networks or devices include:

- Computer viruses
- Denial-of-service attacks
- Malware (malicious code)

Computer as a tool

When the individual is the main target of cybercrime, the computer can be considered as the tool rather than the target. These crimes generally involve less technical expertise. Human weaknesses are generally exploited. The damage dealt is largely psychological and intangible, making legal action against the variants more difficult. These are the crimes which have existed for centuries in the offline world. Scams, theft, and the likes have existed even before the development in high-tech equipment. The same criminal has simply been given a tool which increases their potential pool of victims and makes them all the harder to trace and apprehend.

Crimes that use computer networks or devices to advance other ends include:

- Fraud and identity theft (although this increasingly uses malware, hacking or phishing, making it an example of both "computer as target" and "computer as tool" crime)
- Information warfare
- Phishing scams
- Spam
- Propagation of illegal obscene or offensive content, including harassment and threats

The unsolicited sending of bulk email for commercial purposes (spam) is unlawful in some jurisdictions.

Phishing is mostly propagated via email. Phishing emails may contain links to other websites that are affected by malware. Or, they may contain links to fake online banking or other websites used to steal private account information.

Obscene or offensive content

The content of websites and other electronic communications may be distasteful, obscene or offensive for a variety of reasons. In some instances these communications may be illegal.

The extent to which these communications are unlawful varies greatly between countries, and even within nations. It is a sensitive area in which the courts can become involved in arbitrating between groups with strong beliefs.

One area of Internet pornography that has been the target of the strongest efforts at curtailment is child pornography, which is illegal in most jurisdictions in the world.

Online harassment

Whereas content may be offensive in a non-specific way, harassment directs obscenities and derogatory comments at specific individuals focusing for example on gender, race, religion, nationality, sexual orientation. This often occurs in chat rooms, through newsgroups, and by sending hate e-mail to interested parties. Harassment on the internet also includes revenge porn.

There are instances where committing a crime using a computer can lead to an enhanced sentence. For example, in the case of United States v. Neil Scott Kramer, Kramer was served an enhanced sentence according to the U.S. Sentencing Guidelines Manual §2G1.3(b)(3) for his use of a cell phone to "persuade, induce, entice, coerce, or facilitate the travel of, the minor to engage in prohibited sexual conduct." Kramer argued that this claim was insufficient because his charge included persuading through a computer device and his cellular phone technically is not a computer. Although Kramer tried to argue this point, U.S. Sentencing Guidelines Manual states that the term computer "means an electronic, magnetic, optical, electrochemically, or other high-speed data processing device performing logical, arithmetic, or storage functions, and includes any data storage facility or communications facility directly related to or operating in conjunction with such device."

Connecticut was the U.S. state to pass a statute making it a criminal offense to harass someone by computer. Michigan, Arizona, and Virginia and South Carolina have also passed laws banning harassment by electronic means.

Harassment as defined in the U.S. computer statutes is typically distinct from cyberbullying, in that the former usually relates to a person's "use a computer or computer network to communicate obscene, vulgar, profane, lewd, lascivious, or indecent language, or make any suggestion or proposal of an obscene nature, or threaten any illegal or immoral act," while the latter need not involve anything of a sexual nature.

Although freedom of speech is protected by law in most democratic societies (in the US this is done by the First Amendment), it does not include all types of speech. In fact spoken or written "true threat" speech/text is criminalized because of "intent to harm or intimidate", that also applies for online or any type of network related threats in written text or speech. The US Supreme Court definition of "true threat" is "statements where the speaker means to communicate a serious expression of an intent to commit an act of unlawful violence to a particular individual or group".

Drug trafficking

Darknet markets are used to buy and sell recreational drugs online. Some drug traffickers use encrypted messaging tools to communicate with drug mules. The dark web site Silk Road was a major online marketplace for drugs before it was shut down by law enforcement (then reopened under new management, and then shut down by law enforcement again). After Silk Road 2.0 went down, Silk Road 3 Reloaded emerged. However, it was just an older marketplace named Diabolus Market, that used the name for more exposure from the brand's previous success.

Documented cases

- One of the highest profiled banking computer crime occurred during a course of three years beginning in 1970. The chief teller at the Park Avenue branch of New York's Union Dime Savings Bank embezzled over $1.5 million from hundreds of accounts.

- A hacking group called MOD (Masters of Deception), allegedly stole passwords and technical data from Pacific Bell, Nynex, and other telephone companies as well as several big credit agencies and two major universities. The damage caused was extensive, one company, Southwestern Bell suffered losses of $370,000 alone.

- In 1983, a 19-year-old UCLA student used his PC to break into a Defense Department International Communications system.

- Between 1995 and 1998 the Newscorp satellite pay to view encrypted SKY-TV service was hacked several times during an ongoing technological arms race between a pan-European hacking group and Newscorp. The original motivation of the hackers was to watch Star Trek reruns in Germany; which was something which Newscorp did not have the copyright to allow.

- On 26 March 1999, the Melissa worm infected a document on a victim's computer, then automatically sent that document and a copy of the virus spread via e-mail to other people.

• In February 2000, an individual going by the alias of MafiaBoy began a series denial-of-service attacks against high-profile websites, including Yahoo!, Dell, Inc., E*TRADE, eBay, and CNN. About 50 computers at Stanford University, and also computers at the University of California at Santa Barbara, were amongst the zombie computers sending pings in DDoS attacks. On 3 August 2000, Canadian federal prosecutors charged MafiaBoy with 54 counts of illegal access to computers, plus a total of ten counts of mischief to data for his attacks.

• The Stuxnet worm corrupted SCADA microprocessors, particularly of the types used in Siemens centrifuge controllers.

• The Russian Business Network (RBN) was registered as an internet site in 2006. Initially, much of its activity was legitimate. But apparently, the founders soon discovered that it was more profitable to host illegitimate activities and started hiring its services to criminals. The RBN has been described by VeriSign as "the baddest of the bad". It offers web hosting services and internet access to all kinds of criminal and objectionable activities, with individual activities earning up to $150 million in one year. It specialized in and in some cases monopolized personal identity theft for resale. It is the originator of MPack and an alleged operator of the now defunct Storm botnet.

• On 2 March 2010, Spanish investigators arrested 3 in infection of over 13 million computers around the world. The "botnet" of infected computers included PCs inside more than half of the Fortune 1000 companies and more than 40 major banks, according to investigators.

• In August 2010 the international investigation Operation Delego, operating under the aegis of the Department of Homeland Security, shut down the international pedophile ring Dreamboard. The website had approximately 600 members and may have distributed up to 123 terabytes of child pornography (roughly equivalent to 16,000 DVDs). To date this is the single largest U.S. prosecution of an international child pornography ring; 52 arrests were made worldwide.

• In January 2012 Zappos.com experienced a security breach after as many as 24 million customers' credit card numbers, personal information, billing and shipping addresses had been compromised.

• In June 2012 LinkedIn and eHarmony were attacked, compromising 65 million password hashes. 30,000 passwords were cracked and 1.5 million EHarmony passwords were posted online.

• December 2012 Wells Fargo website experienced a denial of service attack. Potentially compromising 70 million customers and 8.5 million active viewers. Other banks thought to be compromised: Bank of America, J. P. Morgan U.S. Bank, and PNC Financial Services.

• April 23, 2013 saw the Associated Press' Twitter account's hacked - the hacker posted a hoax tweet about fictitious attacks in the White House that they claimed left President Obama injured. This hoax tweet resulted in a brief plunge of 130 points from the Dow Jones Industrial Average, removal of $136 billion from S&P 500 index, and the temporary suspension of AP's Twitter account. The Dow Jones later restored its session gains.

• In May 2017, 74 countries logged a ransomware cybercrime, called "WannaCry"

• Illicit access to camera sensors, microphone sensors, phonebook contacts, all internet-enabled apps, and metadata of mobile telephones running Android and IOS were reportedly made accessible by Israeli spyware, found to be being in operation in at least 46 nation-states around the world. Journalists, Royalty and government officials were amongst the targets. Previous accusations of cases of Israeli-weapons companies meddling in international telephony and smartphones have been eclipsed in the 2018 reported case.

Combating computer crime

Diffusion of cybercrime

The broad diffusion of cybercriminal activities is an issue in computer crimes detection and prosecution. According to Jean-Loup Richet (Research Fellow at ESSEC ISIS), technical expertise and accessibility no longer act as barriers to entry into cybercrime. Indeed, hacking is much less complex than it was a few years ago, as hacking communities have greatly diffused their knowledge through the Internet. Blogs and communities have hugely contributed to information sharing: beginners could benefit from older hackers' knowledge and advice. Furthermore, hacking is cheaper than ever: before the cloud computing era, in order to spam or scam one needed a dedicated server, skills in server management, network configuration, and maintenance, knowledge of Internet service provider standards, etc. By comparison, a mail software-as-a-service is a scalable, inexpensive, bulk, and transactional e-mail-sending service for marketing purposes and could be easily set up for spam. Jean-Loup Richet explains that cloud computing could be helpful for a cybercriminal as a way to leverage his attack – brute-forcing a password, improve the reach of a botnet, or facilitating a spamming campaign.

Investigation

A computer can be a source of evidence (see digital forensics). Even where a computer is not directly used for criminal purposes, it may contain records of value to criminal investigators in the form of a logfile. In most countries Internet Service Providers are required, by law, to keep their logfiles for a predetermined amount of time. For example; a European wide Data

Retention Directive (applicable to all EU member states) states that all e-mail traffic should be retained for a minimum of 12 months.

Methodology of cybercrime investigation

There are many ways for cybercrime to take place, and investigations tend to start with an IP Address trace, however that is not necessarily a factual basis upon which detectives can solve a case. Different types of high-tech crime may also include elements of low-tech crime, and vice versa, making cybercrime investigators an indispensable part of modern law-enforcement. Methodology of cybercrime detective work is dynamic and is constantly improving, whether in closed police units, or in international cooperation framework.

Legislation

Due to easily exploitable laws, cybercriminals use developing countries in order to evade detection and prosecution from law enforcement. In developing countries, such as the Philippines, laws against cybercrime are weak or sometimes nonexistent. These weak laws allow cybercriminals to strike from international borders and remain undetected. Even when identified, these criminals avoid being punished or extradited to a country, such as the United States, that has developed laws that allow for prosecution. While this proves difficult in some cases, agencies, such as the FBI, have used deception and subterfuge to catch criminals. For example, two Russian hackers had been evading the FBI for some time. The FBI set up a fake computing company based in Seattle, Washington. They proceeded to lure the two Russian men into the United States by offering them work with this company. Upon completion of the interview, the suspects were arrested outside of the building. Clever tricks like this are sometimes a necessary part of catching cybercriminals when weak legislation makes it impossible otherwise.

President Barack Obama released in an executive order in April 2015 to combat cybercrime. The executive order allows the United States to freeze assets of convicted cybercriminals and block their economic activity within the United States. This is some of the first solid legislation that combats cybercrime in this way.

The European Union adopted directive 2013/40/EU. All offences of the directive, and other definitions and procedural institutions are also in the Council of Europe's Convention on Cybercrime..

It is not only the USA and the European Union who are introducing new measures against cybercrime. ON 31 May 2017 China announced that its new cybersecurity law takes effect on this date.

Penalties

Penalties for computer-related crimes in New York State can range from a fine and a short period of jail time for a Class A misdemeanor such as unauthorized use of a computer up to computer tampering in the first degree which is a Class C felony and can carry 3 to 15 years in prison.

However, some hackers have been hired as information security experts by private companies due to their inside knowledge of computer crime, a phenomenon which theoretically could create perverse incentives. A possible counter to this is for courts to ban convicted hackers from using the Internet or computers, even after they have been released from prison – though as computers and the Internet become more and more central to everyday life, this type of punishment may be viewed as more and more harsh and draconian. However, nuanced approaches have been developed that manage cyber offenders' behavior without resorting to total computer or Internet bans. These approaches involve restricting individuals to specific devices which are subject to computer monitoring or computer searches by probation or parole officers.

Awareness

As technology advances and more people rely on the internet to store sensitive information such as banking or credit card information, criminals increasingly attempt to steal that information. Cybercrime is becoming more of a threat to people across the world. Raising awareness about how information is being protected and the tactics criminals use to steal that information continues to grow in importance. According to the FBI's Internet Crime Complaint Center in 2014, there were 269,422 complaints filed. With all the claims combined there was a reported total loss of $800,492,073. But cybercrime does yet seem to be on the average person's radar. There are 1.5 million cyber-attacks annually, that means that there are over 4,000 attacks a day, 170 attacks every hour, or nearly three attacks every minute, with studies showing us that only 16% of victims had asked the people who were carrying out the attacks to stop. Anybody who uses the internet for any reason can be a victim, which is why it is important to be aware of how one is being protected while online.

Intelligence

As cybercrime has proliferated, a professional ecosystem has evolved to support individuals and groups seeking to profit from cybercriminal activities. The ecosystem has become quite specialized, including malware developers, botnet operators, professional cybercrime groups, groups specializing in the sale of stolen content, and so forth. A few of the leading cybersecurity companies have the skills, resources and visibility to follow the activities of these individuals and group. A wide variety of information is available from these sources which can be used for defensive purposes, including technical indicators such as hashes of infected files or malicious IPs/URLs, as well as strategic information profiling the goals, techniques and campaigns of the profiled groups. Some of it is freely published, but consistent, on-going access typically requires subscribing to an adversary intelligence subscription service. At the level of an individual threat actor, threat intelligence is often referred to that actor's "TTP", or "tactics, techniques, and procedures," as the infrastructure, tools, and other technical indicators are often trivial for attackers to change. Corporate sectors are considering crucial role of artificial intelligence cyber security.

Hacker

A computer hacker is any skilled computer expert that uses their technical knowledge to overcome a problem. While "hacker" can refer to any skilled computer programmer, the term has become associated in popular culture with a "security hacker", someone who, with their technical knowledge, uses bugs or exploits to break into computer systems, usually in the context of some illicit activity.

Definitions

General Definition

Reflecting the two types of hackers, there are two definitions of the word "hacker":

1. an adherent of the technology and programming subculture; see hacker culture.

2. someone who is able to subvert computer security. If doing so for malicious purposes, the person can also be called a cracker.

Today, mainstream usage of "hacker" mostly refers to computer criminals, due to the mass media usage of the word since the 1980s. This includes what hacker slang calls "script kiddies", people breaking into computers using programs written by others, with very little knowledge about the way they work. This usage has become so predominant that the general public is largely unaware that different meanings exist. While the self-designation of hobbyists as hackers is generally acknowledged and accepted by computer security hackers, people from the programming subculture consider the computer intrusion related usage incorrect, and emphasize the difference between the two by calling security breakers "crackers" (analogous to a safecracker).

The controversy is usually based on the assertion that the term originally meant someone messing about with something in a positive sense, that is, using playful cleverness to achieve a goal. But then, it is supposed, the meaning of the term shifted over the decades and came to refer to computer criminals.

As the security-related usage has spread more widely, the original meaning has become less known. In popular usage and in the media, "computer intruders" or "computer criminals" is the exclusive meaning of the word today. (For example, "An Internet 'hacker' broke through state government security systems in March.") In the computer enthusiast (Hacker Culture) community, the primary meaning is a complimentary description for a particularly brilliant programmer or technical expert. (For example, "Linus Torvalds, the creator of Linux, is considered by some to be a hacker.") A large segment of the technical community insist the latter is the "correct" usage of the word (see the Jargon File definition below).

Representation of Hackers in Mainstream Media

The mainstream media's current usage of the term may be traced back to the early 1980s. When the term was introduced to wider society by the mainstream media in 1983, even those in the computer community referred to computer intrusion as "hacking", although not as the exclusive definition of the word. In reaction to the increasing media use of the term exclusively with the criminal connotation, the computer community began to differentiate their terminology. Alternative terms such as "cracker" were coined in an effort to maintain the distinction between "hackers" within the legitimate programmer community and those performing computer break-ins. Further terms such as "black hat", "white hat" and "gray hat" developed when laws against breaking into computers came into effect, to distinguish criminal activities from those activities which were legal.

Representation of Hackers in Network News

However, network news use of the term consistently pertained primarily to the criminal activities, despite the attempt by the technical community to preserve and distinguish the original meaning, so today the mainstream media and general public continue to describe computer criminals, with all levels of technical sophistication, as "hackers" and do not generally make use of the word in any of its non-criminal connotations. Members of the media sometimes seem unaware of the distinction, grouping legitimate "hackers" such as Linus Torvalds and Steve Wozniak along with criminal "crackers".

As a result, the definition is still the subject of heated controversy. The wider dominance of the pejorative connotation is resented by many who object to the term being taken from their cultural jargon and used negatively, including those who have historically preferred to self-identify as hackers. Many advocate using the more recent and nuanced alternate terms when describing criminals and others who negatively take advantage of security flaws in software and hardware. Others prefer to follow common popular usage, arguing that the positive form is confusing and unlikely to become widespread in the general public. A minority still use the term in both senses despite the controversy, leaving context to clarify (or leave ambiguous) which meaning is intended.

However, because the positive definition of hacker was widely used as the predominant form for many years before the negative definition was popularized, "hacker" can therefore be seen as a shibboleth, identifying those who use the technically-oriented sense (as opposed to the exclusively intrusion-oriented sense) as members of the computing community. On the other hand, due to the variety of industries software designers may find themselves in, many prefer not to be referred to as hackers because the word holds a negative denotation in many of those industries.

A possible middle ground position has been suggested, based on the observation that "hacking" describes a collection of skills and tools which are used by hackers of both descriptions for differing reasons. The analogy is made to locksmithing, specifically picking locks, which is a skill which can be used for good or evil. The primary weakness of this analogy is the inclusion of script kiddies in the popular usage of "hacker," despite their lack of an underlying skill and knowledge base.

Sometimes, "hacker" is simply used synonymously with "geek": "A true hacker is not a group person. He's a person who loves to stay up all night, he and the machine in a love-hate relationship... They're kids who tended to be brilliant but not very interested in conventional goals[...] It's a term of derision and also the ultimate compliment."

Fred Shapiro thinks that "the common theory that 'hacker' originally was a benign term and the malicious connotations of the word were a later perversion is untrue." He found that the malicious connotations were already present at MIT in 1963 (quoting The Tech, an MIT student newspaper), and at that time referred to unauthorized users of the telephone network, that is, the phreaker movement that developed into the computer security hacker subculture of today.

Types

Hacker culture

Hacker culture is an idea derived from a community of enthusiast computer programmers and systems designers in the 1960s around the Massachusetts Institute of Technology's (MIT's) Tech Model Railroad Club (TMRC) and the MIT Artificial Intelligence Laboratory. The concept expanded to the hobbyist home computing community, focusing on hardware in the late 1970s (e.g. the Homebrew Computer Club) and on software (video games, software cracking, the demoscene) in the 1980s/1990s. Later, this would go on to encompass many new definitions such as art, and Life hacking.

Security related hacking

Security hackers are people involved with circumvention of computer security. Among security hackers, there are several types, including:

White hats are hackers who work to keep data safe from other hackers by finding system vulnerabilities that can be mitigated. White hats are usually employed by the target system's owner and are typically paid (sometimes quite well) for their work. Their work is not illegal because it is done with the system owner's consent.

Black hats or crackers are hackers with malicious intentions. They often steal, exploit, and sell data, and are usually motivated by personal gain. Their work is usually illegal. A cracker is like a black hat hacker, but is specifically someone who is very skilled and tries via hacking to make profits or to benefit, not just to vandalize. Crackers find exploits for system vulnerabilities and often use them to their advantage by either selling the fix to the system owner or selling the exploit to other black hat hackers, who in turn use it to steal information or gain royalties.

Grey hats include those who hack for fun or to troll. They may both fix and exploit vulnerabilities, but usually not for financial gain. Even if not malicious, their work can still be illegal, if done without the target system owner's consent, and grey hats are usually associated with black hat hackers.

Motives

Four primary motives have been proposed as possibilities for why hackers attempt to break into computers and networks. First, there is a criminal financial gain to be had when hacking systems with the specific purpose of stealing credit card numbers or manipulating banking systems. Second, many hackers thrive off of increasing their reputation within the hacker subculture and will leave their handles on websites they defaced or leave some other evidence as proof that they were involved in a specific hack. Third, corporate espionage allows companies to acquire information on products or services that can be stolen or used as leverage within the marketplace. And fourth, state-sponsored attacks provide nation states with both wartime and intelligence collection options conducted on, in, or through cyberspace.

Overlaps and differences

The main basic difference between programmer subculture and computer security hacker is their mostly separate historical origin and development. However, the Jargon File reports that considerable overlap existed for the early phreaking at the beginning of the 1970s. An article from MIT's student paper The Tech used the term hacker in this context already in 1963 in its pejorative meaning for someone messing with the phone system. The overlap quickly started to break when people joined in the activity who did it in a less responsible way. This was the case after the publication of an article exposing the activities of Draper and Engressia.

According to Raymond, hackers from the programmer subculture usually work openly and use their real name, while computer security hackers prefer secretive groups and identity-concealing aliases. Also, their activities in practice are largely distinct. The former focus on creating new and improving existing infrastructure (especially the software environment they work with), while the latter primarily and strongly emphasize the general act of circumvention of security measures, with the effective use of the knowledge (which can be to report and help fixing the security bugs, or exploitation reasons) being only rather secondary. The most visible difference in these views was in the design of the MIT hackers' Incompatible Timesharing System, which deliberately did not have any security measures.

There are some subtle overlaps, however, since basic knowledge about computer security is also common within the programmer subculture of hackers. For example, Ken Thompson noted during his 1983 Turing Award lecture that it is possible to add code to the UNIX "login" command that would accept either the intended encrypted password or a particular known password, allowing a backdoor into the system with the latter password. He named his invention the "Trojan horse". Furthermore, Thompson argued, the C compileritself could be modified to automatically generate the rogue code, to make detecting the modification even harder. Because the compiler is itself a program generated from a compiler, the Trojan horse could also be automatically installed in a new compiler program, without any detectable modification to the source of the new compiler. However, Thompson disassociated himself strictly from the computer security hackers: "I would like to criticize the press in its handling of the 'hackers,' the 414 gang, the Dalton gang, etc. The acts performed by these kids are vandalism at best and probably trespass and theft at worst. ... I have watched kids testifying before Congress. It is clear that they are completely unaware of the seriousness of their acts."

The programmer subculture of hackers sees secondary circumvention of security mechanisms as legitimate if it is done to get practical barriers out of the way for doing actual work. In special forms, that can even be an expression of playful cleverness. However, the systematic and primary engagement in such activities is not one of the actual interests of the programmer subculture of hackers and it does not have significance in its actual activities, either. A further difference is that, historically, members of the programmer subculture of hackers were working at academic institutions and used the computing environment there. In contrast, the prototypical computer security hacker had access exclusively to a home computer and a modem. However, since the mid-1990s, with home computers that could run Unix-like operating systems and with inexpensive internet home access being available for the first time, many people from outside of the academic world started to take part in the programmer subculture of hacking.

Since the mid-1980s, there are some overlaps in ideas and members with the computer security hacking community. The most prominent case is Robert T. Morris, who was a user of MIT-AI, yet wrote the Morris worm. The Jargon File hence calls him "a true hacker who blundered". Nevertheless, members of the programmer subculture have a tendency to look down on and disassociate from these overlaps. They commonly refer disparagingly to people in the computer security subculture as crackers and refuse to accept any definition of hacker that encompasses such activities. The computer security hacking subculture, on the other hand, tends not to distinguish between the two subcultures as harshly, acknowledging that they have much in common including many members, political and social goals, and a love of learning about technology. They restrict the use of the term cracker to their categories of script kiddies and black hat hackers instead.

All three subcultures have relations to hardware modifications. In the early days of network hacking, phreaks were building blue boxes and various variants. The programmer subculture of hackers has stories about several hardware hacks in its folklore, such as a mysterious 'magic' switch attached to a PDP-10 computer in MIT's AI lab, that when turned off, crashed the computer. The early hobbyist hackers built their home computers themselves, from construction kits. However, all these activities have died out during the 1980s, when the phone network switched to digitally controlled switchboards, causing network hacking to shift to dialing remote computers with modems, when pre-assembled inexpensive home computers were available, and when academic institutions started to give individual mass-produced workstation computers to scientists instead of using a central timesharing system. The only kind of widespread hardware modification nowadays is case modding.

An encounter of the programmer and the computer security hacker subculture occurred at the end of the 1980s, when a group of computer security hackers, sympathizing with the Chaos Computer Club (which disclaimed any knowledge in these activities), broke into computers of American military organizations and academic institutions. They sold data from these machines to the Soviet secret service, one of them in order to fund his drug addiction. The case was solved when Clifford Stoll, a scientist working as a system administrator, found ways to log the attacks and to trace them back (with the help of many others). 23, a German film adaption with fictional elements, shows the events from the attackers' perspective. Stoll described the case in his book The Cuckoo's Egg and in the TV documentary The KGB, the Computer, and Me from the other perspective. According to Eric S. Raymond, it "nicely illustrates the difference between 'hacker' and 'cracker'. Stoll's portrait of himself, his lady Martha, and his friends at Berkeley and on the Internet paints a marvelously vivid picture of how hackers and the people around them like to live and how they think."

Bibliography

- A Murray, Information Technology Law: The Law and Society (3rd edn 2016)
- A Murray, Information Technology Law: The Law and Society (3rd edn 2016)
- Balkin, J., Grimmelmann, J., Katz, E., Kozlovski, N., Wagman, S. & Zarsky, T. (2006) (eds) Cybercrime: Digital Cops in a Networked Environment, New York University Press, New York.
- Barlow, John P. "A Declaration of the Independence of Cyberspace".
- Bera, Poonam. "Presentation of electronic evidence in court in light of the Supreme Court judgment in Anvar P. K. vs. P.K Basheer & ors. Read more: Presentation of electronic evidence in court in light of the Supreme Court judgment in Anvar P. K. vs. P.K Basheer & ors". ipleaders.in. iPleaders. Retrieved 6 December 2014.
- Bowker, Art (2012) "The Cybercrime Handbook for Community Corrections: Managing Risk in the 21st Century" Charles C. Thomas Publishers, Ltd. Springfield.
- Brenner, S. (2007) Law in an Era of Smart Technology, Oxford: Oxford University Press
- Broadhurst, R., and Chang, Lennon Y.C. (2013) "Cybercrime in Asia: trends and challenges", in B. Hebenton, SY Shou, & J. Liu (eds), Asian Handbook of Criminology (pp. 49–64). New York: Springer (ISBN 978-1-4614-5217-1)
- Chang, L.Y. C. (2012) Cybercrime in the Greater China Region: Regulatory Responses and Crime Prevention across the Taiwan Strait. Cheltenham: Edward Elgar. (ISBN 978-0-85793-667-7)

- Chang, Lennon Y.C., & Grabosky, P. (2014) "Cybercrime and establishing a secure cyber world", in M. Gill (ed) Handbook of Security (pp. 321–339). NY: Palgrave.
- Code and Other Laws of Cyberspace, The Future of Ideas, and Free Culture by Lawrence Lessig
- Computer Law: Drafting and Negotiating Forms and Agreements, by Richard Raysman and Peter Brown. Law Journal Press, 1999–2008. ISBN 978-1-58852-024-1
- Csonka P. (2000) Internet Crime; the Draft council of Europe convention on cyber-crime: A response to the challenge of crime in the age of the internet? Computer Law & Security Report Vol.16 no.5.
- Cyber Rights by Mike Godwin
- Easttom C. (2010) Computer Crime Investigation and the Law
- E-Commerce and Internet Law: Treatise with Forms 2d edition, by Ian C. Ballon
- Emerging Technologies and the Law: Forms and Analysis, by Richard Raysman, Peter Brown, Jeffrey D. Neuburger and William E. Bandon, III. Law Journal Press, 2002-2008. ISBN 1-58852-107-9
- Fafinski, S. (2009) Computer Misuse: Response, regulation and the law Cullompton: Willan
- Free Speech Implications Of Blocking Blog Posts In India, taken from Aaron Kelly Internet Law Firm, Retrieved December 05, 2011.
- Gibson, Owen (March 23, 2006). "Warning to chatroom users after libel award for man labelled a Nazi". The Guardian.
- Glenny, Misha, DarkMarket : cyberthieves, cybercops, and you, New York, NY : Alfred A. Knopf, 2011. ISBN 978-0-307-59293-4
- Grabosky, P. (2006) Electronic Crime, New Jersey: Prentice Hall
- Halder, D., & Jaishankar, K. (2011) Cyber crime and the Victimization of Women: Laws, Rights, and Regulations. Hershey, PA, USA: IGI Global. ISBN 978-1-60960-830-9
- Halder, D., & Jaishankar, K. (2016). Cyber Crimes against Women in India. New Delhi: SAGE Publishing. ISBN 978-9385985775.
- Jaishankar, K. (Ed.) (2011). Criminology: Exploring Internet Crimes and Criminal behavior. Boca Raton, FL, USA: CRC Press, Taylor and Francis Group.
- McQuade, S. (2006) Understanding and Managing Cybercrime, Boston: Allyn & Bacon.

Index

N

O

P

R

S

T

V

W

❑❑❑